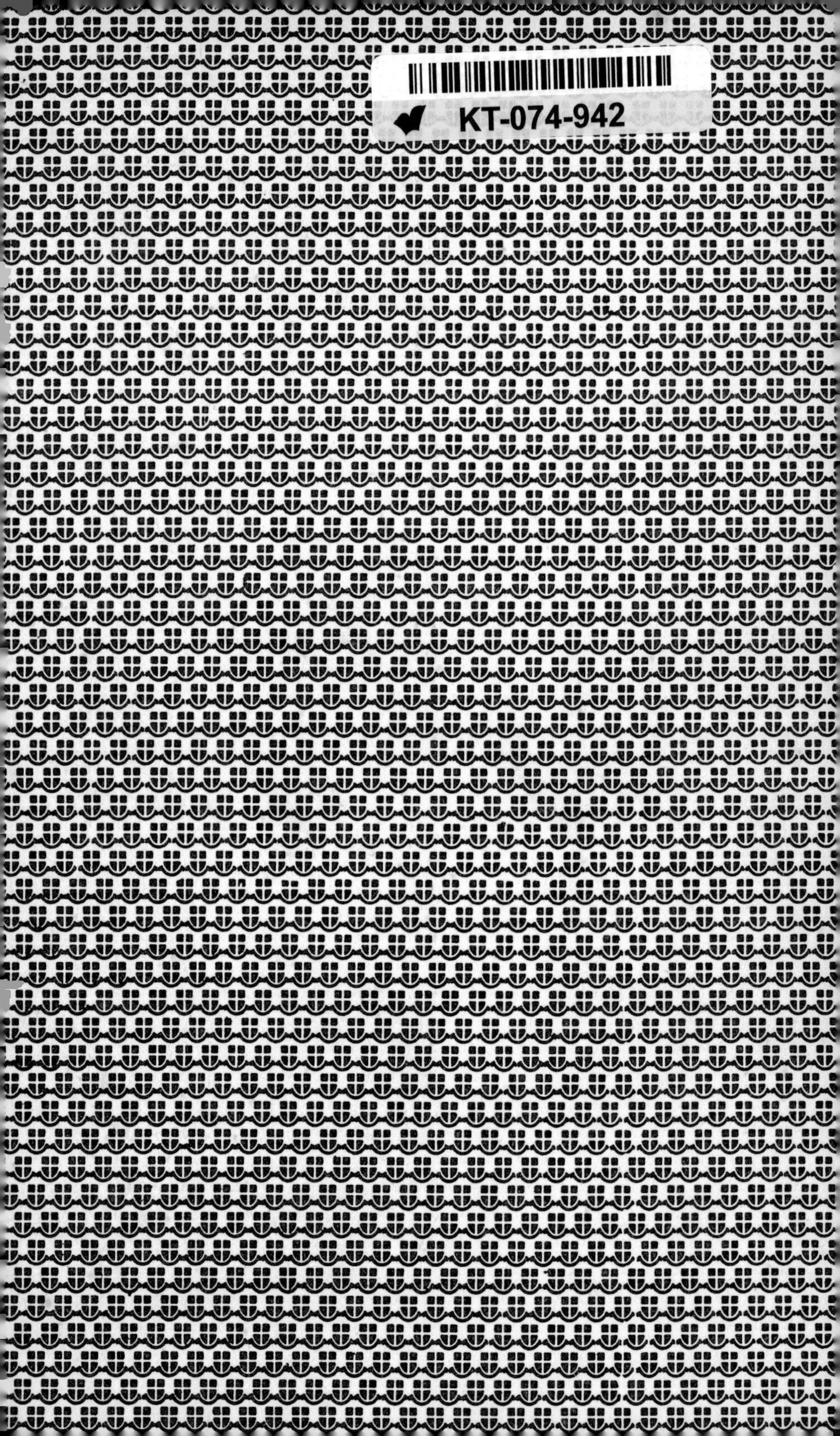

THE LIFE AND WORKS OF

JOSEPH HALL

1574 – 1656

The true Picture of the Right Reuerend father in God
IOSEPH HALL Bishop of NORWICH ∴ Samuell ∴ Waker ∴

Reproduced by courtesy of the British Museum

THE LIFE AND WORKS OF JOSEPH HALL

1574 – 1656

T. F. Kinloch

S T A P L E S P R E S S

STAPLES PRESS LIMITED
Mandeville Place, London

STAPLES PRESS INCORPORATED
70 East 45th Street, New York

FIRST PUBLISHED 1951

This Book is set in the 'Monotype' Times New Roman series

Made and printed in England by
STAPLES PRINTERS LIMITED
at their St Albans, Herts, establishment

Contents

To

NORMAN H. BAYNES

PREFACE

The most recent life of Hall was written by G. Lewis and published in 1886. Since then a good deal has been written concerning him both in this country and in America. His Latin satire, for instance, *Mundus alter et idem* (translated by John Healey in the beginning of the seventeenth century under the title *The Discovery of a New World*) edited with valuable notes by Huntington Brown, of Harvard, was republished in 1937: and what promises to be the definitive edition of his verse was published as recently as 1949 by the Liverpool University Press for A. Davenport. Yet though there have been several monographs and numerous articles on various aspects of his work, no attempt has been made until now to give an account of each of his varied activities and of all his written work.

It would take far too much space to name all the books to which the present writer is indebted. A few, however, must be named. Masson's great *Life of Milton*. His edition of the sixth volume of the *Register of the Privy Council of Scotland*, with its invaluable notes. The writings of such men as E. M. W. Tillyard, C. S. Lewis, C. M. Bowra, Logan Pearsall Smith and D. Saurat who did so much in days when impotent hands were stretched forth to rob him of his glory, to call attention to those great qualities in Milton which make his finest prose magnificent, his noblest verse sublime. Laud's works and Baillie's letters, Calderwood's *History of the Kirk of Scotland*, Professor Willey's *The Seventeenth Century Background*, Professor J. S. Neale's writings on the Elizabethan Age, and in particular his *Elizabethan House of Commons*. E. S. Schuckburgh's *History of Emmanuel College*, Blomefield's *History of Norfolk*, Jebb's *Theophrastus*. Goeter's brilliant *Vorbereitung des Pietismus*. The works of William Perkins, the 'Father of Pietism in England', as Heppe calls him. Heppe's *Geschichte des Pietismus*. The writings of English casuists like Ames (Amesius), Baxter and Jeremy Taylor. All these, together with various accounts of the life and character of James I and his two sons Henry and Charles, have thrown some light on Joseph Hall, his life and times.

I have received personal assistance from Sir Ivor Atkins in regard to Hall's connexion with Worcester Cathedral, and from the late Bishop Hensley Henson in regard to the Synod of Dort.

To two others I wish to express my thanks, my niece Aileen Turner who typed my manuscript, and Felix Franks who read the proofs.

T. F. KINLOCH

Wolverhampton,
1951

NOTE (*a*) Throughout this book the letter P. denotes the edition of Hall's works by Josiah Pratt in ten volumes, London, 1808; the letter W. that of Philip Wynter's edition in ten volumes, Oxford, 1863.

(*b*) Save in a few exceptional instances no attempt has been made in this book to reproduce Hall's archaic spelling.

(*c*) All quotations from Donne are taken from Alford's edition of Donne's works, London, 1839.

I – LIFE

In the evening of his days Hall wrote a short autobiography. He did this, he tells us in characteristic fashion, 'not out of a vain affectation of his own glory; but out of a sincere desire to give glory to God' whose 'wonderful Providence' had guided and guarded him throughout a long and chequered career. From this source we learn that he was born in Ashby-de-la-Zouch (Leicestershire) on July 1st, 1574, and that his father was bailiff[1] to 'that truly honourable and religious Henry Earl of Huntingdon, President of the North'. Under this distinguished nobleman Hall's father 'had the government' of Ashby.

In modern England peers have become numerous; death duties and heavy taxation have made such inroads on their fortunes that an earldom has lost much of the distinction it once possessed. In Elizabeth's time it was otherwise. Then earls were few; their wealth and influence great. Amongst such nobles Henry, third Earl of Huntingdon, was one of the greatest. Descended, on his mother's side, from Edward IV, it seemed quite possible, at one time, that he might ascend the English throne; for in October 1562, when Elizabeth lay between life and death, and men were wondering who would succeed to the Crown, there were those in the Council who thought that the Earl of Huntingdon should become king. Those who put forward this view were strongly Protestant, men who abhorred the fires of Smithfield, and were determined that never again should a 'Catholic' monarch rule over them. Had Elizabeth died in 1562, and had this section of the Protestant party succeeded in their designs, the whole course of English history might have been altered. In any case the State religion would have been of a much more Protestant character than that which it afterwards assumed.

The Earl of Huntingdon, it is said, had little worldly ambition and no desire to secure an earthly crown;[2] but, like other Puritans (if that term may be used here to denote the left-wing reformers), he was anxious above all things that the religion of England should not be a compromise between Protestantism and Catholicism.[3] With such might-have-beens we are not concerned. The fact remains that Huntingdon became, under Elizabeth, President of the North; governed the northern parts of England, exercised great influence,

[1] He probably entered Huntingdon's service in a much more menial capacity. Marston described Joseph Hall as a 'swineherd's brat'.

[2] For the great influence exerted by the 'great Earl' and his four brothers, all ardent Puritans, especially in Leicestershire, see J. S. Neale, *The Elizabethan House of Commons*, page 39 ff.

[3] Knappen, *Tudor Puritanism*, pages 183–4.

and used that influence unsparingly to protect those ministers of the National Church who disliked the Elizabethan Settlement, who longed to see the Church less 'Catholic' and more 'Protestant', who, in a word, desired to reform it on Genevan lines. Huntingdon died in debt, and it has been said that one of the reasons for this was his generous support of the Puritan cause.

Among the men who won his favour and gained his support, was Antony Gilby to whom he gave the living of Ashby-de-la-Zouch. Gilby was amongst the most distinguished of the Marian exiles; and during the 'Frankfort Troubles', when the English refugees were bitterly divided on the question as to whether they should continue to use the second Edwardian Prayer Book, or abandon it for the Genevan Order, Gilby warmly espoused the latter view. In 1556, before he returned to England, he published *A Brief Treatise of Election and Reprobation with Certain Answers to the Objection to the Adversaries of this* (*Genevan*) *Doctrine.*[1] He had also some share in the translation of the Geneva Bible.[2] Returning to England in 1558 or 1559, he secured Huntingdon's favour and protection and soon afterwards published what has been described as 'the outstanding controversial work of the period'. The praise is justly earned: lack of space alone prevents us from devoting to this little book the attention it deserves. Its title is: *A Pleasant Dialogue/ Betweene a souldier of Barwicke,/and an English Chaplaine. Wherein/ are largely handled, and laide open,/such reasons as are brought in/ for maintenance of popishe/Traditions in our/English Church.* To this are added 'a hundred and twenty particular corruptions yet remaining in our saide Church. . . .' Two ex-soldiers, formerly comrades-in-arms, meet in Berwick and discuss the condition of the Elizabethan Church. Miles has lost a leg and his occupation: unlike many others he is too proud to beg. Bernard, Sir Bernard, as he is now called, who had lost a finger and an eye in the wars, has become domestic chaplain to a peer. Miles remains a sturdy Protestant who longs for his Church to be set free from every vestige of Anti-Christ. He is a far abler man than his comrade and has much the better of the argument. Bernard had become a typical Elizabethan priest of the almost entirely illiterate kind that abounded in those days. He does his best to justify the Elizabethan compromise, with its copes and surplices and all the rest of the Roman paraphernalia which Protestants abhorred. Unlike Hall, Gilby avoids all trace of sarcasm when speaking of Rome. He is in deadly earnest, and writes with a greater sense of responsibility, less anxiety to display dialectical subtlety, more earnest desire to establish truth as he understands it. At times the

[1] Knappen, op. cit., page 142.
[2] Knappen, op. cit., page 144.

argument is interrupted by apostrophe. Gilby makes passionate appeals to bishops and laity alike to have done with all that savours of Rome, and to practise the simple rites of the Continental Reformers

The dialogue was published in London on May 10th, 1566. Gilby says it was ready written for publication about seven years earlier, and that he had delayed its publication in the hope that things would be mended. In 1566 he felt that it was almost hopeless to expect from Queen and bishops the reforms he so ardently desired.

Antony Gilby, then Vicar of Ashby, was at once an able man and an out-and-out Puritan who, just because he was a thorough Puritan, enjoyed the protection, support and favour of Henry, third Earl of Huntingdon.

To his mother, Hall tells us, he owed a greater debt than to anyone else. She had borne twelve children and her health had suffered in consequence. 'She was continually exercised', says her son, 'with the affliction of a weak body.' This, in turn, gave rise to a somewhat morbid view of life. She often suffered 'from a wounded spirit which caused her such agony that again and again she recounted with passion that the greatest bodily sicknesses were but flea-bites to those scorpions'. Thanks to Antony Gilby she was set completely free if not from her physical ailments, at least from her spiritual afflictions. In her son's eyes Mrs Hall had no reason to fear comparison either with 'Aleth the mother of that just Honour of Clareval, or with Monica, or indeed with any other of those pious matrons antiently famous for devotion'. No friend could visit her without being edified. All his days, Hall tells us, he blessed his mother's memory for 'those divine passages of experimental divinity' which he had heard from her mouth. She spent much time in devotional exercises 'from which she came forth with a countenance of undissembled mortification'. Her favourite themes were 'temptations, desertions, and spiritual comforts'. 'Never', says Hall, 'have any lips read to me such feeling lectures of piety: neither have I known any soul, that more actually practised them.' Such is the tribute, the noble tribute, which Hall pays to his mother's memory. It is almost certain that Mrs Hall revealed more of this side of her character to her son Joseph than she did to any other; for he had been dedicated in infancy to the service of the Church and she did her best to fit him for his future calling.

Such then were the influences which affected Hall throughout his boyhood (we must remember that he was a precocious child). The great Earl, friend and supporter of all Puritans, who subsequently procured a Fellowship at Emmanuel for his youthful protégé:

Antony Gilby, an intimate friend of the family, confidant of Mrs Hall, with whom she discussed her spiritual problems, and Mrs Hall herself who habitually spoke what German Pietists came to call 'The language of Canaan'. In later life Hall had many hard things to say of the Puritan party. In the quarrels that ensued, he defended what one may call the 'central Anglican position' with vehemence, skill, and not a little bitterness; yet all through life he bore upon him the marks of his Puritan upbringing. What influence Gilby's ecclesiastical opinions had upon him, it is impossible to say; for, apart from this reference in the autobiography, we meet with Gilby only once in Hall's numerous works; and there he is treated in that slightly supercilious way which Hall so often used when dealing with those for whose opinions he had no great affection. Yet it may well be that Hall owed to Gilby, in part, at least, the Calvinism which he never abandoned even when Arminianism gained favour with so many of the Episcopate; his belief in the efficacy and necessity of preaching – in this he differed from many, perhaps from most, of the Anglican party; and the slight importance which he attached to ritual observance – in this he differed profoundly from Laud and his 'Anglo-Catholic' followers. But whether or not he remembered with affection the simple form of worship which obtained in Ashby Parish Church, whether or not he was impressed by Gilby's preaching and by Gilby's Puritan views of the Church, if only for a season, there can be no doubt that all through life Joseph Hall remained his mother's son. Ever abstemious in matters of meat and drink, ever a lover of sober apparel and dignified behaviour, ever intensely diligent, 'scorning delights and living laborious days', ever conscious that he was but a pilgrim and a stranger in a wicked and rather dreary world, he, too, loved to brood over 'temptations, desertions, and spiritual comforts'.

He had, it is true, a strong sense of duty and was never known to shrink from the dust and sweat of the arena. Over and over again he was engaged in controversy, for he loved his Church and his king; and in those days there were many who sought to undermine the absolute authority claimed by each. Yet, in spite of all this, there can be little doubt that had the times in which he lived been more propitious, he would have given proof that the form of Calvinism to which he was most attracted was not that of the vigorous active extrovert; it was rather that form which shades off almost imperceptibly into the 'Precisionism' of Dutchmen like Lodenstein, or the 'Pietism' of Germans like Spener and Francke. In all this he was the true son of his puritanical and somewhat morbid mother.

Like other boys of his class, Hall attended the local grammar school.[1] There he laid the foundation of that excellent knowledge of Latin and Greek which distinguished him even in an age when the classics were so much better known than they are today. It is almost certain that he acquired a thorough knowledge of the outlines of Calvinistic theology from the admirable if long-winded Latin catechism of Dean Nowell.

EARLY MANHOOD

On leaving school it was Hall's ardent desire to go to Cambridge; but his father's means were limited and his family large – 'whose not very large cistern was to feed many pipes beside mine' – and it seemed as if he would have to be satisfied with a less expensive training for the ministry. Indeed, arrangements were almost completed for placing him in the care of a tutor, the 'public preacher of Leicester', who guaranteed to teach him in seven years as much of the 'Arts, Languages, and grounds of Theoretical Divinity as he would acquire from the carefullest tutor in the strictest College of the University'. When things looked blackest for the ambitious boy, when all hope of academic distinction seemed at an end, help came. An elder brother offered to sacrifice his patrimony for Joseph;[2] eventually, however, the necessary funds were provided by a friend of the family. Hall, now 15 years of age, matriculated in 1589. He entered Emmanuel, the strictest and most puritanical college in Cambridge. Dr Chaderton, the Master, had been specially chosen by Mildmay, the founder of the College, for his puritanical views. Hall's tutor was Antony Gilby's son. At Cambridge his career was one of great distinction. He became a scholar of his college, took his B.A. in 1592–93, his M.A. in 1596; became B.D. in 1603, and D.D. in 1610.

Fifteen hundred and ninety-five was one of the most memorable years in his life. Then he was elected fellow of his college, partly through the influence of the Earl of Huntingdon. Let us hear the account of this in his own words:

> 'Then was I, with a cheerful unanimity, chosen into that Society; which if it had any equals, I dare say had none beyond it, for good order, studious carriage, strict government, austere piety. I spent six or seven years more, with such contentment, as the rest of my life hath in vain striven to yield.'

Unless we regard this statement as a mere *cri du cœur* from an old man who, like so many others, was a *laudator temporis acti*, it demands attention. It was written when Laud was dead, when Hall was at least 70. Under Laud's influence Joseph Hall had drifted

[1] The atmosphere of the school was strongly Puritan.
[2] While he was at Cambridge it seemed that he would be unable to complete his studies. Once more help came and he remained.

from his earlier moorings, and approached or seemed to approach Laud's own position. Yet no sooner was *Episcopacy by Divine Right*, whose every paragraph was written under Laud's strict supervision, published (1640) than Hall began to modify the extreme views on the absolute necessity of episcopacy expressed therein. Indeed it was precisely this vacillation on Hall's part, which led Masson, like his hero Milton, to regard Hall as a trimmer who set his sails to catch each favouring breeze. Faced by Laud's inflexible will and clear-cut convictions Hall seems to have – for a time – taken up a position which he felt unable to maintain. Though a convinced Episcopalian all his life he did not feel able, save for a brief interval during which he was Laud's spokesman, to exclude from the One Catholic and Apostolic Church, those who did not accept the necessity of Episcopal Ordination.

Looking back on the whole course of a long life Hall tells us that his happiest days were spent in Emmanuel College. No 'Anglo-Catholic' could possibly have made such a statement. Let us for a moment try to describe the atmosphere of the college which Hall so dearly loved. 'The prevailing tone of the place', says Schuckburgh, the historian of Emmanuel, 'was throughout Chaderton's mastership distinctly that of advanced Puritanism.'[1]

On the gateway of Emmanuel, founded only five years before Hall entered it, is this inscription: *Sacrae Theologiae Studiosis Gualterus Mildmaus An^o^ Domini 1584*. In the nineteenth statute Mildmay says, 'The one object which I set before me in erecting this college was to render as many as possible fit for the administration of the Divine Word and Sacraments.'[2]

> 'All other Colleges in Cambridge do strictly observe, according to the laws and ordinances of the Church of Englande, the form of public prayer prescribed in the Communion Booke. In Emmanuel College they do follow a course of public prayer, after their own fashion, both Sondaies, Holy Daies and workie daies.'[3]

In 1604 we are told they sat at Communion, though some knelt.[4]

Emmanuel College, then, was not intended to be a seat of humanistic culture; it was meant to be a seminary founded for the express purpose of preparing men for the sacred ministry. The whole spirit of the place was definitely puritanical: the main study, Calvinistic Theology. It is of this college, by far the most Puritan college in the University at a time when Puritanism was a great national move-

[1] Schuckburgh, *History of Emmanuel College*, page 52.
[2] Schuckburgh, op. cit., page 23.
[3] Bass Mullinger, *History of the University of Cambridge*, page 313, quoting from Baker MSS., VI 85, 86.
[4] Schuckburgh, op. cit., page 85.

ment,[1] Hall speaks when he tells us that his happiest days were spent within its walls.

During the time in which he held his fellowship, Hall gave the 'Rhetoric Lecture' two years in succession in the 'Public Schools'. His lectures, he tells us, were 'well attended and well applauded'. But, like most of those who came to Emmanuel, Hall had not gone to Cambridge to deliver lectures on rhetoric; he had gone to fit himself for the ministry. He was ordained priest at Colchester on December 14th, 1600. Once he had taken Holy Orders, he tells us:

> 'I was no niggard of that talent which my God had entrusted to me; preaching often, as occasion was offered, both in country villages abroad, and at home in the most awful auditory of the University.'

To complete the picture Hall gives of his life at Cambridge one further fact requires to be mentioned. A feature of university life in those days was the 'Public Disputation'. In these, says Hall, 'I was often called upon to engage with no ill success'. He assures us that he

> 'never durst appear in any of those exercises of scholarship, till he had from his knees looked up to heaven for a blessing, and renewed his actual dependence upon that Divine hand'.

Here then we have a portrait, self-painted, of a young Cambridge don in a strict puritanical college, who asked God's help and blessing on every task he was asked to perform. Yet if this were all we knew of Joseph Hall, we should certainly have an incomplete and possibly an erroneous conception of the man. We shall find in due course that there were certain incidents in his life which he was eager to forget, which so far as he could he was determined to conceal. Two of these occurred after he left the university: of each we shall have to speak later on. One was a youthful effort; the other the fruit of his old age. Two years after he took his B.D. Hall wrote a Latin satire. It first professed to see the light of day in Frankfort but most probably it was published in London. Later on it was republished in Hanau; a year later (1608) it was turned into English by one John Healey. This work, *Mundus alter et idem*, appeared anonymously. The reason is obvious. Milton said that it was altogether unworthy

[1] Schuckburgh, op. cit., VIII.

'In the house of pure Emmanuel
I had my education,
Where my friends surmise
I dazzled my eyes
With the light of revelation.
Boldly I preach
Hate a cross, hate a surplice,
Mitres, copes and rochets;
Come, hear me pray,
Nine times a day,
And fill your soul with crotchets.'
(*Dick Corbet's Song.*)

of a Christian, still more of a divine. In none of his later works does Hall refer to this book. He was most anxious to have it entirely forgotten; for it was altogether out of keeping with that picture of a devout and saintly man who lived as ever in the Great Taskmaster's eye which Hall wished to leave behind him. Between thirty and forty years later, when Milton cut him to the quick with one of the most savage attacks ever made on an English bishop, Hall, with the aid of his son Robert (an archdeacon) – or, as some would have it, Robert, with his father's assistance – published a vile and entirely unwarranted attack on Milton's moral character. To this wicked and malicious tract he made no further reference. Whether he repented of the lies he condoned, if he did not invent them, we cannot tell. Certainly he made no public apology. We shall return to this in a later chapter. Meanwhile we are concerned with something far less regrettable; yet with something that Hall did his utmost to forget and conceal.

While still a don at Cambridge he published a slim volume entitled *Virgidemiarum*. It was published anonymously, of course, and so far as the present writer is aware, Hall never acknowledged the work after he was 30 (unless we take into account a reference to it in one of the tracts in which he replied to Milton). Its opening words are these:

> 'I first adventure: follow me who list
> And be the second English satirist.'

A year later, this volume was followed by another. Shortly afterwards (June 1st, 1599) an edict signed by the Archbishop of Canterbury and the Bishop of London, was issued to the effect that 'noe Satyres be printed hereafter'. Three days later several volumes of satires were publicly burned, though Hall's were spared ('These were staied'). To these satires, many of which are witty and amusing, which reveal an amazing knowledge of all sections of contemporary life, especially on what is sometimes termed 'its seamy side', Hall makes no subsequent reference after 1603. One of his admirers, writing in the Dictionary of National Biography, has to admit that in these satires 'some passages border on scurrility'.

There is a Jekyll and Hyde complex in most men; and one cannot but feel that this complex existed in Joseph Hall. Again and again we shall see that he knew how to practise a discreet silence and an economy of truth. He was exceedingly sensitive to public opinion and he was determined to make the public believe that he was as ingenuous as he was undoubtedly devout. Hence his dismay when Milton revealed his early indiscretions and showed that Joseph Hall had not always been exactly what the admirers of his devotional writings had taken him to be.

'At Emmanuel,' says Schuckburgh, 'Hall does not appear to have given his chief attention to theology.'[1] From one of his contemporaries we have an interesting glimpse of the impression made by him (if only on one man) during his Emmanuel days. This man had turned Catholic: Hall and another fellow of Emmanuel, Bedell by name, argued with him about his conversion. The black sheep who had wandered from the Protestant fold liked Bedell, but complained of the bitterness shown by Hall 'whom I esteemed either my friend or a modester man; whose flaunting epistle I have not answered, because I could not soil my hands with a poetical railer'.[2]

Hall leaves Cambridge

At this time, Blundell's School in Tiverton, well-built and well-endowed, was in need of a headmaster. The Lord Chief Justice was asked to secure the services of a suitable man for the post. He appealed to his friend Dr Chaderton, Master of Emmanuel, who selected Joseph Hall and took him up to London for an interview with the Lord Chief Justice. The interview was of a cordial character, the result to both parties highly satisfactory; for the judge secured the services of an able man, and Hall the promise of a handsome salary, for duties chiefly of a supervisional character, which, he was told, would make small demands on his time. But no sooner had he accepted the judge's offer than he was met in the street by a man who gave him a letter from Lady Drury in which she offered him the living of Halstead[3] in Suffolk. Chaderton told Hall that, as he had already accepted the post at Tiverton, it was his obvious duty to refuse the living of Halstead; but Hall persuaded him that the 'call' to Halstead had come from God, and eventually the judge agreed that one of Hall's Emmanuel friends should go to Tiverton in his stead.

There can be little doubt that Hall was deeply attached to Lady Drury, that he really admired that 'right virtuous and worthy Lady, of dear and happy memory'; but it is perfectly obvious that his relations with her husband, Sir Robert, were of a much less cordial character. At first Sir Robert was certainly prejudiced against Hall.

> 'A witty and bold atheist [Lilly by name[4]] by reason of his travails and abilities of discourse and behaviour, had so deeply insinuated himself into my patron Sir Robert Drury, that there was small hopes, during his entireness for me to work any good upon that Noble Patron of mine, who, by the suggestion of this wicked detractor, was sett off from me before he knew me.'

[1] We shall see how true this is when we deal with his satires.
[2] Schuckburgh, op. cit., 42.
[3] Often spelt 'Hawstead'.
[4] Supposed to be the Euphuist.

The rest of the story throws such an interesting sidelight on one aspect of Hall's character, that it deserves to be given in his own words.

> 'Hereupon, I confess, finding the obduredness and hopeless condition of that man, I bent my prayers against him; beseeching God daily, that he would be pleased to remove, by some means or other, that apparent hindrance of my faithful labours, who gave me an answer accordingly; for this malicious man, going hastily up to London to exasperate my patron against me, was then and there swept away by the pestilence, never returned to do any further mischief. Now the coast was clear before me; and I gained every day the good opinion and favourable respects of that Honourable Gentleman and my worthy neighbours.'

Certain characteristic features which will reappear again and again in Hall's later works, are here revealed for the first time in this story.

(1) In many respects he was a hard man. He had no pity for the Lord's enemies. Like the Psalmist of old, he hated them with a perfect hatred.

(2) Somehow or other every opponent with whom he had to deal – and they were many – was inspired, always by unworthy, and often by distinctively evil motives.

(3) A firm conviction that despite his human frailties, he was a faithful servant of the Lord, and in return enjoyed the Lord's favour and protection.

(4) Few men ever lived who desired more ardently, esteemed more highly and, one might add, sought more eagerly, 'the good and favourable respects' of their neighbours in general, and of influential men in particular, than Joseph Hall.

During the seven years (1601–08) he spent at Halstead, Hall gradually built up a reputation both as a preacher and as a writer. In 1606 he published the first sermon he preached at Paul's Cross. His appearance there marked him out as one of the leading preachers of the day. A year earlier he issued the first volume of that long series of 'Meditations' by which he hoped to be remembered in later days, perhaps even in later ages. Then too he made his first appearance as an authority on divinity in his *Brief Sum of the Principal Points of Religion.* Yet all this, which may be justly regarded as rightly falling within the ambit of his sacred calling, by no means exhausted his boundless energy or satisfied his literary ambition. There was the Latin satire, of which we have spoken, of which he spoke so seldom, if ever. But, in addition, he introduced into England two forms of composition which he claimed had never appeared before in our literature. The first of these was the *Epistle*, an essay in all but name, by means of which a variety of subjects could be discussed in an interesting manner. The other was the *Character-Sketch* based on the work of Theophrastus. Each will be dealt with later. Three other points deserve attention.

His Marriage

We give the story in his own words in order that our readers may realize that in Joseph Hall, despite his undoubted holiness, there was a strain of egoism from which he never altogether escaped.

> 'The uncouth solitariness of my life, and the extreme incommodity of that single housekeeping, drew my thoughts, after two years, to condescend to the necessity of a married estate: which God no less strangely provided for me; for walking from the Church on Monday in the Whitsun-week, with a grave and reverend Minister, Mr Grandidge, I saw a comely and modest gentlewoman standing at the door of that house where we were invited to a wedding-dinner; and enquiring of that worthy friend whether he knew her, "Yes," quoth he, "I know her well, and have bespoken her for your wife." When I further demanded an account of that answer he told me she was the daughter of a gentleman whom he much respected; that, out of an opinion had of the fitness of that match for me, he had already treated with her father about it; whom he found very apt to entertain it; advising me not to neglect the opportunity, and not concealing the just praises of the modesty, piety, good disposition, and other virtues that were lodged in that seemly presence. I listened to the motion, as sent from God, and, at last, upon due prosecution, happily prevailed; enjoying the comfortable society of that meet help for the space of forty-nine years.'

Hall visits the Low Countries

Hall readily accepted an invitation from Sir Edmund Bacon (kinsman of the illustrious Francis) to accompany him on a diplomatic mission to the Low Countries. For he regarded it as a splendid opportunity at once of extending his knowledge of the world – like Dante *che tutto vedea,* he was ever a keen observer of his fellow men – and of acquiring at first hand a more intimate acquaintance with the Roman Church in action. Despite the fact that he was dressed as a layman and formed part of Bacon's retinue, his eagerness to learn, his readiness to enter into theological discussion, the firmness with which he defended the tenets of the Anglican Church, his fluent and graceful Latin, his skill in controversy in which he defeated most of his adversaries aroused suspicion, especially among the Jesuits who realized that he was something other than an English gentleman travelling for pleasure. His inquisitiveness in regard to Roman beliefs and practices threatened to involve him in serious and most unpleasant consequences – 'some perilous issue', as he puts it – but for

Sir Edmund, who did his best to curb Hall's insatiable curiosity, who cast his diplomatic mantle over him, and – to use Hall's expression – 'both by his eye and tongue took me off'.

Resolves to Leave Halstead

In 1608, Hall was 34 years of age. He knew that his abilities were immeasurably greater than those of the average country parson, that he was acknowledged to be one of the ablest and most learned preachers of his time, that he had literary gifts of no mean order, and that year by year his reputation as a writer of devotional literature was steadily increasing. He felt the time had come for him to make a definite decision. There were two alternatives. On the one hand he could settle down at Halstead for the rest of his life. (At this time and for long after, he was convinced that his stay on earth was to be brief.) In that case he would continue to preach thrice a week to a handful of villagers and a few of the neighbouring gentry. No doubt some of these careful compositions would occasionally be heard in a very different pulpit, at Paul's Cross, for instance, where he was ever assured of a warm welcome from a splendid congregation. Then too, he had discovered a new means of treating his village sermons in such a way that their substance could be conveyed to a wide circle of readers. Regarding these sermons as so much rough ore, he could smelt them down and thus extract the metal they contained. Such is his own simile. In other words, he took his sermons, melted them down, recast them in a different mould, stripped them of every word that could be regarded as superfluous, and gave them to the world as a *Contemplation*. It was in this way that the whole of his long series of *Contemplations upon the Principal Passages in the Holy Story* was produced. For such wares, Hall felt, there was at once a ready market and an urgent need. For whilst many learned men were at once able and willing to produce innumerable works on dogmatics, apologetics, casuistry and all such subjects, to say nothing of the endless flood of controversial literature that poured from the press, there was a real shortage of books of a devotional character.[1] In an age which took as keen an interest in theological and ecclesiastical questions as their

[1] Hall's estimate of the *demand* for such literature is correct; his estimate of the *supply* is entirely wide of the mark. Heppe, in his work *Geschichte/des Pietismus und der Mystik/in der Reformirten Kirche/namentlich der Niederlande* proves his statement by a long list of books.

> 'England war in der ersten Hälfte der siebzehnten Jahrhunderts mit pietistischen Schriften geradezu *uberflüthet*, indem dem schriftsellerischen Eifer der Theologen das brennendste Verlangen der Gemeindeglieder nach erbaulichen, ascetischen Schriften entsprach.' (Page 49.)

Hall always ignored his fellow practitioners. He *must* have known some of their devotional writings. Nowhere does he refer to any.

descendants did in economics, there were a hundred who appealed to the head for one who addressed the heart. To make such an appeal to heart and conscience lay, so Hall felt, well within his powers; and surely there was no place in which there was more opportunity for peaceful meditation than a quiet Suffolk village.

On the other hand it was obvious that the salary he received was inadequate to provide for his own needs and the needs of what promised to become a good-sized family. But Drury persisted in withholding a portion of his stipend – it was exactly £10 – which Hall knew was due to him. This alone, apart from the fact that Drury could be generous to those, like Donne, whom he really cared for, would seem to support the contention we have previously made that there was never any real intimacy or true affection between Drury and Hall; and much as Hall desired (and needed) that extra £10, it was lack of appreciation and affection on the part of one whom he regarded as his superior which grieved him most.

On the other hand, he might leave Halstead, obtain a much more lucrative living, which, with the aid of the influential friends he had recently acquired, might prove a stepping-stone to some important position in the Church, which would afford ample opportunity for the exercise of the unusual ability he was persuaded he possessed. At this time he was offered the 'public preachership' in Bury St Edmunds and he resolved to use this as a counter in bargaining with Drury. If Drury promised to pay him the extra £10, which was the source of constant friction between them, he would, he tells us, remain in Halstead to the end of his days: if Sir Robert refused then his only course was to accept this, or some better appointment. As he lay in bed one morning thinking of all this 'a strong motion was suddenly glanced into his thoughts of going to London'. He called on Sir Robert at his mansion in Drury Lane, stayed with him over the week-end, broached the subject of his call to Bury St Edmunds, heard Drury's view that it was not worth serious consideration, found him, however, adamant on the question of the £10 increment to his stipend and preached, presumably in the mansion, on Sunday. Sir Robert enjoyed the sermon and chancing to meet Lord Denny (later Earl of Norwich) mentioned his approval of the sermon he had just heard. Denny replied that he had read Hall's works, admired them greatly, and said that he would like to meet their author. Hall stayed a day or two longer in Drury Lane. He was 'full of cold and distemper', but to this apparently Drury paid little attention. However, a man called Gurney, an acquaintance rather than a friend, called to see him. Gurney was tutor to the Earl of Essex and, apparently at the Earl's instigation, told Hall that his 'Meditations' were highly esteemed at the Court of Prince Henry, and asked him to preach before His Royal Highness at Richmond on the following Sunday. Hall was taken aback, for this was perhaps the last thing he expected. He 'strongly pleaded his indisposition of body and inpreparation for any such work; together with his bashful fears, and utter unfitness for such a presence'. But Gurney refused to take 'no' for an answer. The rest of the story is best told in Hall's own words.

> 'He made way for me to that awful pulpit; and encouraged me by the favour of his Noble Lord, the Earl of Essex. I preached. Through the favour of my God, that sermon was not so well given as taken; insomuch as that Sweet Prince signified his desire to hear me again the following Tuesday. Which done, that labour gave me more contentment than the former; so as that Gracious Prince both gave me his hand and commanded me to his service.'

In other words he made Hall one of the twelve chaplains, each of whom was in attendance for a month at a time.

On his return to London, Hall met his patron who noticed that men of rank were paying attention to his chaplain. 'It is evident,' said he, 'that sooner or later some one will persuade you to leave Halstead.' In reply Hall told him, 'that it was in his power to prevent this; that if he would but pay him his proper salary' (i.e. give him the extra £10 which was in dispute) 'he would never stir from him'. Instead of meeting this offer with ready approval, Drury explained that it was always possible to make a small income adequate to one's needs by cutting down one's expenses. Hall pointed out that as things were he could only make both ends meet by doing literary work. Even this, however, failed either to mollify Sir Robert or to unloose his purse strings. 'Shortly,' says Hall, 'some harsh and unpleasing answer so disheartened me, that I resolved to embrace the first opportunity of my removal.' Almost at that very moment a message came from Denny (afterwards Earl of Norwich) inviting Hall to come and see him. Hall went.

> 'No sooner came I hither, than, after a glad and noble welcome, I was entertained with the earnest offer of Waltham. The conditions were, like the mover of them, free and bountiful. I received them as from the munificent hand of my God: and returned, full of the cheerful acknowledgments of a gracious Providence over me.'

Drury now offered to pay Hall his proper stipend; but the offer came too late. Hall tells us he returned home 'happy in a new master' (i.e. Prince Henry) 'and in a new patron' (Norwich, who eventually became his intimate and lifelong friend): 'betwixt whom I divided myself and my labours, with much comfort and no less acceptation'. He was now free from all financial anxiety and had set his feet on the ladder of prosperity, which brought him – what he so dearly loved and prized so highly – the favour of his king, important duties, at home and abroad, to the height of a clergyman's ambition, the mitre and the pastoral staff of a bishop.

WALTHAM ABBEY

Shortly after he was instituted to the living of Waltham, Hall was invited by Prince Henry to become his principal domestic chaplain and to reside permanently at Court. But though the Prince promised to 'obtain for him such preferments, as should yield him full contentment' he felt compelled to decline the offer, and remained at Waltham for twenty-two years. There can be little doubt that Joseph Hall, Vicar of Waltham Cross, was a much happier man than Joseph Exon or Joseph Norvic. Yet we must not conclude from this that in the seventeenth century a distinguished Anglican divine, with a royal patron, would remain satisfied with an income derived from a single parish.

In 1808 the Rev Josiah Pratt collected Hall's numerous writings and published them in ten volumes. This work he dedicated to the 'Right Reverend Father in God, George Prettyman Tomline, D.D., Lord Bishop of Lincoln, *and Dean of St Paul's*'. In one respect at least Hall resembled that worthy divine. He too was a pluralist. From 1611 to 1626 he was Archdeacon of Nottingham; from 1616 to 1627 he was Dean of Worcester. In addition to this he was for a short time Prebendary of Willenhall in the Collegiate Church of St Peter's, Wolverhampton, then closely connected with the Deanery of Windsor.[1] To do him justice, however, it must be said that he obtained this post through Prince Henry's influence in order to regain for the Church some of its patrimony which had been alienated by the Leveson family. At the end of a long and no doubt costly

[1] The following note taken from an article in the *Wolverhampton Antiquary*, Vol. I, page 305 ff, by a distinguished local antiquary, G. P. Mander, throws an interesting light on the state of religion in Wolverhampton in those days.

'At the beginning of the century Wolverhampton had no preachers. The two poor curates . . . who carried on the work of the large parish were scornfully regarded as "notorious drunkards and dissolute men". The Canons were chiefly non-resident or had preferment in the neighbourhood which had a call upon them.'

After Hall had regained the endowments usurped by the Leveson family he surrendered the Prebendary of Willenhall to the Rev Richard Lee, who for the next twenty-five years performed his task, says Hall, 'with great mutual contentment and happy success'. Describing the state of his parish in 1624 Lee said, 'I never knew any part of the Kingdom, where Rome's snakie brood roosted and rested themselves more warmer and safer, and with greater countenance than in our country'. Unfortunately for Lee (and his fellow workers in the district) Laud had them ejected because Lee (and his clerical friends) 'favoured Puritanic practices'. Laud was executed in 1645. On his death the Committee for Plundered Ministers restored Lee as a 'minister' in his old parish in January 1646. Instead of his prebendary valued at £40 per annum, he was given a salary of £100 per annum derived from rents of the Collegiate Church. He died soon afterwards, either in 1647 or 1648.

law-suit in chancery, Hall succeeded in restoring to St Peter's Church the revenues which the Leveson family had appropriated to themselves. No sooner had the Courts decided in his favour than Hall resigned his prebend and addressed himself to His Majesty, with a petition for the renewing of the charter of that church (St Peter's, Wolverhampton); and the full establishment of the 'lands, rights, liberties, thereto belonging'. This, he tells us, he 'easily obtained from those gracious hands'. No one pretends that 'pluralism' was confined to the Elizabethan Church. It was all too common in medieval times and Cardinal Wolsey was a notorious pluralist. None the less, though it continued for more than a century and a half after Hall's death, it was condemned by many, even in Hall's time. Nor is it surprising that when Milton delivered a fierce attack upon this manifest evil, Hall put up a singularly feeble defence. Obviously the fact that he could not render service at one and the same time in Waltham, Nottingham and Worcester did not trouble his conscience.

In his *History of Norwich* (page 180) Augustus Jessop tells us that a few years previous to the period with which we are now dealing there was only one member of the chapter who even pretended to reside in Norwich. Even when he became Bishop of Exeter Hall tells us that 'it pleased God to make up the competency of that provision, by the unthought of addition of the Rectory of St Breok within that Diocese'. As a pluralist Hall could not compete with his famous – in some ways his notorious – contemporary Dr Williams – James's favourite chaplain – who at one and the same time was Bishop of Lincoln, Dean of Westminster and Lord Chancellor of England. None the less, it is not without interest to note than one who was regarded as pre-eminently devout, who gained this reputation by a long series of pamphlets which dealt with the most exalted aspects of the spiritual life, was little more disturbed by some of the manifest evils of his time than his more ambitious and wordly contemporaries. In one respect he was far more conscientious than most, indeed perhaps more conscientious than any; and that was in regard to his preaching. It is well known that King James disliked 'read sermons', and men have sometimes asked how it was possible for preachers like Hall and Donne to produce the lengthy sermons studded as they were with Latin and Greek quotations in which the king delighted. Hall leaves us in no doubt in regard to his own procedure. At Waltham, as at Halstead, he preached (for about an hour) three times a week,

> 'yet never durst I climb into the pulpit to preach any sermon, whereof I had not before, in my poor and plain fashion, penned every word in the same order, wherein I hoped to deliver it; although, in the expression, I liked not to be a slave to syllables'.

Whilst at Waltham, Hall not only became more and more intimate with Prince Henry, he steadily grew in favour with King James; and on three occasions was chosen by his royal master to occupy a post of some distinction.

He Visits France

He was in attendance on the Earl of Carlisle 'who was sent upon a Noble Embassy, with a gallant retinue into France'. From this expedition, Hall returned with two lasting memories. One, of a 'miserable distemper of body, which ended in a *Diarrhaea Biliosa*, not without some beginning, and further threat of dysentry'. He was very ill; and at one time it looked as though he would never see England again. The other memory which he took home with him was of the great kindness shown him by Peter Moulin, a distinguished Huguenot divine. This kindness, and the friendship to which it led, Hall never forgot; and it undoubtedly influenced his views in regard to the 'catholicity' of the non-episcopal Huguenot Church.

Before he left for France Hall received a promise from the king that he would be made Dean of Worcester; yet – such were the ways of Anglican clergy in those days – it seemed unlikely that he would obtain the Deanery; for, in his absence, another 'was by his potent friends put into such assurance of it, that I heard where he took care for the furnishing that ample house'. However, King James kept his word, and the gentleman who had 'taken care for the furnishing of the Deanery' never occupied it; for, to quote Hall's own words,

> 'God fetched it about for me, in that absence and nescience of mine: and that reverend and better deserving Divine was well satisfied with greater hopes, and soon after exchanged this mortal estate for an immortal and glorious.'

Thus all ended well, and Joseph Hall, through God's blessing – so he regarded the whole transaction – became Dean of Worcester.

Perth

In 1617 King James revisited his native kingdom. One of his dearest desires was to force the Scots to abandon the Presbyterian form of Church government and to adopt an Episcopal form similar to that which obtained in England. He had cherished this desire for many years and had gone a considerable way to reaching his goal. Now he felt able, by means of his subservient (Scottish) Privy Council, to take a further step and to signify the way in which the Scots were to worship in future. Hence the Five Articles of Perth which decreed that henceforth the Scots were to kneel at Communion, to have their babies baptized in public within a week of their birth, to observe as solemn festivals Easter, Whitsuntide and Christmas, to catechize diligently and to present those who had been properly instructed to the bishop. In order to persuade the Scottish clergy, if that were possible, he took along with him a number of Anglican divines. Hall was of their number and so was Laud. Hall made himself very popular with the Scottish clergy with whose views he had more sympathy than Anglicans like Laud approved. They criticized his conduct and what, from Hall's point of view, was far more dangerous, their criticism was carried back to England. Hall, whose dearest earthly desire was to be popular with the king, took fright, persuaded Lord Doncaster to recall him to London, had an audience with the king, explained that he was a loyal Episcopalian, wrote down the substance of what he had said to His Majesty and published it. So all was well once more. No doubt his reconciliation with the king – if such it may be termed – was made all the more easy since James and Hall agreed in their profound suspicion of Laud whom both disliked.

The Synod of Dort (1618–19)

During the reigns of Elizabeth and James I, the influence of Calvin on England was very great. 'When James I died in 1625 Calvinism was still the prevailing belief of religious Englishmen.'[1] With a few distinguished exceptions, those who taught theology in the universities and those who held important positions in the Church were Calvinists. Abbot, the Archbishop of Canterbury, like James himself, was a convinced Calvinist. Soon after James's death a change came over the scene – Laud had much to do with it: yet to explain the change would require a long and complicated exposition; for there were few Englishmen who could name the date and place of their conversion, and say with Hales, '*There* I bid John Calvin goodnight'.[2] But England was not the only country in which members of the Reformed Church revolted against Calvin's remorseless logic. Indeed the most famous and perhaps the most influential of such rebels was a Dutch theologian called Arminius (1560–1609).

In Holland Arminius had many adherents, as he had many bitter opponents. Disputes concerning predestination, election, the part played by free will in man's redemption, became so widespread and so embittered that at length a synod was held in Dort, to arrange, if possible, a settlement of the dispute, and to define the position, not only of the Dutch, but of all the Reformed Churches in regard to this mysterious subject. To this synod divines from various foreign Churches were invited: to this synod certain English divines

[1] H. H. Henson, *English Religion in the Seventeenth Century*. London, 1903.
[2] *The Golden Remains of John Hales*, preface.

were sent. For James was keenly interested in this synod, and before his deputies left for Holland he gave them a list of instructions.

> 'They were to inure themselves to the practice of the Latin tongue, that when occasion offered they might deliver their minds with more readiness and facility: they were always to act together, and in every way to promote ecclesiastical peace.'[1]

According to Henson the States 'paid them an allowance of no less than £10 sterling a day, which they spent in keeping a table general, where any fashionable foreigner was courteously and plentifully entertained'.[2] Fortunately we have a brilliant account of the proceedings of the synod; for Sir Dudley Carleton, English Ambassador at the Hague, sent his chaplain,[3] John Hales, to Dort, and the letters[4] which he sent to the ambassador have been preserved.

It is obvious that James chose his deputies with extraordinary care. They were all distinguished men and accomplished theologians. They won the admiration of the whole assembly by the moderation, the clarity, the succinctness of their speeches. They exerted a steadying influence on an assembly in which passion often ran high; of which the president, despite his ability, was at times less than just to say nothing of far from courteous, to those who represented the Arminian point of view.

There is no need to dwell at length upon the synod, since we are only concerned with one of the English deputies – Dr Joseph Hall. The part he played was far less important than that of the Bishop of Llandaff who 'led the deputation', and revealed himself as a man possessed at once of unusual ability and tact. As a matter of fact Hall was ill during most of the time he spent in Dort.

> 'Mr Dean of Worcester is very crazy and sickly of late, and keeps his chamber, neither hath he been in the Synod some of these last sessions.'[5]

He left Dort on January 8th, 1619, and even after he returned to England we find him writing Carleton in the following terms:

> 'From Waltham, April 25th. Since my return I have been twice dead in general rumour, and my dignity (i.e. the Deanery of Worcester) is sued for; yet I still rub out; and hope for as much health as I have lost.'

From Hales we learn that when Hall left Dort the *Praeses* of the synod, the assessors and the secular scribe waited upon him, thanked

[1] H. H. Henson, op. cit., page 29.
[2] H. H. Henson, op. cit., page 29.
[3] 'He was a man, I think, of as great a sharpness, and subtility of wit, as ever this, or, perhaps, any nation bred.' – Bishop Pearson (preface to *The Golden Remains*).
[4] To be found in *The Golden Remains*. Hales attended eighty-four sessions of the synod. After February 7th his place was taken by Balcanqual, who remained until April, when the synod ended.
[5] Hales to Carleton, early in December.

him for his services, expressed the hope of his speedy recovery and asked him to convey to James their gratitude for all that he had done for them through his deputies. He adds:

> 'Mr Dean at his departure had an *honorarium* bestowed on him by the States. Heinsius the Scribe came to his lodging and presented him in the name of the States with *munusculum* as he calls it. What or how much it was no man knows.
>
> 'When in April 1619 the Synod ended, the States presented every English deputy with a golden medal, and added £200 for the expenses of their return journey.'[1]

One feature of the Synod of Dort was a series of Latin sermons by outstanding divines. Out of compliment to England, whose divines were more honoured than those of any other foreign Church (*exteri* as they were called), the first of these sermons was delivered on November 19th by Joseph Hall. When the second Latin sermon was delivered a month later, the preacher began by expressing his delight that he should speak '*post eruditissimum virum Josephum Hallum Decanum Wigornae meritissimum*'.

Those who desire to know what Hall said on this occasion may read the sermon in his collected works. Here we give the summary which Hales sent to Carleton. The views expressed are so characteristic of the preacher (and of his royal master) that they deserve attention:

> 'Upon Thursday Nov. 19th the Synod met together, Mr Dean of Worcester made in the Synod-House a polite and pathetical Latin sermon; the portion of Scripture he chose for his theme was the 17th verse of the 6th of Ecclesiastes, *noli esse justus nimium, neque esto sapiens nimis*. After a witty coming upon his text, how it should come that Righteousness and Wisdom, which are everywhere commended unto us, should here seem to receive a check, he showed how men might seem to be too just; First the Seculars, when sitting in place of Justice they stood too strictly in keeping the Letter of the Law, and by inflicting too heavy punishments, when in equity lighter would serve; next in the second word *sapiens nimis* he taxt the Divines for presuming too far in prying into the Judgments of God, and so came to reprove the curious disputes which our age hath made concerning Predestination; that this Dispute for its endlessness was like the Mathematical line, *divisibilis in semper divisibilia*; that it was in Divinity, as the Rule of *Cos* is in Arithmetick. For the ending of these disputes his advice unto the Synod was, that both parts contending should well consider of St Paul's discourse in the ninth of the Romans, and for their final determination both should exhibit unto the Synod, a plain perspicuous and familiar paraphrase of that Chapter. For if the meaning of that Discourse were once perfectly opened, the question were at an end. For hence he came to exhort them to stand to the former determinations which had hitherto most generally past in the Reformed Churches, in these points: and told

[1] H. H. Henson, op. cit., page 29.

> them that it was an especial part of his Majesties Commission to exhort them to keep unalter'd the former Confessions. How fit it was to open so much of their Commission, and thus to express themselves as a party against the Remonstrants (i.e. the Arminians) your Honour (i.e. Carleton) can best judge. . . . After this he brought a very pathetical conclusion, consisting of a vehement exhortation to peace and union, and so he ended.'

In some respects the Synod of Dort may be regarded as the opposite number of the Council of Trent. Each was profoundly interested in the question of justification by faith: in each there was deep division of opinion. In the former the Calvinist won an overwhelming victory over his Arminian opponent; in the latter the Jesuit triumphed at the expense of those who like Protestants and Jansenists upheld the views of Augustine, and as they believed, St Paul. Yet while there is resemblance, the difference is profound. The decisions reached at Trent are binding on every faithful Catholic for all time to come. It is otherwise with the decrees of the Synod of Dort. 'The conclusions of that synod', said Laud, 'have no authority in this country, and, it is hoped, never will.' Even by English-speaking Presbyterians, who form the vast majority of that body in the world today, the Westminster Confession – liberally interpreted – is regarded as authoritative: whilst, save by ecclesiastical historians, Dort is almost completely ignored.

Thus James's well-meant effort came to nought. In England, after Dort, instead of peace there was renewed warfare. Angry divines persisted in proclaiming their views on the most mysterious of all subjects, and in denouncing those who differed from them, till James gave orders that all such preaching should come to an end, and that the clergy instead of pretending to explain the incomprehensible acts of God, should devote their attention to the spiritual edification of their flocks.

Yet after all no royal fiat could bring such a debate to a speedy end. In all ages determinist and libertarian have been opposed to one another; in future ages their irreconcilable differences are almost certain to continue. In the seventeenth century the banners under which the rival parties fought bore the names of Calvin and Arminius.

Our main concern, however, is not with Dort, but with Joseph Hall. Thirty years after his return from the synod we find him writing to his friend Bishop Davenant in the following terms:

> 'I will live and die in the Suffrage of that Synod of Dort; and I do confidently avow that those other opinions (i.e. the Arminian views of Laud and others) cannot stand with the doctrine of the Church of England.'

Davenant replies:

> 'I know that no man can embrace Arminianism in the doctrines of *predestination and grace* but he must desert the articles agreed on by the Church of England; nor in the point of *perseverance*, but he must vary from the received opinions of our best approved doctors in the English Church.'[1]

Hall may have wavered in his views as to the necessity of episcopacy. On the other burning question of the day he was as firm as a rock. Like most of the bishops and the vast majority of the laity of his time he was an out-and-out Calvinist.

Bishop of Exeter

'Now there arose up a new king over Egypt which knew not Joseph.'

So long as James reigned Joseph Hall was assured of royal favour and support. With the accession of Charles the situation was completely changed; for almost at once Laud became a great influence in affairs of State and head of the Church in all but name.

James had always mistrusted Laud; and that for two reasons. He disliked his Arminian theology and the excessive importance he attached to ritual. He realized, moreover, that no man was more calculated to thwart his purpose of uniting the Church of England and the Church of Scotland on an episcopalian basis than William Laud. When at long last he yielded to the solicitations of his friend and chaplain Dr Williams, and made Laud Bishop of St David's, the old king, who was not lacking in a certain shrewdness, told Williams that he would live to rue the appointment (he did), and expressed his own fears of what would happen when Laud attempted, as he surely would, to *thrust* episcopacy on the Scots by force. 'He knoweth not the stomach of that people.'

In 1622, when hunting in Hampshire, Archbishop Abbot accidentally killed a gamekeeper. His enemies insisted that hunting was no fit sport for a clergyman, and that homicide, even when involuntary, precluded an archbishop from exercising the functions of his office. James, who maintained that 'an angel might have miscarried after this sort', was forced to appoint a commission to settle the question. The ten commissioners were equally divided, and the king gave his casting vote in the archbishop's favour. He did more. He signed a formal pardon and dispensation. In spite of this, however, Abbot was so distressed at what he had done that though he attended James in his last illness and took part in the coronation of his son, he virtually withdrew from public life altogether; and when he refused to license the assize sermon preached by Dr Robert Sibthorp at Northampton on February 16th, 1626/27, which proclaimed the duty of absolute non-resistance to royal demands however arbitrary,

[1] Hall's works (W., X 526).

Charles deprived him of his functions as primate and put them into commission. The old man did not die until 1633; but throughout the last six years of his life Laud virtually governed the Church of England. It is well known that Laud presented Charles on his accession with a certain document. It contained a list of all the important clergy in the Church of England. In one column headed *O* were the names of the 'orthodox' who were marked out for promotion: in another headed *P* were the names of those whom Laud regarded as 'Puritan' who were at best to be passed over, at worst to be punished.

Like James, Hall was at one time suspicious of Laud, and in return Laud was suspicious of Hall. And yet for some reason or other Laud was determined to make Hall a bishop. It may be that there were few clergymen in England who approached Hall in ability and distinction. It may be that Laud was prepared to overlook Hall's Calvinism in view of the fact that from his own standpoint Hall's attitude to Romanists and Dissenters was essentially sound. It may be that as he remembered Hall's puritanical upbringing and his all too favourable view of continental churches and divines, he felt confident that his own indomitable will was strong enough to direct a man of a much more pliable nay even vacillating disposition in the path he was required to follow. In any case we read the following note:[1] 'Matters to move His Majesty for, viz. Dr Hall (for) Ely or Bath and Wells.'

A little later Laud offered Hall the See of Gloucester. This he refused 'with much humble deprecation'. Soon afterwards, however (1627), a new offer was made and accepted. ''Tis known,' said Laud, when defending himself against the charge of promoting none but those of his own way of thinking, 'I preferred Bishop Hall to Exeter.'[2]

With what feelings Hall entered on the duties of his new office we do not know. He had no reason to expect promotion at Laud's hands. For many years the two had not seen eye to eye with one another. At one time, it is almost certain, he regarded Laud very much as James regarded him, as a wrong-headed, narrow-minded martinet born to disturb the peace of Israel. We find him, for instance, writing to Laud in the following terms:

> 'I would I knew where to find you: today you are with the Romanists, tomorrow with us; our adversaries think you ours, and we theirs; your conscience finds you with both and neither. How long will you halt in this indifference?'[3]

He may or may not have recalled an old tag which he had learned

[1] *Calendar of State Papers Domestic*, Supplement D XXV, 21, November 6–16.
[2] Laud's works IV, 297.
[3] Neal II, 152.

at school: *Timeo Danaos et dona ferentes.* We cannot tell. Let us therefore hear his own account of the matter.

> 'Beyond all expectation it pleased God to place me in that Western Charge.'

Then he continues,

> 'which, if the Duke of Buckingham's letters, he being then in France, had arrived but some hours sooner I had been defeated of'.

Buckingham, the king's favourite – the only man, it is said, he ever trusted – was opposed to Hall's appointment. And Buckingham was Laud's friend too. Perhaps Laud himself was dubious of the wisdom of his choice. In any case he kept close watch on Hall's proceedings. 'Some, that sat at the stern of the Church,' says Hall, 'had me in great jealousy for too much favour of Puritanism.' Laud's spies were busy. They reported that Hall was not suppressing 'Lecturers', i.e. Puritan preachers hired by those who preferred their sermons to the services of the established Church; that he was not insisting on the clergy reading the Royal Declaration about the Book of Sports. (To Puritans this order to 'desecrate the Sabbath' by sporting and revelling after Sunday service was iniquitous.) So numerous were the complaints, so well were such criticisms of the newly appointed bishop received at Court that, to use Hall's words,

> 'the billows went so high that I was three several times upon my knee to His Majesty, to answer these great criminations. Under how dark a cloud I was hereupon I was so sensible, that I plainly told the Lord Archbishop of Canterbury, that rather than I would be obnoxious to those slanderous tongues of his misinformers, I would cast up my rochet.'

Hall maintained that up to the last year he spent in Exeter he had no trouble in managing his diocese; that those who disturbed his peace came from without. The fact of the matter was that he had early learned to 'yield to authority' and that – perhaps against his better judgment – he carried out Laud's instructions. In any case, in 1633 Laud writes to the king in the following terms:

> 'For Exeter, where, according to many complaints that had been made here above, I might have expected many things out of order; I must do my Lord the bishop this right, that for your majesty's instructions, they have been carefully observed.'

In 1637 and 1638 the accounts are equally satisfactory. Hall had not the strength of character possessed by Archbishop Abbot who opposed King James on the question of the Essex divorce, and forbade the reading of the king's declaration about Sunday sports, in Croydon Church. He knelt to receive the king's rebuke; he obeyed the Primate, for he was a man of peace. He believed it to be his duty to obey those who were set over him in Church and State. He was not a Luther. He never said – he never could have said, '*Hier stehe ich. Ich kann nicht anders. Gott hilfe mir, Amen*'.

Of how Joseph Hall, who had been reared in a Puritan home and spent his happiest years in a Puritan college, intervened in the dispute between the king and the Scots; of how he wrote a book entitled *Episcopacy by Divine Right* whose every paragraph was submitted to Laud and carefully scrutinized by him before it was published; of how when Laud was arrested Hall wrote another pamphlet, *An humble Remonstrance to the High Court of Parliament by a dutiful son of the Church*; of how this 'Humble Remonstrance', though described by its author as 'meek and gall-less' was regarded by its enemies as 'neither humble nor a remonstrance'; of how Baillie said of it 'The king likes it well, but all else pities it as a most poor piece': of all this we shall hear in a subsequent chapter. The rest of the story is quickly told.

The king showed his appreciation of Hall's services by making him Bishop of Norwich. But the appointment was to bring him little benefit and much unhappiness. For Parliament had made up its mind to do away with bishops. Angry crowds were crying in the streets 'Down with bishops!' The country was weary of Laud and the Star Chamber. One was soon to die; the other to be abolished. Because the Canons (much too Laudian for Parliament at once in their theology and in their insistence on the duty of unquestioning obedience to an absolute king) were produced after Parliament had risen they were condemned as treasonous. In spite of Williams's efforts bishops were expelled from the House of Lords. Bishops were fined great sums of money (though these were not always exacted). In due course the office of bishop was abolished. Hall was assigned a pension of £400 a year (a considerable sum in those days). He tells us he had difficulty in getting even a part of it. His wealth was sequestered. He had to leave his palace. He retired to what he called his 'cottage at Heigham' a mile or two from Norwich. He complained of its size. And to one who had lived in two palaces and before that had at his disposal the great deanery of Worcester, no doubt 'The Dolphin' – though by no means small – seemed a tiny house. His wife, who died in 1652, had a little money of her own; his books continued to sell, even during the Interregnum. But for this, it is said 'he would have been in want of bread'.[1] He continued to preach as opportunity offered. Those who care to do so may still read the sermon which he preached on his eightieth birthday. He even continued to ordain. But in the closing years of his life his activity was chiefly confined to the production of books and pamphlets of a devotional character. These flowed from his pen in a never-ending stream. Over and over again he said 'This is the last book I shall

[1] Jessop, 'History of Norwich' in *Diocesan Histories*.

write'. Over and over again he produced another. He died at Heigham in his eighty-third year on September 8th, 1656.

That Joseph Hall was one of the most distinguished clergymen of his time, there can be no doubt. Jessop says that he was the most distinguished and highly esteemed bishop in England when he came to Norwich in 1641. That perhaps is not saying very much, for bishops at that time were at a heavy discount. But Hall has had admirers ever since. For though he was not a genius like Donne or a saint like Lancelot Andrewes, he was a man of great ability, and of yet greater industry. He was a pioneer in more than one branch of literature, and though he never coined an immortal phrase by which to be remembered, he never wrote a slovenly sentence. Though in all his innumerable pages he never expressed a single idea which some one greater than himself had not conceived long before he was born, he was master of a style at once lucid, concise and attractive: and after all most men are remembered not so much by what they say as by the way in which they say it. Perhaps the best description of Hall's writings is still that of Fuller:[1] 'He was commonly called our English Seneca for his pure, plain, and full style. Not ill at *controversies*, more happy at *comments*, very good in his *characters*, better in his *sermons*, best of all in his *meditations*.'

Before turning to Hall's writings, it may be fitting here to say a word about his character. The purveyor of devotional literature is often apt to identify his own spiritual achievements with the lofty ideals he sets before his readers. From this temptation Hall did not altogether escape. None can deny that he sought to view things *sub specie aeternitatis*; that he taught himself to regard every event in his life, every object that caught his attention, as a means of spiritual edification. He knew that he was esteemed by many, and despite his many protestations of humility there is little doubt that he felt that he was not altogether unworthy of their esteem. Yet, though he himself apparently did not realize it, his character like that of most other men was marred by serious flaws. Living as he did in an age when the key to promotion in the Church, like the key to success in literary effort, lay in the hands of a powerful patron, he early acquired the art of turning a graceful compliment. At times the compliment degenerated if not into fulsome flattery at least into undeserved adulation. When, for instance, he published *A Recollection of Treatises*, in 1615, and dedicated it to the king, he expressed himself in the following terms:

> 'None can be so blind, or enuious, as not to graunt, that the whole Church of God upon earth, rests her-selfe principally (next to her stay above) upon Your Majestie's royall supportation.'

[1] *Worthies*, page 144.

This flattery of powerful patrons, of whom he had many, was offset by the arrogant tones in which he so often addressed his adversaries. He not only underrated Romanist, Brownist, Presbyterian, he made it obvious that he despised them. To those who ventured to oppose him he often attributed, and that quite wrongfully, unworthy motives. Robinson, he said, became a sectary merely because he failed to obtain preferment in Norwich; Milton composed the famous prayer which ends 'Come forth from thy royal chambers O Prince . . .' merely because he sought to gain the hand of a wealthy widow. Hall was an old man before he learned, as we believe he eventually did, to forgive his enemies.

Soon after he was imprisoned in the Tower he wrote to a friend:

> 'Shortly then, knowing nothing by myself, whereby I have deserved to alienate any good heart from me, I shall resolve to rest securely upon the acquitting testimony of a good conscience, and the secret approbation of my Gracious God: who shall one day cause mine innocence to break forth as the morning light, and shall give me beauty for bonds; and, for a light and momentary affliction, an eternal weight of glory.'

This is the way in which Hall habitually regards himself. A few months pass. Hall is stunned by Milton's savage attack. He and his son Robert determine to give Milton tit-for-tat. They scour Cambridge and London for scandalous stories with which to bring baseless charges against Milton's chastity. They publish a venomous pamphlet. Early in 1641 Joseph Hall might boast that he had 'the acquitting testimony of a good conscience, and the secret approbation of his Gracious God': before the year was out he had proved to the world that when 67 years of age, despite his many prayers and spiritual endeavours, he was not yet of that noble but select number who when reviled revile not again. Far from it. Like most men, though unlike his great contemporary John Donne, he never acknowledged his faults or confessed his sins, in public. And just because he was so discreet, and knew so well how to keep silent when silence was of service to reputation, one can never feel quite certain that his self-portraiture is accurate and complete. To us, though not perhaps to himself, his faults are obvious; yet his many virtues far outnumber them. He was a good man; he tried hard to become a saint. According to the measure of his ability he did his utmost to show his fellow men the way wherein they should go, and to help them forward on that journey which is so difficult and painful for us all.

II – SERMONS

I

Of Hall's innumerable sermons[1] only forty-three survive; of these no fewer than twenty were preached before the Court. It is therefore natural that we should say a word of his attitude towards the king.

James had his good points. He was genial and kindly, firmly resolved to save his country from the ravages of war. At the same time he lacked all sense of dignity; his figure was ungainly, his tongue too big for his mouth. His table manners left much to be desired. His court was one of the coarsest and most corrupt in Europe; and he is commonly believed – though the charge has never yet been proved – to have been addicted to a vice which according to the Apostle Paul should not even be named among us. Like many other Scotsmen he took a keen interest in theology, and liked listening to doctrinal sermons especially if they were freely interspersed with Latin tags. In his later days, his favourite preacher was Donne, as all through life his favourite chaplain was Bishop Williams. Next to these in favour came Joseph Hall. Indeed, it is doubtful if any two men in England were more fully agreed in regard to theology, the theory of government in Church and State, and the way in which divine service should be conducted than Joseph Hall and his royal master.

Time was when James had declared that the Anglican Eucharist was nothing better than the Roman Mass without 'the liftings' (i.e. the elevation of the Host) when he had derided the Genevan practice of keeping 'Pasch and Yule'. But these days were over. He had long since grown weary of the forthright utterances of Scottish preachers who denounced him to his face; had come to believe, with Hall, that 'the Spouse of Christ cannot be without her chains and borders'; had learned to prefer the more ornate Anglican service to the stern simplicity of the Genevan rite. Above all he had welcomed the change from the Hildebrandine Church of Scotland in which he was only 'God's silly vassal' to the Erastian Church of England, of which he was now Supreme Governor, under God.

That James was conceited there can be no doubt; he was vain at once of his learning and his wisdom. All courtiers and many if not most of the clergy invited to preach before him took advantage of this and lost no opportunity of ministering to his vanity. Here and

[1] All quotations from sermons are taken either from Pratt's edition (P.) or Wynter's edition (W.).

there one found a man who realized the spiritual danger to which he was exposed when preaching to the king. On one occasion, for instance, Donne said:

> 'Every man that comes with God's message hither brings a little Amaziah of his own (See Amos vii., 10) in his bosom, a little whisperer in his own heart that tells him, *this is the king's chapel, and it is the king's court*, and these woes and judgments, and the denouncers and proclaimers of them are not so acceptable here.'[1]

No such words ever crossed Hall's lips. 'My will', he said, 'hath ever learned to give place to Authority.' Early in life, he had learned like Agag to walk delicately.

Neither Hall nor Donne can be excused for the flattery they offered to their king. In one sermon, for instance, Donne spoke of 'our incomparable King James, the learnedest king, that any age hath produced.'[2] Hall went further. In a sermon preached at Paul's Cross on the tenth anniversary of James's accession, he spoke of the king's 'learning and knowledge wherein he exceedeth all his one hundred and five predecessors'. He then went on to say that the 'King's Justice in governing matched his knowledge of how to govern', praised his 'piety and firmness in religion', claimed that he had 'becalmed the world like Augustus', maintained that 'Rome never had such an adversary' and ended by saying that in England 'government had never before been so happy or so easeful'.[3] In view of all this we are not surprised to learn that when preaching to the king and court he described his Majesty as 'our dread sovereign', 'our Constantine', 'our Solomon', 'our Gideon'.

In the very sermons in which James is addressed in these flattering terms, the morals and manners of the court are vigorously denounced, the injustice and mismanagement which abounded in the country passionately condemned. Yet there is no suggestion that if the easy-going, good-natured king, whose power was admitted by every hearer to be absolute, had chosen to bestir himself he could have banished the drunkard, the blasphemer, the profligate from his court, and transferred the power bestowed on worthless favourites to abler and more upright men.[4]

[1] Sermon XXVI, 354.
[2] Donne's works, page 428.
[3] W., V 106, 7.
[4] Compare this estimate of James with that of a later writer:

> 'It is certain that no king could die less lamented or less esteemed than he was. . . . The great figure that the Crown of England made in Queen Elizabeth's days was so eclipsed, if not totally darkened in his, that he became the scorn and derision of his age; and, while hungry writers flattered him out of measure at home, he was despised by all abroad as a pedant without true judgment, courage or steadiness, subject to his favourites, and delivered up to the counsels, or rather corruptions, of Spain.' – Bishop Burnet's *History of His Own Times*.

II

It has been said that in the eighteenth century the Anglican preacher addressed his hearers in terms which one sensible man of the world might have used in talking to another: in the seventeenth century he always spoke as one who had authority. This authority he claimed to derive from two sources. By James's time, many of the clergy and almost all the hierarchy had come to believe in the doctrine of Apostolic Succession and claimed that Anglican Orders were as valid as those of Rome. True, a large number of the clergy were ignorant men, their morals little if any better than those of their parishioners; yet amongst the hierarchy were men who were universally regarded as amongst the most learned of their time. The learning, so much admired, so essential, as it was believed, in those who kept watch and ward over the Anglican Church when highly skilled representatives of the Counter-Reformation were seeking to undermine it, was chiefly confined to Patristics and the Bible. Hence it is that the printed sermons of a seventeenth-century divine are studded with italics. Occasionally we meet with a Greek word, more rarely with a Hebrew word printed in Hebrew characters. Nearly always however the citation is in Latin; very often even when the words are taken from Holy Scripture, almost always when a Father is quoted, even though he belonged to the Eastern Church and wrote in Greek. To us this display of erudition seems at once ostentatious and superfluous, for in ninety-nine cases out of a hundred the Latin tag is followed by an English translation. We must remember, however, that in those days every boy who went to a grammar school had a knowledge of Latin that few possess today. It was not Ciceronian Latin: it resembled in some respects that of the university orator who has to speak of things of which Cicero never dreamed.

At times quotations served as a guarantee of orthodoxy. Canterbury was anxious to show that she esteemed ancient patristic doctrine at least as highly, perhaps even more highly, than did Rome. The doctrine taught in England, it was claimed, was the doctrine taught centuries before. 'God loves not innovations,' says Donne,[1] 'old doctrines, old disciplines, old words and forms of speech in his service God loves best.' Joseph Hall leaves us in no doubt as to the fact that in this respect he agreed with Donne. At the same time it is well to remember that this is a very different view from that expressed by Bishop Ponet in 1550 when, preaching before Edward VI, he said:

> 'The antiquity of a ceremony or rite does not justify its preservation. That our ancestors have done anything is no reason why we should do it. By this reason, if our forefathers denied Christ, we must also deny Christ.'

[1] Sermon LXII, page 299.

Quotations from the Fathers are numerous, but they are far outnumbered by quotations from the Bible. If the English schoolboy of those days knew far more Latin than most men know today, his knowledge of the Bible was far more thorough than any the average churchgoer can now claim to possess. 'Almost every man', says Donne,[1] '(God be blessed for it) is so accustomed to the text of Scripture, as that he is more affected with the name of David, or St Paul, than with any Seneca or Plutarch.' One single example out of dozens may serve to show how Hall (like other preachers of his time) could assume that a congregation would readily understand and appreciate allusions to characters in the Bible. He is paraphrasing the words of Aquinas in which he tells us that there are nine ways in which we may participate in evil. This is how he does it.

> 'Shortly, if we would save ourselves from the sin of the time, we may not command it, as Jezebel did to the elders of Jezreel; we may not advise it, as Jonadab did to Amnon; we may not consent to it, as Bathsheba did to David; we may not sooth it, as Zidkijah did to Ahab; we may not further it, as Joab did to David; we may not forbear to dissuade it, as Hirah the Adullamite to Judah. . . .'[2]

Hall did not claim to be an original thinker; in fact he boasted that he introduced no novelties and simply handed on to his hearers the doctrine he had received from the Church. Yet there can be little doubt that to all intents and purposes the doctrines which he sought to impress on men's hearts and minds were those of Calvin. To Hall as to most Anglicans of his generation Calvin was the prince of modern commentators. He was the man who stated the doctrinal views of the Reformed Church with a force and clarity to which no other theologian could lay claim. Even when Calvin's influence on England began to decline; when men found favour with Charles (and, in his later days, though to a far less extent, with James) by expressing Arminian views, Hall stuck to his old position. He died, as he had lived, a firm believer in that moderate Calvinism which characterized the English Church in the days of Elizabeth.

Yet if one had asked him whence he derived his views of God and man, he would have pointed neither to Calvin nor to the Early Fathers; he would have replied that he got them from the Bible. To him, as to all his contemporaries in the English Church, the Bible was the Word of God; the sacred writers merely His penmen. In other words he firmly believed in the doctrine of literal inspiration.

Most of the Early Fathers and their medieval followers maintained that scripture to be rightly and fully understood had to be interpreted in a mystical sense. The plain natural sense of scripture, or at least of the many passages in the Old Testament from which but little

[1] IV, 415.
[2] P., V 389; W., V 422.

edification is to be derived, was of small importance compared with the mystical meaning that was supposed to underly it. In this way it was possible for St Bernard to interpret a passionate oriental love song ('The Song of Solomon') as an account of the spiritual communion that exists between the devout soul and Christ. Yet a casual glance at any of the Fathers is enough to show that as often as not this method of interpretation leads to puerilities which at times amuse, at times disgust a modern reader. For, as Dr Scott said, in his criticism of John Mason Neale, who sought to revive it in the nineteenth century, 'At this rate, you may prove any doctrine from any text; everything is reduced to uncertainty, as if the Scripture had no determinate meaning, till one was arbitrarily imposed by the imagination of men'.

Whatever effect the Renaissance had on men's religious opinions, it conferred one lasting benefit on students of scripture. It taught them to seek a text as free from error as man could make it, and to interpret this text in the fairest and most faithful manner, in other words to discover, so far as that was possible, the exact terms in which an ancient writer had expressed himself, the exact meaning he sought to convey. Hall accepted the Renaissance view, but he combined it with the theory of literal inspiration. Hence, like most men of his time, he had to try to reconcile the sentiments attributed to God in the less edifying and more barbaric parts of the Old Testament with the picture given of God by the author of the fourth gospel. It was no easy task. Indeed it is difficult for those who live after the doctrine of development has won the day, after the main work of biblical criticism has been done, to estimate the difficulties with which Hall and his contemporaries were faced. We must frankly acknowledge that there is a deep cleavage between the way in which men like Hall and Donne read the Bible, and the way in which it is read by educated people at the present time. Hence it is that there are many passages in each of these preachers which awaken little response in us; for even if we concede the truth, the eternal truth in some of their statements, we cannot admit that this truth has been obtained by legitimate deduction from a particular text or group of texts. Yet after all, what applies to them applies with almost equal force to much of the rabbinical exegesis of St Paul. Often enough the statement made by the Apostle is equally true and convincing: the strange argument by which it is reached and defended leaves us entirely unmoved.

In one sermon Donne tells us that he had but two themes in all his preaching: Mortality and Immortality. None who knows his writings needs to be reminded of the fact that no English preacher has ever approached him in the moving and eloquent terms in which he spoke concerning death.[1] In the same way there is in Hall one central doctrine, proclaimed, developed by St Paul, Augustine and John Calvin. It is this: Man is a fallen creature. The greatest of humanists, if one may use such an expression with reference to genius so many-sided, so all-embracing as that of Shakespeare, has spoken thus of man:

> 'What a piece of work is a man! How noble in reason! how infinite in faculty! in form, in moving, how express and admirable! in action how like an angel! in apprehension how like a god! the beauty of the world! the paragon of animals!'

Surely it is not too far-fetched to suggest that Hall had this very passage in mind when he said:

> 'There is nothing more wretched than a mere man. We may brag what we will; how noble a creature man is above all the rest; how he is the lord of the world, a world within himself, the mirror of majesty, the visible model of his Maker; but, let me tell you, if we be but men, it had been a thousand times better for us to have been the worst of beasts.'[2]

In the same sermon he says:

> 'Let us not flatter ourselves, Honourable and Beloved: we are all born wolves, bears, tigers, swine, one beast or other. It must needs be a notable change, if of beasts we become men; of men saints.'[3]

'The best fruits of nature', he said on another occasion, 'are but glorious sins; the worst are horrible abominations.'[4] 'If ye be but men, it had been better ye had never been.'[5] If this be the case in spite of all that humanists urge against it, the first duty of a Christian preacher is to awaken men from their sleep of false security, to convince them that they are sinners, to teach them to say: 'Let the rest of our enemies do their worst, only from the evil of our own hearts, good Lord deliver us.'

When we come to consider Hall's satires we shall be impressed by the fact that it is remarkable that a very young man who had lived a sheltered life as student or as don in a strict puritanical college should have possessed such an extensive knowledge of the sins and follies of his time. Meanwhile we have to deal with the fact that there was no living preacher who dealt so often and in such detail with the sins which prevailed in his day and generation. For this we suggest there were three reasons. In the first place, Hall's view of the functions of the ministry. Secondly, the strong puritanical strain in his character. And lastly the fact that as his first published work was satire, so all through life he retained not a little of the satirical spirit.

(1) Unlike the great Scottish preacher, Dr Chalmers, Hall did not

[1] E.g. Vol I, Sermon XII, page 241 ff.
[2] P., V 292; W., V 305.
[3] P., V 291; W., V 304.
[4] P., V 348; W., V 373.
[5] P., V 419; W., V 458.

attach much importance to 'the expulsive power of a new affection'. On the contrary he was convinced that 'before Truth and Righteousness could be established, Falsehood and Wickedness must be destroyed'. The true method of Christian practice, he maintained, is 'first destructive, then astructive'.

> 'Wherefore', he cries, 'hath God put the two-edged sword of the Spirit into the mouths of us his Ministers, but that we should lay about us zealously, in season and out of season, to the hewing down of the overgrown abominations of this sinful age?
>
> 'It is the warrantable and necessary duty of St Peter and all his evangelical successors, when they meet with a froward generation, to call it so. . . . Why do not we follow Peter in the same steps, wherein Peter followed Christ, and Christ his forerunner, and his forerunner the prophets? Who should tell the times of their sins if we be silent?'[1]

Because other preachers neglected this duty, Hall felt keenly that he himself was called upon to perform it. Perhaps he was confirmed in this by the feeling that he had the gifts for its performance in abundant measure. The clergy, he once said, should be 'properly trained so as to deal with evil'; they needed both 'counsel and strength' for 'strength without counsel is like a blind giant, and counsel without strength is like a quick-sighted cripple'. When Joseph Hall girded on his sword to fight with evil, he felt within him the strength of a giant; and he was quite certain that he was not blind.

(2) In the time of King James, as we have already seen, the term Puritan was used in a twofold sense. On the one hand it was used to describe those who desired change at once in the form of worship which obtained in the English Church, and the method in which it was governed. On the other hand it was used to describe those who took a serious, even a somewhat austere, view of life. To begin with, Hall was probably a Puritan in both senses, but he soon came to dislike the Puritan mode of worship and the form of Church government which such Puritans desired to introduce. On the other hand he remained a Puritan in the second sense in which the term was used: he followed the way of life of a Puritan, and a rather strict Puritan at that, all his days.

In early manhood he was delicate and never expected to reach a ripe old age. All through life he was most temperate in his habits. He tells us that he never rose from table without feeling that he could have eaten more. He differed entirely from that bishop who, having to entertain a Scottish minister whom James had summoned to his presence, explained that clerical life in England was much less austere than it was in Scotland. 'After a meal,' he said, 'we refresh ourselves for an hour or two by a game of cards and conversation.' After a

[1] P., V 385; W., V 417.

meal Hall rested for a little, then straightway he returned 'to his book'. It is easy to see why such a man, delicate in constitution, ascetic in habit, was disgusted with the gluttony and drunkenness of his time. There is no sin which he denounced with such vigour and such frequency as drunkenness. It was evidently widely prevalent in those days. 'What street shall a man walk in, and not meet with a drunkard?'[1] To Hall it seemed almost incurable. 'All the world cannot reclaim a drunkard.' None the less he never lost an opportunity of denouncing it. Next only to drunkenness he abhors gluttony and smoking (which he detested as intensely as did his royal master).

> 'In vain shall the vassals of appetite challenge to be the servants of God.'[2]
>
> 'Think not that ye can climb up to heaven with full paunches; reeking ever of Indian smoke, and the surfeits of your gluttonous crammings and quaffings.'[3]

Convinced as he was that it is 'a sad and austere thing to be a Christian',[4] we are not surprised to hear that he desired 'to bring austere abstinence and sober moderation into fashion'.

Like many another moralist Hall disliked the fashions of the day. 'I am sure,' he said, 'from our outward fashions of attire, we need no other dissuasive, than their ugliness and misbecoming.' He is especially severe on women. Some were 'plaster-faced Jezebels'; others were 'wanton dames' who appeared in church with breast 'bare almost to the navel'.[5] He hated 'feathers, peruques, wires, locks, frizzles, powders and such trash'. Of pride in women he says:

> 'The woman was first proud, and it sticks by her ever since. She is none of the daughters of Eve, that inherits not her child's part in this sin. Neither is this feminine pride less odious, less dangerous: rather the weakness of the sex gives power and advantage to the vice; as the faggot-stick will sooner take fire than the log.'[6]

One last quotation, though Hall speaks here rather as a satirist than as a Puritan. Speaking of the transformation of character which is required of us if we are to enter heaven he says:

> 'I see transformations enough everywhere: God knows, too many. I see men transformed into women, in their effeminated dispositions: women transformed to men, in their affectation of masculine boldness and fashions: I see men and women transformed into beasts of all kinds; some, into drunken swine; others into cruel tigers; others into rank goats; others into mimic apes; yea I see these beasts transformed again into devils; in the delight they take in their sin, in their mischievous tempting of others to sin.'

[1] Sermon XIX, P., V 283; W., V 295.
[2] XXVI, 359; W., V 385.
[3] P., V 360; W., V 386.
[4] P., V 359; W., V 385.
[5] P., V 492; W., V 545.
[6] P., V 301; W., V 315.

The enormous stress which Hall laid on the sins of the flesh, is the outcome of that puritan strain in his character to which we have called attention. The Church has always taught – Hall knew this just as well as any man in England – that sins of the flesh, however deplorable, are venial in comparison with the sins of the spirit – malice, uncharitableness and the like. Yet just because he himself disliked feasting and merry-making, because he himself preferred sober garments to brighter and more fashionable attire, he laid disproportionate emphasis on a particular form of sin, whilst certain other sins, which he could have easily detected in each of his royal masters, escaped unscathed. Yet in fairness to Hall it must be admitted that he does not confine his denunciations to the sins of which we have hitherto spoken. In one passage he speaks of the oppression of the poor almost in the tones of an Amos:

> 'What grinding of faces, what racking of rents, what enclosing of Commons, what engrossing of commodities, what griping exactions, what straining the advantages of greatness, what unequal levies of legal payments, what depopulations, what violences abound everywhere.'

Then having once more denounced drunkenness, especially in the clergy, he returns to complete his indictment. He goes on to speak of

> 'bribery and corruption in the seats of judicature: perjuries at the bar: partiality and conniving in magistrates: disorders in those that should be teachers: sacrilege in patrons: simoniacal contracts in unconscionable Levites: oaths: profaneness: cozening in bargains: breaking of pledges: flattering: pride in both sexes but especially in the weaker: contempt of God's messengers: neglect of His ordinances: violation of his days'.

The long list ends with these words: 'We may be forgiven. O Lord forgive.'

(3) We have already seen that Hall claimed to be the earliest English satirist: we now observe that as he never entirely escaped from the puritanical influences of his boyhood and early manhood, there are many passages in his sermons which go to prove that in his denunciation of sin the fervour of a Hebrew prophet was often blended with the spirit of an English satirist. Nowhere is this more clearly seen than in the numerous passages in which he pours out scorn upon the Roman Church.

> 'Let me have no faith if ever playbook were more ridiculous than their Pontifical, and Book of Holy Ceremonies.'[1]

The Pope is 'that Romish Usurper; Peter's successor in nothing but in denying his Master'. The Romanist laity are

[1] Sermon III, 53. P., V 53; W., V 62.

> 'like silly calves which go wherever their dams lead them. Blind obedience is their best guide. Are they bidden to adore a God, which they know the baker made? they fall down upon their knees, and thump their breasts; as beating the heart, that will not enough believe in that pastry-deity'.[1]

Joseph Hall was not the only bishop who expressed himself in such trenchant terms. The point to notice, however, is that his invective is not only bitter, it is contemptuous. In Hall's eyes Romanism was not only false and sinful; it was foolish. None but a fool, he thought, would ever dream of worshipping 'a breaden god'.

There can be little doubt that Hall regarded the drunkard, the glutton, the gaily apparelled courtier, with profound contempt. Though he himself would have said that his heart was filled with 'holy indignation' and with that alone, that he was but following in the footsteps of Amos and Isaiah, the fact remains that most of the sins he so vehemently and so scornfully condemned were sins that made no appeal to him. It is hard to avoid the suspicion that in Joseph Hall there was at least a slight trace of the disposition to

> 'Compound for sins we are inclined to
> By damning sins we have no mind to'.

In secrecy and solitude, Hall, who was truly devout, may have resembled Lancelot Andrewes whose *Private Devotions* (written in Greek) were found at his death 'all slubbered with tears'. Be that as it may, in his public utterances he rarely if ever makes mention of his own sins or refers to the fact that he is a sinner. There is, so far as the present writer remembers, but one exception to this rule. In his powerful sermon on *The Fall of Pride* he tells us 'that there is much affinity between knowledge and pride'. Starting low down in the social ladder he had risen to high estate. A friend of kings and princes, he had many admirers. He was one of the most distinguished members of the English Church. He had done well in life. And there is reason to believe that he not only regarded his success with natural complacency; but was tempted to despise men who were less successful and less gifted than himself. All this suggests that Joseph Hall was tempted by pride, that in his private litany there was this petition: 'From the sin of pride, which has much affinity with knowledge, in respect of which there is a flaw even in the most holy, Good Lord deliver us.' The truth of all this will be felt more clearly, perhaps, if for a moment we compare Hall with his great contemporary John Donne. Like Hall, Donne had won fame as a satirist; yet in after life he said:

[1] XVII. P., V 258; W., V 265.

> 'We make satires; and we look that the world should call that wit; when God knows that that is in great part, self-guiltiness, and we do but reprehend those things which we ourselves have done, we cry out upon the illness of the times, and we make the times ill....'[1]

Compare this with Hall's reticence. Like Simon, who once invited Jesus to his house, Hall had led what the Prayer Book describes as a godly, righteous and sober life. Like the Magdalene, Donne had given way to the lusts of the flesh; had wandered like the Prodigal into the far country. He felt that he had sinned much: he knew that he had been forgiven and that he loved much. 'I date my life', he said, 'from my ministry; for I received mercy as I received the ministry, as the Apostle says.'[2] So overwhelmed was Donne with the sense of the unspeakable mercy which God had shown him, that he broke forth into these words:

> 'Were I to live a hundred years, I would ask no other marrow to my bones, no other wine to my heart, no other light to mine eyes, no other art to my understanding, no other eloquence to my tongue, than the power of apprehending for myself, and the power of deriving and conveying upon others by my ministry, the mercy, the early mercy, the ever lasting mercy of yours, and my God.'[3]

In spite of all their vehemence and skill it is doubtful if the words which Hall employed in passionate denunciation of sin, filled with righteous indignation, as they undoubtedly are, will ever have such power to persuade sinners to abhor evil and to turn to good as these noble words of Donne: to say nothing of the immortal words of the great Apostle when he describes himself as the chief of sinners, who, despite his sins, had received mercy.

'Truth hath no room, till falsehood be removed.'[4] If goodness can be established only after evil has been destroyed, it is equally certain that truth can never be established until error has been overthrown. In Hall's eyes, as one might have supposed, the chief obstacle to the triumph of religious truth, was the doctrine of the Roman Church. Hence his controversial writings; hence, too, the fact that almost every one of his printed sermons includes an attack on Rome. There was, however, another evil to be overcome, and that was schism. Not content with writing letters and pamphlets in which schism was denounced, he constantly appealed to the Government to suppress it by force, and in many sermons hurled anathemas against those who presumed to leave the Established Church. He admitted – he had to admit – that he lived 'in a cold and hollow age, wherein the religion of many was but a fashion, and their piety gilded superstition',[5] that the Church of England included amongst her members

[1] CVIII, 484.
[2] CVI, 454.
[3] CVII, 454.
[4] I, 4.
[5] (I). P., V 17; W., V 18.

many who attended church and received the sacrament once a year ('it matters not how corrupt their hearts, how filthy tongues, how false hands they bring') simply because they were legally compelled to do so; yet, he was convinced that the remedy for this did not lie in 'Separation'. 'We are not tied to avoid the service of God, for the commixture of lewd men; as the foolish Separatists have fancied.'[1]

> 'Let our Recusants, whether out of heresy or faction, make what slight account they please of these holy assemblies, surely the keeping away from the Church is the way to keep out of heaven.'

The only way indeed in which an Englishman could make sure of entering heaven, was to be a faithful member of the Established Church, to accept without criticism or complaint the doctrines she taught; the rites she practised.

> 'It is a bold word, but a true one, "Ye shall never wear his long white robe, unless his servants, your ministers, bring it and put it on". He, that can save you without us, will not save you but by us. He hath not tied himself to means; man, he hath. He could create you immediately to himself; but he will have you begotten by the immortal seed of your spiritual fathers. Woe be to you, therefore, if our word hath lost the power of it in you! You have lost your right in heaven. Let us never come there, if you can come thither ordinarily without us.'

There are perhaps two main reasons for the intensity of the zeal shown by Hall in his attempts to remove evil. A very slight acquaintance with Donne's sermons is sufficient to convince us that he preached 'as a dying man to dying men': that his interest in the grave, to which time's rolling stream bears us so swiftly, is little less than morbid. On his eightieth birthday Hall preached a sermon in which he told his hearers that whilst 80 was a great age to those who looked forward, to him, who looked back, 'it seemed so short that it was gone like a tale that is told, or a dream by night, and looked but like yesterday'.[2] A quarter of a century earlier, when he was as yet in his prime, he told his hearers that 'it was a great way to heaven, and we have but little time wherein to reach it'. 'What shadows we are', said Burke, 'and what shadows we pursue.' More than a century earlier Hall had expressed much the same idea. 'What a flower, a vapour, a smoke, a bubble, a shadow, a dream of a shadow our life is.' The brevity of human life was constantly in Hall's mind. The other thought, ever present, was that he lived in an evil world, was born to trouble as the sparks fly upward. 'If there were any other way to be saved and to get to heaven', said Donne, 'than by being born into this life, I would not choose to come into this world.'[3]

[1] XXXVIII, 389.
[2] (XLII). P., V 582; W., V 651.
[3] CVII, 456.

'O England, England,' cries Hall in one of his latest sermons, 'too like to thy sister Israel, in all her spiritual deformities, if not rather, to thy sister Sodom. Lo thou art haughty as she; and hast committed all her abominations.'[1]

Like many another old man, Hall was inclined to be a *Laudator temporis acti*, to feel that the world was steadily going from bad to worse; that 'it was no good sign, if we be loth to go to our Father's home'. But long before he drew near the gates of death he left no doubt in men's minds that his view of man's life on earth was dark and gloomy. But for his belief in eternal blessedness in the world to come, he would have been ready to agree with Byron (and Donne):

> 'Count o'er the joys thine hours have seen
> Count o'er thy days from anguish free
> And know whatever thou has been
> 'T is something better not to be.'

> 'In the few minutes of our life, how are our drachms of pleasure lost in our pounds of gall! Anguish of soul, troubles of mind, distempers of body, losses of estate, blemishes of reputation, miscarriages of children, miscasualties, unquietness, pains, griefs, fears take up our hearts; and forbid us to enjoy, not happiness, but our very selves; so as our whole life sits, like Augustus, *inter suspiria et lachrymas*, between sighs and tears: and all these hasten us on to our end; and, woe is me, how soon is that upon us!'[2]

If England were to be saved, it was essential that the errors of Romanist and schismatic should be suppressed, not only by reasoned argument; but also by the exercise of physical force. Yet even this was inadequate. A further condition had to be fulfilled. Those who transgressed the law must be 'made to smart'. When we remember the way in which Hall spoke of the torments of the damned, we are quite prepared to believe that he offered no protest against the cruel and vindictive sentences which were then passed on those who offended against the laws of Church and State.

> 'Thus justice hath stocks for the vagrant; whips for harlots; brands, for petty larzons; ropes, for felons; weights, for the contumaciously silent; stakes, for blasphemous heretics; gibbets, for murderers; the hurdle, the knife, and the pole, for traitors; and upon all these engines of justice, hangs the garland of peace. . . . Ye never see Justice painted without a sword: when that sword glitters with use, it is well with the public: woe be to the nation, where it rusts! There can be no more acceptable sacrifice, than the blood of the flagitious. . . . The blood of traitors shed by the sword of Justice, is a well of oil to fatten and refresh the Commonwealth. . . . No marvel, if one of those four things, which Isabel of Spain was wont to say she loved to see, were "A thief upon the ladder". Even through his halter might she see the prospect of peace.'

[1] P., V 565; W., V 631.
[2] P., V 417; W., V 455.

But after all, the destruction of evil and the uprooting of error is merely negative, but an essential preliminary to the process of reform. Nature abhors a vacuum.

> 'When the unclean spirit is gone out of a man . . . he returns to the house whence he had gone out, and finding it empty, swept, and garnished, he goes out and returns bringing with him seven other spirits more wicked than himself. They enter in and dwell there, and the last state of that man is worse than the first.'[1]

Therefore religious truth must be instilled into the minds of Englishmen: and by religious truth Hall undoubtedly meant orthodox opinion. We have already seen reason to believe that for him at least orthodox opinion meant that moderate (or modified) Calvinism which was the hall-mark of the Elizabethan Church. Never, one may say with confidence, was so much theology taught in England. For not only did everyone *have* to attend the parish church and listen week by week to the dogmas expounded by duly authorized ministers of the National Church; in every grammar school the boys were drilled in Nowell's Latin catechism. On Sunday the schoolmaster took his pupils to church. On their return to school, the younger boys were expected to know the 'heads' of the sermon; the elder boys were asked to give a résumé of what the preacher had said. It is impossible to believe that boys could really understand the intricate dogmas they were taught; still less that they could relate them to actual life. None the less it is certain that schoolmaster and preacher alike did his utmost to make boys familiar with the theological terms in which such dogmas were expressed. To the men of that time, this seemed to be of vital importance. 'He hath not learned to spell', wrote Donne,[2] 'that hath not learnt the Trinity; not learnt to pronounce the first word, that cannot bring three persons into one God.'

In emphasizing the dogmatic character of so many of Hall's sermons, we must not be understood to suggest that a preacher so able as he undoubtedly was, could not distinguish between a sermon and a lecture. 'To what purpose', he once asked, 'should I read a Metaphysical Lecture to Courtiers?'[3] Unlike the ancient Greeks he did not identify knowledge with virtue. None the less he laid such stress on the possession of religious knowledge, as to give it a place in the religious life out of all proportion to its importance.

Two results, one immediate, one more remote, followed from the extraordinary emphasis laid on dogmatic orthodoxy by men like Donne and Hall.

(*a*) So often did they tell their hearers that the Pope was not infallible and that Rome misinterpreted the Scriptures, that from the

[1] Matt. xii, 43–5.
[2] CVIII, 24.
[3] (XI). P., V 184; W., V 175.

first there were many Englishmen who believed that the criticism passed on Rome by Anglican bishops and divines, might be applied to themselves. For if it were true that the Gospel message was intended for all, that Scripture contained the sole rule of faith and duty; if, as Anglican preachers admitted, the most learned divines differ in their interpretation of Scripture; if, in the last resort, man has to depend on the light of conscience and the guidance of the Holy Spirit: then it was quite possible that 'the babes' might be right, that 'the wise and prudent' might be wrong. In any case, no Englishman who came under the influence of the Reformation, regarded a preacher, even though he were a saintly bishop or a learned divine, as the devout Romanist regarded the most ignorant and sinful priest. Wherever blind faith and implicit obedience gave place to Bible study, and the exercise of private judgment, differences of opinion were bound to arise. In England they *did* arise. Men questioned episcopal views in regard to the way in which God was to be worshipped, the Church was to be governed, the words of Scripture were to be understood.

As early as 1628 we find Hall speaking with contempt of the religious views of laymen and the sermons of unqualified preachers.

> 'There is an audacious and factious liberty of this loose film; which not only untutored scholars take to themselves under the name of *libertas prophetandi*, pestering both presses and pulpits with their bold and brainsick fancies; but unlearned tradesmen, and tattling gossips too; with whom, deep questions of divinity, and censures of their teachers, are grown into common table-talk; and preremptory decisions of theological problems is as ordinary as backbiting their neighbours.'[1]

To some extent, we can, of course, sympathize with Hall. 'A little learning is a dangerous thing.' Those who possess it often draw false conclusions from premises which they do not understand. The professional is apt to look with suspicion on the amateur; the university man on one who is more or less self-taught. All the same Hall was to learn to his bitter cost that there were laymen in England who could argue about theology as ably as himself. One of these, however unorthodox his views, was John Milton. That then, was the first result of the prominence given to theology (as distinguished from religion) in church and school. Anglican and Puritan fought to the death.

(*b*) The second was this. Within the short space of twenty years the king (a devout Anglo-Catholic) lost his head, the Archbishop of Canterbury was executed, the use of the Prayer Book forbidden. All this Joseph Hall saw and bewailed. Had he lived six years longer he would have seen the monarchy restored, the Act of Uniformity

[1] P., V 367; W., V 394.

passed, two thousand puritan clergy ejected from their livings. All this led to the inevitable swing of the pendulum. And just as in Germany the perennial stream of polemical sermons in Lutheran pulpits, in which preachers spent so much time in defending their own doctrines and in launching bitter attacks on the views of their Romanist and Calvinist opponents, drove men to seek peace, either in Pietism – a form of intense evangelicalism and biblicism – or in Rationalism: so in England, the national Church, having got rid of Puritans, sank into that deep spiritual torpor, from which she was aroused at long last by the Methodist movement and the Evangelical revival. Educated men turned away, with increasing impatience, from a religion of dogmatic authority, whose exponents professed to lay bare the hidden Counsels of the Almighty, and took refuge in what they called Natural Theology, a form of rationalism, which professed to expound that creedless, undogmatic form of religion, which many in those days claimed to be the real religion of all sensible men.

Hall's Technique

Having dealt with the substance of Hall's preaching, we must now consider the way in which he presented his message to his hearers. In those days the average length of a sermon was an hour, though it was often much longer; and it was not easy then, as it is not easy now, for any speaker to retain the close attention of his hearers for so long a period. Like Donne, Hall resisted a temptation to which many succumbed. He refused to introduce 'novelties' and he abstained from any display of wit.

> 'If your curiosity extort more than convenient ornament, in delivery of the word of God, you may have a good oration, a good panegyric, a good encomiastic, but not so good a sermon.'[1]

Hall was intensely conservative. 'The old way, saith the Prophet, is the good way: every novelty carries suspicion in the face of it.'[2] Therefore we are not surprised to hear him condemn the new style of preaching which some were seeking to introduce:

> 'Certainly there cannot be a more certain argument of a decayed and sickly stomach, than the loathing of wholesome and solid food, and longing after fine *quelques choses* of new and artificial composition. For us; away with this vain affectation in the matters of God. Surely, if aught under heaven go down better with us than the savoury viands of Christ and Him crucified; of faith and repentance, and those plainly dressed, without all the lards and sauces of human devices; to say no worse, our souls are sick, and we feel it not.[3]
>
> 'I have heard some preachers, that have affected a pleasantness

[1] Donne, Vol. IV, 414–5.
[2] P., V 467; W., V 515.
[3] P., V 207; W., V 202.

> of discourse in their sermons; and never think they have done well, but when they see their hearers smile at their expressions. . . . Surely jigs at a Funeral, and laughter at a Sermon, are things prodigiously unseasonable. It will be long, my Beloved, ere a merry preacher shall bring you to heaven.'[1]

Hall's sermons, then, are and were intended to be, grave and dignified. Like Donne, he felt convinced that 'Extemporal, unpremeditated sermons, that serve the popular ear, vent, for the most part, doctrines that disquiet the Church'.[2]

(1) Many men have won popular favour through what may be described as *motto preaching*. That is to say they have selected a few striking words of Scripture, and professed to find in them a theme which they developed without further reference to their text. They have done this because there is no form of preaching which makes such heavy demands alike on preacher and hearer, as that which is termed 'expository preaching'. Every one of Hall's sermons is of an expository character. If then, Hall eschewed so many means of winning popularity, if he refused to deal with 'attractive subjects', to introduce novelties of any kind; if he rejected every opportunity of appearing witty and clever; if on every occasion he handled great themes in a grave manner; how, it may be asked, did he win favour with those who heard him preach? In the first place, he showed great skill in the selection of his text and the opening words of his sermon. On one occasion, for instance, when he preached in Gray's Inn, his subject was *The Great Imposter*; his text, 'The heart is deceitful above all things';[3] his opening words:

> 'I know where I am; in one of the great Phrontiseries of Law and Justice. Wherefore serve Law and Justice, but for the prevention or the punishment of fraud and wickedness? Give me leave, therefore, to bring before you, Students, Masters, Fathers, Oracles of law and justice, the greatest cheater and Malefactor in the world: our own Heart.'[4]

On another occasion, when preaching before the rich merchants of London on behalf of a charity, the title of his sermon was *The Righteous Mammon*; his text, 1 Tim. vi. 17, 18, 19: 'Charge them that are rich in this world . . .'; his opening words:

> 'These things, which are excellent and beneficial in their use, are dangerous in their miscarriage. It were lost labour, for me to persuade you how good riches are: your pains and your cares are sufficient proofs of your estimation; and how deadly the abuse of them is, many a soul feels, that cannot return to complain. There is nothing more necessary therefore for a Christian heart, than to be rectified in the managing of a proper estate, and to learn so to be happy here, that it may be more happy hereafter; a task, which

[1] P., V 210.
[2] Donne, IV 442.
[3] Jer. xvii. 9.
[4] P., V 132; W., V 158.

> this Text of ours undertakes; and, if ye be not wanting to it and yourselves will be sure to perform. What should I need to intreat your attention, Right Worshipful and Beloved, to a business so near concerning you? The errand is God's; the use of it yours.'[1]

The Thirty Years' War is being waged. Hall preaches before the Court. His subject is Saint Paul's combat; his text 1 Cor. xv. 32: 'If after the manner of men, I have fought with beasts at Ephesus': his opening words:

> 'Our Saviour foretold us, that these last days should be quarrelsome. All the world doth either act, or talk of fighting. Give me leave therefore, to fall upon the common theme of the times; and to tell you of a Holy Combat.'[2]

These examples, which could be easily multiplied, may serve to show Hall's method. He asks himself, as it were, What is the message which I must take to this particular congregation, at this particular time? What text of Scripture best suggests it? How can I expound my text in the most profitable and convincing manner? One example must serve to show how Hall tried, on occasion, to impress his text on the minds of his hearers, by the use of paradox. He was the last of a series of bishops who were asked to prepare the Court for the National Fast which Charles appointed in 1628. His subject was *The Christian's crucifixion with Christ*; his text, 'I am crucified with Christ: nevertheless I live; yet not I, but Christ liveth in me'. (Gal. ii. 20). This is how he begins:

> 'He, that was once tossed in the confluence of two seas, was once no less straitened in his resolutions betwixt life and death; Neither doth my text argue him in any other case here; as there, he knew not whether he should choose; so here, he knew not whether he had. *I am crucified*; there he is dead: *yet I live*: there he is alive again: *yet not I*: he lives not: *but Christ in me*: there he more than lives. This holy correction makes my text full of wonders; full of sacred riddles. (1) The living God is dead upon the Cross. (2) St Paul, who died by the sword, dies on the Cross. . . .'[3]

Finally one example must suffice to show the way in which at times (though not often) he sought to arouse the interest of his hearers by stirring up their curiosity. He is preaching a very long sermon before the Court. It was divided into two parts, and a year elapsed between the delivery of the first part and the delivery of the second. His subject is: *The Impress of God*; his text Zech. xiv. 20:

> 'In that day shall be written upon the bridles (or bells) of the horses, Holiness unto the Lord: and the pots of the Lord's house shall be like the bowls before the altar.'

His opening words are these:

[1] P., V 99; W., V 118.
[2] P., V 319; W., V 337.
[3] P., V 355; W., V 380.

> 'If any man wonder whither this discourse can tend; let him consider that of Tertullian, *Ratio divina in medulla est, non in superficie*. These Horses, if they be well managed, will prove like those fiery horses of Elijah, to carry us up to heaven: these Bells, like those golden Bells of Aaron's robe; these Pots, like that *Olla pulmenti* of the prophets after Elisha's meal: and these Bowls, like that blessed and fruitful navel of the Church.'[1]

(2) In his analysis of the text, Hall is always simple. As against the Puritan preachers of the next generation, who divided their texts into a number of 'heads', and each head into a number of 'points', he rarely has more than three heads, and these are never too much subdivided. The heads are given very early in the course of the sermon and thus the hearers are enabled to follow the argument step by step. In his analysis Hall displays great skill. His divisions seem simple and natural. Closer inspection reveals the fact that their excellence is largely due to the art which conceals art. Hall did not like to see men taking notes of his sermons (a common practice in those days). Yet anyone who cared to do so would have very little difficulty in reproducing the outline which the preacher had in front of him when he wrote out his sermon.

(3) One of the characteristics of Hall's preaching which makes his sermons attractive to a modern reader, and must have helped to maintain interest in those who heard them, is that he never uses an abstract noun when a concrete noun will serve his purpose. To use a distinction that was once common in logic, he always prefers the inductive to the deductive method. That is to say, he prefers to speak of those who exhibit various aspects of a virtue in their lives, rather than to analyse the virtue as an abstract concept. He is able to do this because he has such a magnificent knowledge of the Bible. In addition, however, he is able to draw on an apparently inexhaustible supply of illustrations from his Commonplace Books. In this respect ecclesiastical history is perhaps his richest mine; but he makes use of classical history, English history and books of travel. There are some references to Chaucer and other English poets, though these are far less numerous than references to the Classics – even these are not very common. Occasionally he makes use of a story which he has been told or has read in some book, when it suits his purpose. In addition to all this, although his sermons, like those of all his contemporaries, are filled with Latin quotations from the Fathers, they contain passages of English as simple and beautiful as that of Bunyan: and, when he tries to do so, he can paint a picture almost as vivid as one painted by Defoe.[2]

[1] Cant. vii. 2. P., V 47; W., V 54.
[2] E.g. (*a*) The vivid description of refugees from the Plague (1624) (P., V 253; W., V 259); (*b*) The description of Adam and Eve when expelled from Paradise (*Contemplations*, Vol. I).

(4) Hall had a great advantage over many of his contemporaries in his preference for the short sentence to the lengthy paragraph. Anyone who has struggled with the intricacies of German philosophy, will remember how a difficult task was made yet more difficult by the constant use of lengthy periods consisting of an apparently endless sequence of subordinate clauses, each qualifying or amplifying the main statement. Such writing is hard enough to read for oneself: to hear it read aloud by another is for most Englishmen, almost intolerable. In *A Preface to Milton*, C. S. Lewis has shown that the greatness of *Paradise Lost* is not to be sought in isolated lines torn from their context; but in a great mass of verse taken as a whole. Milton disliked Hall's short sentences and compared them to the breathings of an asthmatic. Few will venture to deny the splendour of Milton's prose at its best. Many good judges say that its noblest passages are unequalled for eloquence and grandeur in English literature.[1] But as with his verse, so with his prose. He thinks in periods (not in sentences), whose full beauty is realized not by dwelling on this or that immortal phrase, but by regarding the massive period as a magnificent whole. Yet anyone who listens to a passage of the Areopagitica read aloud, will realize that it demands far closer attention than a prose passage which consists of a series of short complete sentences. Hall was one of the first to abandon the elaborate period for the short simple sentence.

(5) Readers of the Psalter will remember that Hebrew verse is built up on antiphonal lines. A statement is made; a response follows. At times the 'response' merely reiterates, in different words, the opening statement.

> 'For in death there is no remembrance of thee:
> in the grave who shall give thee thanks?'

At times the 'response' presents an antithesis.

> 'The young lions do lack, and suffer hunger:
> but they that seek the Lord shall not want any good thing.'

Hall loves such antithesis and makes constant use of it. No doubt it helped men to remember his sermons.

He is equally fond of aphorisms. He loves to express a great truth in a short, pithy sentence. At times, though not often, 'The English Seneca', as men called him, descends to sententious platitudes: much more frequently he succeeds. Here are a few examples:

(1) The heart of man lies in a narrow room: yet all the world cannot fill it.[2]

(2) If Truth be the mother of Hatred, she is the daughter of Time.

[1] 'His gorgeous prose.' – Tillyard.
[2] P., V 133; W., V 159.

(3) As every obedience serves God, so every sin makes God serve us.
(4) In vain shall ye plead the goodness of your heart, if ye be careless of your heels and elbows.[1]
(5) God himself was the first Herald and shall be the last.[2]
(6) Let the rest of our enemies do their worst, only from the evil of our own hearts, good Lord deliver us.[3]
(7) God will never thank you for keeping his counsel: he will thank you for divulging it.[4]
(8) The best fruits of nature are but glorious sins; the worst are horrible abominations.[5]
(9) The conscience is but God's bailiff.[6]
(10) He that says there is no God, is a vocal atheist: he that lives as if there were no God, is a vital atheist.[7]
(11) The World makes a God of itself; and would be serving any God but the true one.[8]
(12) Every day, therefore, must be a Good Friday of a Christian.

(6) The powers of eloquence possessed by Donne, and in yet greater measure, perhaps, by Milton, were denied to Hall. He was at once incapable of lofty rhetoric, and suspicious of it. The only sermon, perhaps, in which he shows what he might have accomplished had he striven after eloquence, is his sermon on the Passion, where at times, intensity of feeling proves too strong for habitual, deliberate restraint.

To complete the picture we have sought to give of Hall as preacher and to prevent distortion, three further facts must be borne in mind.

(*a*) Every sermon is not moulded on one pattern. In one, for instance which he preached at Paul's Cross on *Pharisaism and Christianity*, the description of the various types of the ancient Pharisees is so elaborate, so overweighted with learning, that the introduction must have wearied many of his hearers. He felt this himself: 'There is no point wherein it is more difficult to avoid variety, yea ostentation of reading.'[9] At the opposite extreme, there is a sermon preached to the lawyers of Gray's Inn on *The Fashions of the World*, which reminds one of nothing so much as the Bible-reading, once popular with the devout in Victorian times.

(*b*) In spite of all his controversial works Hall cherished the vision of one Protestant Church, embracing the various national Churches, united in resistance to the errors of Rome. He hoped that to this end Lutheran and Calvinist – yes, even Zwinglian – might reach agreement in regard to the doctrine of the Eucharist; that in God's good

[1] P., V 208; W., V 204.
[2] P., V 49; W., V 58.
[3] IX, 41.
[4] P., V 206; W., V 201.
[5] P., V 348; W., V 373.
[6] P., V 370; W., V 399.
[7] XXIX. P., V 403.
[8] P., V 285; W., V 297.
[9] P., V 4; W., V 3.

time the Calvinistic Churches of France, Holland and Scotland, might see their way to accept that episcopal form of Church government which had persisted throughout so many centuries. In 1608 he said:

> 'Say the Papists, "One saith I am Calvin's; another Luther's". We disclaim, we defy these titles, these divisions: we are one in truth; would God we were yet more one! It is the lace and fringe of Christ's garment, that is questioned among us: the cloth is sound.'[1]

Yet like all others who have striven for any form of Church reunion, Hall realized the difficulties that stood in the way of realizing his dream.

> 'The God of Heaven, before whom I stand, from whom I speak, knows how oft, how deeply, I have mourned for the divisions of his Church: how earnestly I have set my hand on work on such poor thoughts of reunion, as my meanness could reach: but, when all is done, I still found we may not offer to sell Truth for peace.'

In spite of Laud's efforts to persuade men that ritual was a matter of paramount importance, in spite of the strong pressure that Laud put upon Hall to agree with him, in spite of the fact that Hall's powers of resistance were feeble when compared with the iron will of Laud, there can be no doubt that throughout the whole of his life Hall attached little importance to ritual and was in no way perturbed when he found great variety of ceremonial amongst the different members of the Reformed Church. In 1641 he preached a sermon before the Court on *The Mischief of Faction and the Remedy of it.*

> '"This man is right," ye say, "that man is not right; this sound; that rotten." And how so, Dear Christians? What! for ceremonies and circumstances, for rochets or rounds, or squares? Let me tell you, he is right, that hath a right heart to his God, what forms soever he is for. The Kingdom of God doth not stand in meats and drinks; in stuffs or colours, or fashions, in noises, or gesture; it stands in holiness and righteousness; in godliness and charity; in peace and obedience; and, if we have happily attained unto these, God doth not stand upon trifles and niceties of indifference; and why should we?'[2]

(*c*) Some of Donne's most moving sermons might have been delivered in a Methodist chapel. He did not hesitate to display emotion. He was ready to reveal his most intimate personal experience. In Hall there is none of this. An out-and-out Calvinist, he presents his message in a purely objective manner. Like the Baptist he is content to be only 'a Voice', a voice which proclaims the divine message. As he stands in the pulpit he bids men forget the messenger

[1] P., V 5; W., V 4.
[2] W., V 517.

in the message. As 'man's chief end is to glorify God'; so the preacher's chief end is to speak of God; not of himself.

(*d*) Despite this, however, it is obvious that Hall loved his Saviour and earnestly desired to persuade his fellows to love and trust the Lord.

> 'He is thine, and thou art his; if thy hold seem loosened; his is not. When temptations will not let thee see him, he sees thee and possesses thee: only believe him against sense, above hope; and, though he kill thee, yet trust in him.'[1]

The man who could speak like this was a born preacher. He knew, at once, what to say, and how to say it.

[1] W., V 51.

III – CONTEMPLATIONS

The book on which Hall's fame as a religious writer chiefly, if not almost entirely depends, is entitled *Contemplations upon the Principal Passages in the Holy Story*. Its composition was his main interest during the twenty best years of his life, and it has found more readers and admirers than all his other works put together. It consists of 142 meditations on Old Testament stories and forty-nine on stories from the New Testament.[1]

Hall was convinced that he had found an entirely new method of expounding scriptural truth, which differed at once from the allegorical explanations of the Fathers and the expositions offered by the preachers of his time. As was his wont, he insisted that his work was 'a poor thing': with equal emphasis he maintained that it was 'his own'. 'These thoughts, such as they are, through the blessing of God, I have woven out of myself.' (P., I 37; W., I 43.) He tells us that throughout the greater part of his ministerial career he found his greatest happiness in writing these contemplations. From them he turned reluctantly to undertake the many tasks imposed upon him by his 'Royal Master': to them he returned with zest when these tasks had been faithfully performed. As the claims on his time became more and more exacting, he tells us that he devoted every moment that he could 'beg or borrow' from his other labours to the completion of this work. Whether it was good or bad, profitable or unprofitable, he had done his best.

'The words of the Shunamite to Elisha', says Hall, 'were short, quick, and pithy.' This is as good a description as any of his own work. 'I have so done my task', he says, 'as fearing not affecting length; and as careful to avoid cloying of my reader with other men's thoughts.'

Before writing a contemplation he dealt with its theme in a sermon. Then and then only did he proceed 'to gather the quintessence of those larger discourses into these forms of Meditation'. The sermon he compared to the ore: the meditation to the 'wedge of metal' which emerged from it. In contrast to his sermons, which resemble those of other seventeenth-century preachers in their ostentatious and wearisome display of learning, Hall's *Contemplations* are written in the simplest language. Paragraphs and sentences are equally short. No direct reference is made to any commentator, ancient or modern. There are no Latin quotations, no textual criticism; only a few references to Papists; none to Dissenters. There

[1] For some unexplained reason two sermons are included in the book.

is no reference to Anglican dogma; little, if any direct reference to dogma of any kind at all. It is as though Joseph Hall deliberately shut the door on controversy, on all display of elaborate scholarship, on argument of any kind, in order that he might enjoy uninterrupted communion with his Maker. Believing, as he did, that in the Bible God speaks to the human heart, he was content to listen to the heavenly voice, to meditate on the divine message, to kindle his imagination, to allow his mind to be filled with that sense of admiration and awe which was aroused in Kant by the starry heavens above, and the moral law within, to give grateful and adoring thanks for light received; to ask humbly for grace to follow the path which the divine light revealed. For we must bear in mind that when he first began these contemplations he did so for the good of his own soul. Only after he had proved by personal experience the benefit he had derived from such meditation did he begin to write out his *Contemplations* and publish them in the hope that what had brought so much happiness and comfort to himself might prove of like benefit to his fellow men.

Dante tells us that he heard a voice saying 'Make thou thy vision fully manifest.' 'Seldom if ever', says Hall, 'was knowledge given to keep, but to impart.' 'If these my thoughts shall be approved beneficial to any soul, I am rich. I shall vow my prayers to their success.' He spoke of his work as his 'divine task', the 'issue of time and thoughts', in which his 'joy and crown' would be 'the edification of many'.

More than three hundred years have come and gone since the last of Hall's *Contemplations* was given to the world, and during these three centuries many changes have taken place in men's minds. In his *Elizabethan Background*, Professor Tillyard has shown that in many respects the Elizabethan belonged rather to the medieval than to the modern world. Between his cosmology and ours there is a great gulf fixed. In view of the fact, therefore, that the great majority of the contemplations deal with the Old Testament and were written before the science of biblical criticism came into existence, it is inevitable that one should ask what difference this makes to those who read them now. The answer is not difficult to give. The modern man firmly believes in the doctrine of development; is convinced that if he desires to obtain a true idea of the divine nature, he is well advised to turn to the Fourth Gospel rather than to the Book of Judges. Such an idea is alien to the mind of Joseph Hall.

It may be, as some urge, that the doctrine of the literal inspiration of Holy Scripture is absent from the Thirty-nine Articles and the Westminster Confession; none the less it is certain that Hall like his contemporaries firmly believed that every sentence in the Old Testament was dictated by the Almighty to 'his penmen', as he terms the various authors to whom these writings are ascribed. Thus for Hall the story of the Garden of Eden is not a myth inspired by God, as most Christians now believe. It is the record of an actual occurrence whose historic accuracy is guaranteed by God. In the same way, because we are told in the Old Testament that Elisha made an axe-head swim, and that the sun stood still in Ajalon, we are compelled to believe these stories since their sole author is the Almighty. This view of literal inspiration, which the Bible nowhere claims for itself, leads Hall into many difficulties; compels him in fact over and over again to present us with a sub-Christian view of God.

Sub-Christian Views of God

It is unfortunate that pressure of affairs prevented Hall from devoting as much space to his contemplations on the New Testament as he gave to the Old. This leads to a certain amount of distortion, and one is apt to leave the *Contemplations* with the feeling that Hall does less than justice to the view of God set forth in Christ. His belief in literal inspiration involved him, as we have already said, in many difficulties. In the Old Testament many cruel commands are ascribed to God. Hall's moral sense revolts against them: yet throughout he tries, as did a greater, to justify the ways of God to man. He lived in a cruel age and was far from being a sentimentalist. He knew how men were tortured to wring from them a confession of guilt. 'God's judgments', he says, 'are the rack of godless men; if one strain make them not confess, let them be stretched by one wrench higher, and they cannot be silent.' (P., I 273; W., I 330.) In Hall's time capital punishment was not restricted to murderers. He seldom expresses any pity for the hapless man on the scaffold. He always assumed his guilt. 'There is no less charity than justice', he says, 'in punishing sinners with death: God delights no less in a killing mercy, than in a pitiful justice.' (P., I 109; W., I 131.) 'There cannot be a better sacrifice to God than the blood of malefactors.' (P., I 110; W., I 131.) When the much needed rain followed the killing of the priests of Baal, Hall tells us that 'A few drops of blood have procured large showers from heaven. A few carcasses are a rich compost to the earth.' (P., I 413; W., I 502.) If man sins he must suffer. 'The messengers of God's wrath fly forth at the least beck; and fulfil the will of his revenge upon those, whose obedience would not fulfil the will of his command.' (P., II 69; W., II 143.)

In every religion there is a great deal of anthropomorphism: man, it would seem, can only speak of God in human terms. As truly as God made man in his own image; so ever since man has been making God in his own image. Today we speak of divine retribution; in

Hall's time men spoke of God's revenge. No doubt the two terms are intended to convey much the same meaning; yet to a modern reader the term revenge has a more limited connotation than it bore in Hall's time, and rarely fails to convey a suggestion of personal animosity entirely out of keeping with the nature of God. Despite the plain teaching of the New Testament, Hall's view of literal inspiration led him to say 'An eye for an eye, was God's rule'. (P., I 370; W., I 448.) 'It is happy that God hath such store of plagues and thunderbolts for the wicked; if he had not a fire of judgment, wherewith the iron hearts of men might be made flexible, he would want obedience, and the world peace.' (P., I 274; W., I 331.) 'The view of God's revenge, is so much more pleasing to a good heart than his own, by how much it is more just and full.'

That which apart from revelation would be termed cruelty is not really cruelty at all: it is the vengeance of God. Thus it is that Jael, who murdered a fugitive guest, is praised since it was God who 'put this instinct into her heart, and strength into her hand'. It was God who 'guided Sisera to her tent, and guided the nail through his temples'. (P., I 189; W., I 229.) It was God who ordered the massacre at Jericho in which men and women, infants and sucklings, oxen and sheep, camels and asses were put to death. Were it not that God had an 'old quarrel' with certain people, 'David could not be excused from a bloody cruelty, in killing whole countries, only for the benefit of the spoil; now, his soldiers were at once, God's executioners, and their own foragers'. (P., I 342; W., I 424.)

Such instances are almost innumerable. Let one more suffice. Elijah kills the priests of Baal. This is Hall's comment:

> 'Let no man complain that those holy hands were bloody. This sacrifice was no less pleasing to God, than that other. . . . Far be it from us, to accuse God's commands or executions of cruelty. It was the ancient and peremptory charge of God, that the authors of idolatry and seduction should die the death: no eye, no hand might spare them. . . . It is a merciful and thankworthy severity, to rid the world of the ringleaders of wickedness.' (P., I 487; W., II 50.)

The only relief which Hall can offer to believers in literal inspiration when men say, as say they must, that mass murder either in Old Testament times, or in our own, is an abomination to the Lord, is given in these words:

> 'It is not for the holy severity of God, to stand at the bar of our corrupted judgment. . . . The holy severity of God in the revenge of sin sometimes goes so far, that our ignorance is ready to mistake it for cruelty.' (P., I 83.) 'It is not for us to examine the charges of the Almighty. Be they never so harsh or improbable, if they be once known for his, there is no way but obedience, or death.' (P., II 7; W., II 68.)

'If they be once known for his.' There lies the crux of the whole matter. Because an ancient Jew claimed to know the will of God, and defined that will in such a way that every God-inspired instinct in our being condemns it, we are left with no option but to say: either God *was* cruel and bloodthirsty or the prophet was mistaken. The modern man has no hestitation in making his choice. Unlike Joseph Hall he believes that despite their claim to divine inspiration, Hebrew prophets were over and over again mistaken. St Paul spent much time in arguing that with the death of Christ the old Jewish law was abolished. The modern man believes that with the coming of Christ into the world, a new standard of morality was introduced. 'It was said of old . . . but I say unto you . . .' His doctrine of literal inspiration prevented Hall from realizing the full significance of these and other words of his Master. It is not without interest to reflect that in all ages Christians have found it more easy to grasp the central truths of their faith than to realize their ethical implications.

Our space is limited; and though there are many other characteristic features of the *Contemplations* which deserve attention, we shall content ourselves with the mere mention of two in passing, and with calling attention to a third.

(*a*) In a later chapter we shall have something to say of Hall's angelology: meanwhile we merely note the fact that there are many passages in the *Contemplations* in which this doctrine is expressed.

(*b*) Though Calvin's name is never mentioned there are countless references to his central doctrine. Throughout the *Contemplations* it is a convinced Calvinist who speaks. 'It is no better than theft, to ascribe unto the second causes, that honour which is due unto the first.' (P., I 354; W., I 430.) 'God's choice is not led in the string of human reasons. His holy will is the guide and ground of all his actions.' (P., I 477; W., II 38.) Side by side with this we meet with the paradox to be found in the writings of St Paul as well as in those of John Calvin. Belief in God's election, so far from encouraging us to sit at ease in Zion is a call to action. 'The acts of God must abate nothing of ours; rather must we labour by doing that which he requireth, to further that which he decreeth.' (P., I 400; W., I 486.)

There is a third characteristic of the *Contemplations* to which attention must be drawn: the frequency with which Hall finds a 'Type of Christ' in men who lived before Christ was born. Hall is not unique in this respect. Far from it: he had innumerable predecessors and, until quite recent times, countless successors. No one who has seen the Oberammergau Passion Play can fail to remember how the main action of the drama is constantly interrupted to introduce a scene from the Old Testament or the Apocrypha (as for instance the Sacrifice of Isaac) in which one of the characters reveals something of the spirit of Christ.

(*c*) *Types of Christ*. 'He was not of an age but for all time.' It is hard to believe that the 'groundlings' who first witnessed a Shakespearian tragedy perceived the deep meaning in many passages which later commentators (A. C. Bradley, for instance) have professed to find. It is doubtful if even Shakespeare realized the full glory of the words he wrote. This is the truth contained in the medieval view of the mystical interpretation of Scripture. There is a greater depth of meaning in the Word of God than the prophet through whose lips it was first uttered realized. Something like this lies behind the belief that certain Old Testament characters were 'types of Christ'. They adumbrate qualities which are perfectly revealed in Jesus Christ, and in him alone. The significance of some of their deeds and some of their qualities was not fully realized till Christ appeared and, on the other hand, in some mysterious way, they at once prepared men for his coming, and threw light on the nature of his character when he eventually appeared.

It was once thought that between them the fifteenth-century Renaissance and nineteenth-century biblical criticism had dealt a mortal blow at all such interpretation. But mysticism never dies and it is quite possible that the writings of Rudolf Steiner and his disciples may give a fresh lease of life to views which seemed at one time to have been finally discarded. In any case, Hall and his contemporaries found no difficulty in discovering 'types of Christ' in the Old Testament Scriptures.

> 'I see in Joseph not a clearer type of Christ, than of every Christian because we are dear to our Father, and complain of sins, therefore are we hated of our carnal brethren.' (P., I 49; W., I 59.)

Samson is a 'type of Christ', since through his own death he vanquished his enemies and wrought deliverance for his people.

> 'So didst thou, O blessed Saviour, our better Samson, conquer in dying; and triumphing upon the chariot of the cross, didst lead captivity captive.' (P., I 232; W., I 281.)

The most elaborate specimen of such 'typology' is found in P., I 437; W., I 531, where Hall gives us a long disquisition – much too long to be quoted here – on the first temple as a type of the Christian Church. It begins thus:

> 'But what do we bend our eyes upon stone, and wood, and metals? God would never have taken pleasure in these dead materials, for their own sakes, if they had not a further intendment.'

It ends with a long prayer from which the following sentences are taken:

> 'Let the altars of our clean hearts send up ever to thee, the sweetest perfumed smokes of our holy meditations, and faithful prayers, and cheerful thanksgivings. . . . Lock up thy law and thy manna within us; and speak comfortably to us from thy mercy-seat. . . .'

Unless we are entirely mistaken, then, the views on theology and religion which underlie the *Contemplations* are those which Hall held in common with almost every Elizabethan Calvinist. He towers above his contemporaries and is read today, not because he introduced novel doctrines or presented his fellow men with fresh ideas; but because he had learned to handle familiar ideas in a new way. In this he won success partly because he was master of a characteristic and attractive style; partly because he possessed, and used to full advantage, a knowledge of human nature unequalled by any other religious writer of his time. At the same time he is far more than a mere medium through which orthodox opinion was expressed. He had his own ideas on many subjects. To three of these we wish to call attention.

1 – *The Clergy*

In Hall's time the average Anglican clergyman was often regarded with contempt.[1] 'O God,' he exclaims, 'what shall we say to those notorious contempts, which are daily cast upon thy spiritual messengers?' (P., I 373; W., I 452.) 'Where no respect is given to God's messengers,' he says in another place, 'there can be no religion.' (P., I 242; W., I 291.) 'There can be no greater argument of a foul soul than a dislike of the glorious calling of the priesthood.' (P., I 265.)

In Hall's time the churches were full – the Government saw to that – the effect on men's lives was bitterly disappointing. 'The noise of the Gospel is common; but where is the power of it? It hath a store of hearers but few converts.' (P., II 402; W., I 550.) Then, too, whilst the Romanist laity went regularly to confession, the average Anglican refused to consult his parish priest. Hall maintained that it was the duty of the laity to seek guidance in all difficulties from their ministers.

> 'There cannot but arise many difficulties in us about the ark of God: whom should we consult with, but those which have the tongue of the learned? Even those who are inwardest with God must have use of the ephod.' (P., I 412.)

And yet the people simply would *not* go to their parish priest. The few who did are likened to Zacchaeus when he climbed the sycamore to see Jesus.

> 'Do you see a weak and studious Christian, that, being unable to inform himself, in the matters of God, goes to the cabinet of heaven, the priest's lips, which shall preserve knowledge? there is Zacchaeus in the sycamore.' (P., II 306.)

[1] Donne expresses the same opinion.

Hall found it hard to court displeasure; yet he knew that the preacher of the Gospel is ever bound to meet with opposition.

> 'There must meet in God's ministers courage and impartiality; impartiality, not to make difference of persons; courage, not to make spare of the sins of the greatest. It is a hard condition, that the necessity of our calling casts upon us, in some cases to run upon the spikes of displeasure: prophecies were no burden, if they did not expose us to these dangers.' (P., II 318; W., II 431.)

No doubt the majority of Hall's readers were clergymen. Certainly the great majority of his foreign readers were ministers. He was proud of being a clergyman. In his eyes it was the greatest honour open to man. Thus it is that he resents so strongly 'the contempts cast upon them', and feels so much sympathy with them in their many difficulties. Of the fifty-odd references to clergymen in the *Contemplations* none is so touching as that in which he refers to the faults men found in Christ and John the Baptist.

> 'What can we do, to undergo but one opinion. If we give alms and fast, some will magnify our charity and devotion; others will tax our hypocrisy: if we give not, some will condemn our hardheartedness; others will allow our sense of justice. If we preach plainly, to some it will savour of a careless slubbering, to others of a mortified sincerity; if elaborately, some will tax our affectation, others will applaud our diligence in dressing the delicate viands of God. What marvel is it, if it be thus with our imperfection, when it fared not otherwise with him, who was purity and righteousness itself.'

After a few words on the difference between Christ and his 'austere Forerunner', he ends with a quotation from St Paul. It was, he says, a heroical resolution of the chosen vessel. 'I pass very little to be judged of you, or of men's day.'

II – *The Family*

Only second to Hall's interest in the clergy was his interest in the home. He looked at it from three different standpoints; for he was at once a shrewd observer of human nature, a shepherd of souls and the father of a family.

How should a father treat his children, what should be his chief ambition for them? How does their father affect them? These were questions never far from his thought. In two respects he seems remote from us. Today most men believe that the mother's influence on the child is greater than that of his father. Though in one passage he says, 'The mother, as she is more tender over her son, so by the power of a reciprocal love, she can work most upon his inclination.' (P., I 234). Hall seldom speaks of mothers; almost always he speaks of fathers. Like the ancient Roman he was a firm believer in the patriapotestas. A second difference is in his view of heredity. Modern psychologists are agreed that children do not inherit qualities: they inherit tendencies. Despite this difference in outlook Hall's views on the relation between parent and child deserve attention.

In a famous passage Milton describes the aim of all education in these words:

> 'It is to repair the ruins of our first parents by regaining to know God aright, and out of that knowledge to love him, to imitate him, to be like him, as we may the nearest by possessing our souls of true virtue, which being united to the heavenly grace of faith makes up the highest perfection.'

In much the same spirit, Hall insists that the parent's supreme desire must be to see his children grow up good.

> 'Oh the madness of parents, that care not which way they raise a house; that desire rather to leave their children great, than good: that are more ambitious to have their sons lords on earth, than kings in heaven!' (P., II 430; W., II 585.)
>
> 'If there be anything', he says in another place, 'that, in our desires for the prosperous condition of our children, takes place of goodness, our hearts are not upright.' (P., I 424; W., I 515.)

It is true that we can do little to effect this; for, 'as the greatest persons cannot give themselves children, so the wisest cannot give their children wisdom'. (P., I 449; W., II 3.) Yet there are two things that we *can* do. We can set a good example, and we can refuse to 'indulge' children.

> 'Where the father of the family brings sin home to the house, it is not easily swept out.'

Indulgence of children is a form of cruelty: this is a theme which occurs over and over again in the *Contemplations*. 'For my own part,' says Hall, 'I would rather be a just than a kind father.' He quotes one famous instance in which a father's indulgence brought ruin on his children. It was the case of David.

> 'These two, Absalom and Adonijah, were the darlings of their father. Their father had not displeased them from their childhood; therefore they displeased him in his age. Those children had need to be very gracious, that are not marred with pampering. It is more than God owes to us, if we receive comfort in those children, whom we have over-loved. The indulgence of parents at last pays them home in crosses.' (P., I 240.)

In two other passages much the same thought is expressed:

> 'Indulgent parents are cruel to themselves, and their posterity. Parents need no other means to make them miserable, than sparing the rod.' (P., I 264; W., I 319.)
>
> 'Indulgence of parents is the refuge of vanity, the bawd of wickedness, the bane of children. . . . When the lawlessness of youth knows where to find pity and toleration, what mischief can it forbear?' (P., I 139.)

Yet though Hall is a firm believer in the use of the rod, he is neither a tyrant nor a sadist.

'As it becomes not children to be forward in their choice, so parents may not be peremptory in their denial . . . the one is disobedience; the other may be tyranny.' (P. I, 219; W., I 265.)

'As we, so God also finds it seasonable, to tell his children of their faults, while he is whipping them.' (P., I 209; W., I 253.)

Hall is a convinced believer in the doctrine of original sin. 'Parents may transmit sin: they do. They cannot transmit goodness; for though goodness may be repaired in ourselves, yet it cannot be propagated to others.'

Here is one statement which shows his view alike of the sinful nature that is handed from parent to child, and of the effects of education on children brought up in a worldly home.

'It is not so frequently seen, that the child follows the good qualities of the parent; it is seldom seen, that it follows not the evil. Nature is the soil; good and ill qualities are the herbs and weeds; the soil bears the weeds, naturally; the herbs not without culture. What with traduction, what with education, it were strange if we should miss any of the maldispositions of our parents.' (P., II 320; W., II 449.)

One last quotation must serve to complete this gloomy picture:

'If the conveyance of grace were natural, holy parents would not be so ill suited in their children. What good man would not rather wish his loins dry, than fruitful of wickedness? Now, we can neither traduce goodness, nor chuse but traduce sin. If virtue were as well entailed upon us as sin, one might serve to check the other in our children; but now, since grace is derived from heaven on whomsoever it pleases the Giver, and that evil which ours receive hereditarily from us is multiplied by their own corruption, it can be no wonder, that good men have ill children; it is rather a wonder, that any children are not evil.' (P., I 262; W., I 316.)

Yet lest this gloomy view of life lead to utter despair, Hall adds one qualification.

'As no good is traduced from parents, so not all evil. There is an Almighty hand, that stops the foul current of nature at his pleasure. No idolator can say, that his child shall not be a convert.' (P., II 35; W., I 102.)

To complete the picture, one must mention the fact that Hall insists on implicit obedience, utter docility on the part of the child.

'Children should have no will of their own. As their flesh is their parents', so should their wills be. They do justly unchild themselves without the consent of those, which gave them being. . . . It is both unmannerly and unnatural in a child, to run before, without, against the will of the parent.' (P., II 321; W., II 450.)

III – *Women*

'How many have we known, whose heads have been broken with their own rib!' (P., I 144.)

It is said that Donne had a poor opinion of women. Be that as it may there can be little doubt that if we wish to find an exalted view of women we shall not find it in Joseph Hall. True he loved and admired his mother, was a chaste and dignified husband; but he was no romantic, and when he speaks of women it is generally to find fault with them. He has two favourite names for a wife. One is 'the rib'; the other 'the weaker vessel'. Each is scriptural; and if neither tells us very much about women, both tell us a good deal about Joseph Hall.

> 'They have unlearned the very dictates of nature, that can abide the head to be set below the rib.' (P., II 163; W., II 258.)
>
> 'It is not fit, for a woman to be loud and clamorous. Nothing beseems that sex better, than silence and bashfulness; as not to be too much seen, so not to be heard too far.' (P., II 444; W., II 602).

Hall was in complete agreement with the Apostle. 'Wives submit yourselves unto your own husbands as unto the Lord.'

> 'It is not for a good wife to judge of her husband's will, but to execute it. Neither wit, nor stomach, may carry her into a curious inquisition, into the reasons of an enjoined charge; much less to a resistance: but in a hoodwinked simplicity she must follow, whither she is led; as one that holds her chief praise, to consist in subjection.' (P., II 162; W., II 256.)

Let us now turn for a moment to consider Hall's view of the part that woman has played in history.

> 'Our first mother Eve bequeathed this dowry to her daughters, that they should be our helpers in sin.' (P., I 147; W., I 177.)
>
> 'No one means has so enriched hell, as beautiful faces.' (P., I 149.)

Solomon was undone by women. 'If one woman undid all mankind, what marvel is it, if many women undid one?' (P., I 443; W., I 539), and Moses took a grave risk when he married Zipporah. 'He hath need to be more than man, that hath a Zipporah in his bosom, and would have true zeal in his heart.' England is remote from Palestine: yet in England also woman has proved dangerous.

> 'There were wont to be reckoned three wonders of England: Ecclesia, Femina, Lana. The churches, the women, the wool. Femina may pass still; who may justly challenge wonder for their vanity, if not their persons.' (P., II 371; W., II 513.)

Hall rarely mentions woman without calling attention to her vanity. Yet he believed that though the average woman is at once frail and dangerous, there have been good women.

> 'It is easy to observe that the New Testament affordeth more store of good women than the Old.' (P., II 194; W., II 293.)

In England too, women can be found who are more religious than their husbands.

> 'Husbands shall abuse their authority, if they shall wilfully cross the holy purposes of their yoke-fellows. How much more fit is it

> for them, to cherish all good desires in the weaker vessels! and as we use, when we carry a small light in a wind, to hide it with our lap or hand, that it may not go out. If the wife be a vine, the husband should be an elm to uphold her in all worthy enterprises; else she falls to the ground, and proves fruitless.' (P., I 260; W., I 315.)

If Hall remembers what St Paul said about the subjection of wife to husband, he also remembers the noble passage in which the Apostle declares that as in Christ there is neither Jew nor Greek, bond nor free; so there is neither male nor female.

> 'There is no reason, that sex should disparage, where the virtue and merit is no less than masculine. Surely the soul acknowledgeth no sex; neither is varied according to the outward frame. How oft have we known female hearts in the breasts of men; and, contrarily, manly powers in the weaker vessels.' (P., I 409; W., I 497.)

Hall was far too pedestrian to rise to such heights as the unknown poet who thus sang of love: 'For love is strong as death. . . . Many waters cannot quench love, neither can the floods drown it: if a man would give all the substance of his house for love, it would utterly be contemned.' (Song of Solomon viii. 6, 7.) In his own prosaic way, however, he too sang an epithalamium: 'All the substance of the earth is not worth a virtuous and prudent wife.' (P., I 256; W., I 309.)

In Pratt's edition of Hall's works the *Contemplations* extend to over a thousand pages. Human nature being what it is, few who are not professional students of literature or theology can be expected to read them all. Out of pity for human frailty, a number of men – some of them distinguished – have published selections from the work. Unlike Hooker and Milton, Donne and Sir Thomas Browne, Hall has no 'purple passages' which can be easily detached from their context. Like all other writings, some of the contemplations are more excellent than others; yet the difference between the best and the worst is not pronounced. Then, too, just as no anthology ever satisfied anyone save the compiler; since every reader misses some favourite poem whilst wondering that another poem, which seems to him of far inferior merit finds a place in the collection; so almost any selection from the *Contemplations* will be found to disappoint almost as many readers as it is calculated to please. Shortage of space has rendered this impossible. Out of hundreds of possible examples we shall select a number of sentences, which may claim to be like the words of the Shunamite, 'short, quick, and pithy'. Before doing this, however, we must say a word about Hall's technique; for as we have pointed out over and over again Hall's reputation depends not so much on what he had to say, as on the way in which he said it.

Hall's Technique

1 – *His Mastery of the Sententious*

When St Paul reached Athens he found that 'all the Athenians and strangers which were there spent their time in nothing else, but either to tell or to hear some new thing'. Those who are possessed of this Athenian spirit, whose ruling passion is to discover '*le dernier cri*', '*die neuste Theorie*' will find little to interest them in Joseph Hall. 'Curiosity of knowledge', he says, 'is an old disease of human nature.' Yet there are others, perhaps the great majority, who ask for nothing better than to follow the path their fathers trod, who feel that any kind of change is always disturbing; that as often as not improvement promised ends in bitter disappointment. Conservative by instinct, they refuse to put forth effort to grasp an entirely new idea. From such as these Hall is sure of a warm welcome, since he knows how to express familiar thoughts in neat and pungent terms. If the word 'platitude' did not suggest, as its derivation indicates, a certain flatness, an inability to coin fresh phrases, which is entirely lacking in Hall, one might be tempted to say that his *Contemplations* abound in platitudes. As it is, however, a better description is that he is a master of the sententious. The better one knows him; the more easily one understands why he was called 'The English Seneca'.

Now just as in primitive times men loved to have their experience of life expressed for them in proverbs; so in all ages men have been at once pleased and flattered when they found their own ideas expressed for them in a terse and striking phrase. The popular preacher knows how to put into graceful words the very commonplace ideas he shares with his congregation. The political speaker often wins fame by the ability to utter a familiar commonplace with gravity mingled with enthusiasm. Of all these arts Hall is a master. He constantly employs them.

But he makes use of a second device. Apollo does not always strike his lyre: Achilles does not keep his bow for ever bent. For most men the spiritual atmosphere is like that upper air in which they find it difficult to breathe for long. They find relief in descent from the mountain top to the familiar plain. This every preacher knows. Conscious of man's infirmity he gives rest and refreshment to his hearers by introducing every now and then an anecdote, an illustration, a piece of worldly wisdom. In Hall's *Contemplations* there are many such cases in which the weary pilgrim is allowed to sit down and take his ease. Here are some instances:

(1) Envy and malice can make noon of midnight. (P., II 476; W., II 642.)

(2) Pride is the inmost coat, which we put off last, and which we put on first. (P., II 430; W., II 585.)
(3) The suit is half obtained, that is seasonably made. (P., II 429; W., II 583.)
(4) Who ever knew any earthly thing trusted in, without disappointment? (P., I 188.)
(5) The way not to repine at those above us, is to look at those below. (P., I 129; W., I 155.)
(6) Covetous men need neither clock nor bell to awaken them; their desires make them restless. (P., I 143; W., I 172.)
(7) It is a sign the horse is galled, that stirs too much when he is touched. (P., I 159.)
(8) If discretion do not hold in the reins, good intentions will both break their own necks and the rider's. (P., I 181; W., I 218.)
(9) It is quarrel enough amongst many to a good action, that it is not their own. (P., I 315; W., I 381.)
(10) The fire of a neighbour's house would not so affect us, if it were not with the danger of our own. (P., I 319.)
(11) A weak man's rules may be better than the best man's actions. (P., I 327; W., I 397.)
(12) How severe justicers we can be, to our very own crimes in other's persons. (P., I 381; W., I 462.)
(13) This is one means to fill hell, lothness to displease. (P., II 383.)
(14) No man knoweth the weight of a sceptre, but he that swayeth it. (P., II 388; W., I 533.)
(15) There was never any man that worshipped but one idol. (P., I 204; W., I 247.)
(16) Every cur is ready to fall upon the dog, that he sees worried. (P., II 188; W., II 188.)
(17) We may be as happy in russet as in tissue. (P., II 216; W., II 320.)
(18) We cannot better judge of our hearts, than by what we most fear. (P., II 319; W., II 447.)
(19) The greatest griefs are not most verbal. (P., I 382; W., I 463.)
(20) All the good of wealth or poverty is in the mind, in the use. (P., II 303; W., II 428.)

II – *Skilful Construction of the Opening Paragraph*

A famous orator once said that he took the utmost pains with his opening sentence and his closing paragraph. He wrote out each with care and committed it to memory. The rest of the speech he left to the inspiration of the moment. Like every good preacher Hall tried to gain the attention of his hearers by his opening words. The more one studies the *Contemplations* the more one realizes the pains he took with his opening paragraphs. He deliberately sets himself to gain the attention of his readers, and he nearly always succeeds. Here are a few examples chosen almost at random which may serve to illustrate this statement:

(1) OF ABRAHAM:

> 'It was fit that he which should be the father and pattern of the faithful, should be thoroughly tried; for in a set copy every fault is important, and may prove a rule of error. Of ten trials which Abraham passed, the last was the sorest. No son of Abraham can hope to escape temptations, while he sees that bosom, in which he desires to rest, so assaulted with difficulties.' (P., I 26; W., I 32.)

(2) OF ISAAC:

> 'Of all the patriarchs, none makes so little noise in the world as Isaac; none lived either so privately, or so innocently: neither know I whether he approved himself a better son or husband.' (P., I 37; W., I 44.)

(3) OF JACOB:

> 'Isaac's life was not more retired and quiet, than Jacob's was busy and troublesome. In the one I see the image of contemplation; of action, in the other. None of the patriarchs saw so evil days as he; from whom justly hath the church of God therefore taken her name. Neither were the faithful ever since called Abrahamites, but Israelites.' (P., I 41; W., I 49.)

(4) OF JOSEPH:

> 'I marvel not that Joseph had the double portion of Jacob's land, who had more than two parts of his sorrows: none of his sons did so truly inherit his afflictions; none of them was either so miserable or so great: suffering is the way to glory.' (P., I 49; W., I 58.)

(5) OF ELIJAH:

> 'Who should be matched with Moses in the hill of Tabor, but Elijah? Surely next after Moses, there was never any prophet of the Old Testament more glorious than he.
>
> 'None more glorious: none more obscure. The other prophets are not mentioned without the name of their parent, for the mutual honour both of the father and the son; Elijah, as if he had been a son of the earth, comes forth with the bare mention of the place of his birth. Meanness of descent is no block in God's way, to the most honourable vocations. It matters not whose son he be, whom God will grace with his service.' (P., I 474; W., II 34.)

(6) OF THE AGONY:

> 'What a preface do I find to my Saviour's Passion! A hymn and an Agony; a cheerful Hymn, and an Agony no less sorrowful. A hymn begins, both to raise and testify the courageous resolutions of his sufferings; an Agony follows, to shew that he was truly sensible of those extremities, wherewith he was resolved to grapple.' (P., II 468; W., II 632.)

III – *Use of the First Person instead of the Third*

One of the devices which Hall employed to give a sense of vividness to his narrative, is, every now and then to change the third person for the first. Instead of saying, 'So-and-so did this or that', he says, 'I see so-and-so do something'. With Hall this is a favourite device: it is used over and over again, and serves its purpose well. A few examples may make this statement clearer:

(1) 'But what is this I see? Satan himself with a Bible under his arm, with a text in his mouth.' (P., II 239; W., II 348.)

(2) 'I see none come for his servant, but this one centurion.' (P., II 251; W., II 363.)

(3) 'I never read that Samson slew any, but by the motion and assistance of the Spirit of God.' (P., I 224; W., I 270.)

(4) 'I do not find, where Jesus was ever bidden to any table, and refused.' (P., II 271; W., II 387.)

(5) 'I never find, that Christ entertained any guests, but twice and that was only with loaves and fishes. I sometimes find him feasted by others more liberally. But his domestical fare, how simple how homely it is.'

IV – *Speculations*

Hall constantly turns aside to ask *why* this or that thing was done. Of Christ in the temple he says:

> 'But where wert thou, O blessed Jesus, for the space of these three days? Where didst thou bestow thyself, or who tended thee, while thou wert thus alone at Jerusalem? I know, if Jerusalem should have been as unkind to thee as Bethlehem, thou couldst have commanded the heavens to harbour thee; and if men did not minister to thee, thou couldst have commanded the service of angels; but, since the form of a Servant called thee to a voluntary homeliness, whether it pleased thee to exercise thyself thus early with the difficulties of a stranger, I inquire not, since thou revealest not: only this I know, that hereby thou intendest to teach thy parents that thou couldest live without them; and that, not of indigency, but out of a gracious dispensation, thou wouldest ordinarily depend upon their care.' (P., II 226; W., II 332.)

Other questions of the same sort are asked and answered. Why did the Gadarenes ask Christ to leave them? (P., II 287; W., II 407.) Why were Peter, James and John present at the Transfiguration? Why did Christ write on the ground? (P., II 397; W., II 544.) Why did Christ say to Mary 'Touch me not'?

As may be expected the *Contemplations* on the Old Testament contain many such 'speculations'. We name but four. Why did the Hebrews march round Jericho on the Sabbath? Why did it fall on a Sabbath? Why at the fall of Jericho did the Jews blow on rams' horns instead of on their silver trumpets? Why did David take *five stones* from the brook when he went to meet Goliath? There are many questions of all sorts and some ingenious if not always convincing answers. We can find room for only one more. 'Why did Christ fast?'

> 'And why did it please thee, O Saviour, to fast forty days and forty nights, unless, as Moses fasted forty days at the Delivery of the Law, and Elias at the Restitution of the Law, so thou thoughtest fit, at the Accomplishment of the Law, and the Promulgation of the Gospel, to fulfil the time of both these types of thine; wherein thou intendest our wonder, not our imitation; not our imitation of the time, though of the act.' (P., II 234; W., II 342.)

V – *The Use of Soliloquy*

Hall is fond of what may be termed the 'dramatic method'. He uses it over and over again. By this we mean to imply that Hall tries to enter into the thoughts and feelings of the men whose action he describes, and seeks to express them in the form of a soliloquy. Here is one example: Ahab meets Elijah. Hall says:

> 'Doubtless, Ahab startled to hear of Elijah coming to meet him; as one that did not more hate, than fear the prophet. Well might he think "Thus long, thus far, have I sought Elijah. Elijah would not come to seek me, but under a sure guard, and with some strange commission. His coarse mantle hath the advantage of my robe and sceptre. If I can command a piece of earth, I see he can command heaven".' (P., I 483; W., II 45.)

As may be imagined the Old Testament contains much material that can be dealt with in this way. Such for instance are the soliloquies put into the mouth of the Amalekite who reported the death of Saul to David (P., I 355; W., I 430) and the mingled feelings of the sons of Jesse when they learned that David had been chosen to be king. (P., I 310; W., I 375.) But Hall does not reserve this method to Old Testament characters: he uses it in dealing with the men and women of the New Testament. He even goes so far as to put a soliloquy into the mouth of Christ himself as he watched Peter cut off the ear of Malchus: and it is obvious that if Hall had cared to do so he could have written a play, possibly a tragedy in the manner of the time.

VI – *The Use of Apostrophe*

David sins with Bathsheba. Hall tells the story. This is how he begins:

> 'With what unwillingness, with what fear, do I still look upon the miscarriage of the man after God's own heart!'

Then turning to David, so to speak, he continues:

> 'O holy prophet! who can promise himself always to stand, when he sees thee fallen, and maimed with the fall? Who can assure

> himself of an immunity from the foulest sins, when he sees thee offending so heinously, so bloodily? Let prophane eyes behold thee contentedly, as a pattern, as an excuse of sinning: I shall never look upon thee but through tears, as a woeful specimen of human infirmity. . . .'

In much the same way he addresses Bathsheba. (P., I 376; W., I 455.) Again he apostrophizes David when Absalom is killed. (P., I 402, W., I 488.) Our last quotation shall be from the passage in which Hall deals with Solomon when he is led astray by his foreign wives.

> 'O Solomon, where was thy wisdom, while thine affections run away with thee into so wild a voluptuousness? What boots it thee to discourse of all things, while thou mis-knowest thyself? . . . O Solomon, wert not thou he, whose younger years God honoured with a message and style of love? to whom God twice appeared; and, in a gracious vision, renewed the covenant of his favour, whom he singled out from all the generation of men, to be the founder of that glorious temple, which was no less clearly the type of heaven, than thou wert of Christ, the Son of the ever-living God? Wert not thou that deep sea of wisdom, which God ordained to send forth rivers and fountains, of all divine and human knowledge to all nations, to all ages? Wert thou not one of those select secretaries, whose hand it pleased the Almighty to employ, in three pieces of the divine monuments of Sacred Scriptures? Which of us ever hopes to aspire unto thy graces? Which of us can promise to secure ourselves from thy ruins?' (P., I 444; W., I 540.)

Few modern readers would agree with Hall's conception of David's character, or with his belief that David's son was the author of the Book of Proverbs, Ecclesiastes, and the Canticles. The above quotations have been made only because they are as good specimens as any to be found in the first volume, of the way in which Hall makes use of apostrophe to give life and feeling to his *Contemplations*. In the breast of this dignified divine there was a depth of passion, a power to hate and to adore, to admire and to bewail that one would hardly expect to find.

When, in the second book, in which are to be found all the passages which deal with Christ, apostrophe becomes more and more common, we find on almost every page the expression 'O Saviour!' though that is sometimes replaced by 'O Blessed Jesus!' Such apostrophe reaches a climax, in the noble contemplation which deals with Christ's death on Calvary. There we find Hall consumed with passionate love for his Saviour, with horror at human sin, and unspeakable adoration for the grace of God.

VII – *The Use of Antithesis*

Throughout Hall's work abundant use is made of antithesis. Over and over again we meet with beautifully constructed sentences in which this is revealed. It is a device to which every sententious writer is apt to resort. There are few more sententious writers than Hall: few so fond of the adversative clause, of antithesis. Let one illustration suffice. It is taken from the contemplation which deals with Christ's passion:

> 'In the meantime, whither, O whither dost thou stoop, O thou co-eternal Son of thy Eternal Father! Whither dost thou abase thyself for me? I have sinned, and thou art punished: I have exalted myself, and thou art dejected: I have clad myself with shame, and thou art stripped: I have made myself naked, and thou art clothed with robes of dishonour: my head hath devised evil, and thine is pierced with thorns: I have smitten thee, and thou art smitten for me: I have dishonoured thee, and thou for my sake art scorned: thou art made the sport of men for me, that have been insulted on by devils.' (P., II 485; W., II 653.)

It is true that in this moving passage Hall uses the word 'and' whereas he generally uses 'but'. The form may not be as purely antithetical as one finds in scores of other passages. It is quoted here not only because it draws throughout a vivid contrast between the sinner and his Saviour; but because it is an expression of that sense of adoration and awe that fills Hall's heart whenever he thinks of the redemptive work of Christ.

Such, then, are Joseph Hall's *Contemplations*. Like every other work it does not appeal to every taste. In many ways it is so old-fashioned that some readers turn from it with impatience. But it shows such deep knowledge of the heart, of that side of human nature which does not change, that it has found readers and admirers in every generation since it first saw the light. To such it is one of the few books that can be picked up at any time. It is often in their hands; still oftener, perhaps, beside their beds. For wherever it is opened, the reader finds something of interest, something calculated to make him a wiser and better man.

IV – MEDITATIONS

Though Hall seems to regard the terms 'contemplation' and 'meditation' as synonymous, we propose, for convenience sake, to draw a distinction between them. Throughout this book the term 'contemplation' is confined to that commentary of a unique character which Hall wrote on certain parts of Holy Scripture. On this work, as we have already said, his fame as a religious writer almost entirely depends. In addition to this work which he himself regarded as the most important which came from his pen, he wrote a number of meditations of which we must now give some account. He believed that every object with which he met was capable, if rightly regarded, of raising his thoughts to heaven: that every experience in life is intended to convey a spiritual lesson. Hence his *Meditations* may be divided in the first instance into two classes. There are those which he termed *extemporal*: those which he termed *deliberate*. Such of these 'extemporal' meditations as survive were published by his son Robert, with his father's permission. At the same time their author translated them into Latin and published them simultaneously with the English original, under the title of *Meditatiunculae Subitaneae*. We shall begin with them, for they are of no great importance. We shall then deal with the more elaborate pieces. We shall find that only one or two are what may be described as full-dress meditations which follow the method of the great masters of devotion. The others are much simpler and express in graceful language Hall's own views of Religion and Life.

Such meditations we shall divide into two classes: those written before his downfall and those written after he had been expelled from his bishopric. The former we shall find for the most part to be the moralizings of a man who had not as yet passed through the school of affliction. The writer is indeed a Christian but he is at one and the same time a man of the world profoundly influenced by stoic thought, saturated one might almost say in the teachings of his hero Seneca. The later meditations are of much greater spiritual value. In them there is less of Seneca and more of Christ.

We begin then with the *extemporal* meditations: the *Meditatiunculae Subitaneae*.

(*a*) MEDITATIUNCULAE SUBITANEAE *or* OCCASIONAL MEDITATIONS (1634)

Towards the end of 1634 Hall was so busy with diocesan work that he had little, if any leisure, to devote to his *Contemplations on the*

New Testament Story, which he was eager to complete. One day his son Robert came across a bundle of papers in his father's study. They were records of short meditations which his father had jotted down from time to time. He asked and received permission to publish them. Meanwhile his father decided to issue a Latin version simultaneously with the English original. He did this partly because he desired to 'brush up his Latin'; partly because he felt that some of those who had translated certain of his writings from English into Latin had not been completely successful. He also felt that these *familiares non inutilium cogitationum minutias* might be of service to mankind.

As it is interesting to learn what attracted Robert Hall to this particular form of meditation we quote his own words:

> 'Holy minds have been ever wont to look through these bodily objects at spiritual and heavenly. So Sulpitius reports of St Martin, that, seeing a sheep newly shorn, he could say, "Lo, here is one, that hath performed that command in the Gospel; having two coats, she hath given away one"; and seeing a hogherd freezing in a thin suit of skins ,"Lo," said he, "there is Adam cast out of Paradise"; and seeing a meadow part rooted up; part whole but eaten down; and part flourishing; he said, "The first was the state of fornication, the second of marriage, the third of virginity".'

From this it is obvious that neither father nor son was likely to contribute anything of permanent value through such 'occasional meditations' to mankind; partly because they insisted that every meditation should yield an immediate practical application; partly because their standard of excellence was by no means high.

The 140 'occasional meditations' which Robert discovered and admired are difficult to classify. Many, perhaps most, deal with insects, birds and animals. Flies gather on a galled horse or are consumed in the flame of a candle: cocks fight, dogs bark, larks soar. But there are other sights which catch the good bishop's eye and yield improving thoughts. There is the starry sky, the ever-changing cloud, the rolling thunder; and on earth beneath there are flowers and trees and the infinite variety of human beings. Herbs are dried, corn is fanned, the red hot iron hisses when dropped into water. A man yawns, a harlot is 'carted', a child cries. On one's walk one meets with a blind man, a drunkard, or an open grave: and every time one sees such sights one ought to think of things spiritual and of God. More often than not, when one jots down such a meditation on a sheet of paper one adds a little prayer. The Bishop sees bees fight, meditates on the occurrence and adds these words: 'O God, who art at once the Lord of Hosts and Prince of Peace, give us war with spiritual wickedness, and peace with our brethren.'

We end by quoting two of these meditations so that readers may estimate their value for themselves. Some of them are not without a certain charm. They are published, their author says, for the benefit of his weaker brethren ('weak minds' is the term he employs) to show them how to do for themselves what had proved of such benefit to Joseph Hall throughout the whole course of his life. Undoubtedly there is room for many such teachers for most men are so busy with 'worldly affairs' that all thought of God is often entirely absent from their minds. Yet there are many who find the ladder which Hall set up between heaven and earth of little service. They feel that there is something forced and artificial in many of these meditations. They seem to lack spontaneity. There is a hardness, a prosaic quality in most of them which is entirely absent from the meditations of the great mystics. For help they turn from Hall to men like Blake whose 'Tiger, tiger burning bright' poses the great question, 'Did He who made the lamb make thee?' to Tennyson who felt that if he could but understand the 'little flower in the crannied wall' he would understand God; to Gerard Manley Hopkins with his 'inscape' through which flowers revealed to him the Beauty and the Love of Christ; to Francis Thompson with his vision of Christ walking on the waters 'not of Gennesareth but Thames' or to Wordsworth with his sublime words in which he tells of 'that Presence that disturbed him with the joy of elevated thought'. These and such as these are they who can alone, perhaps, open blind eyes to behold the 'hosts of God' which encamp around the dwellings of the just, can even in some great moment and as it were through a glass darkly enable them to catch a glimpse of that Beatific Vision which alone can satisfy the heart of man.

On the barking of a dog (XXIII):

> 'What have I done to this dog, that he follows me with this angry clamour? Had I rated him, or shaken my staff, or stooped down for a stone, I had justly drawn on this noise, this snarling importunity.
>
> 'But, why do I wonder to find this unquiet disposition in a brute creature, when it is no news with the reasonable? Have I not seen innocence, and merit bayed at, by the quarrelsome and envious vulgar, without any provocation, save of good offices? Have I not felt, more than their tongue, their teeth upon my heels; when I know I have deserved nothing but fawning on? Where is my grace, or spirits, if I have not learned to contemn both?
>
> 'O God, let me rather die, than willingly incur thy displeasure; yea, than justly offend thy godly-wise, judicious conscionable servants: but if humour, or faction, or causeless prejudice fall upon me, for my faithful service to thee; let these bawling curs tire themselves, and tear their throats, with loud and false censures: I go on in a silent constancy; and, if my ear be beaten, yet my heart shall be free.'

On occasion of a red-breast coming into his chamber, and singing:

'Pretty bird, how cheerfully dost thou sit and sing; and yet knowest not where thou art, nor where thou shalt make thy next meal, and at night must shroud thyself in a bush for lodging! What a shame is it for me, that see before me so liberal provisions of my God, and find myself set warm under my own roof; yet am ready to droop under a distrustful and unthankful dulness! Had I so little certainty of my harbour and purveyance, how heartless should I be, how careful, how little list should I have, to make music to thee or myself! Surely, thou camest not hither without a Providence. God sent thee, not so much to delight, as to shame me; but all in a conviction of my sullen unbelief, who, under more apparent means, am less cheerful and confident. Reason and faith have not done so much in me, as in thee mere instinct of nature. Want of foresight makes thee more merry, if not more happy, here, than the foresight of better things maketh me.

'O God, thy Providence is not impaired by those powers, thou hast given me, above these brute things: let not my greater helps hinder me, from a holy security and comfortable reliance on thee.'

Let us now turn to what Hall termed his more 'elaborate' meditations. Let us begin with those which were written when he was comparatively speaking a young man, and let us introduce them by an account of the tract which was written to teach men who desired to do so, how to meditate.

(*b*) THE ART OF DIVINE MEDITATION

We shall do less than justice to the complexity of Hall's character if we fail to remember that in his Cambridge days, he did not (as one might assume from his autobiography) devote his entire attention to religious exercises and the study of theology. In this connexion it is of interest to note that *Meditations and Vows* was followed within four months by a Latin satire published anonymously 'at Frankfort' on June 2nd, 1605. This satire, as we shall learn in due course, is distinguished by its scornful treatment of the Roman Church, and by its attitude at once cynical and contemptuous towards England's besetting sins. Even the most fervent of Hall's admirers will fail to discover in this somewhat scurrilous work, any trace of 'that most excellent gift of charity, the very bond of peace and of all virtues, without which whosoever liveth is counted dead' before God.[1]

In spite of this, however, Hall undoubtedly believed that the great need of his age was not satire: it was devotional literature. Of works on systematic divinity, polemical theology, casuistry and the like there was enough and more than enough; for despite their learning and orthodoxy such works seemed to have little effect on men's lives.

[1] Much the same may be said of Donne's *Ignatius his Conclave* (1611), which John Hayward describes as 'in many respects his most entertaining work in prose'. (*Donne*, edited by John Hayward for the Nonesuch Library, fourth impression, 1942, page 356.)

'Never', says Hall, 'were the brains of men more stuffed, their tongues more stirring, their hands more idle.' (Preface to the *Art of Divine Meditation.*) The great need of the time was for men to read books of meditation and to learn to meditate for themselves. Hall had just published the first 'century' of 300 such meditations: he now proceeds to teach men the art of meditation which is, he assures us 'profitable for all Christians to know and practise'. He further undertakes to give two specimens, 'two large patterns' as he calls them: one on Eternal Life as the End, the other on Death as the Way.

It is not easy to determine how much Hall knew of the works of the great mystics; though it is fair to assume that his reading in this field was less extensive than it was in certain others. He admires a few such writers and occasionally refers to them; though by no means as often, in view of his determination to specialize in devotional literature, as one might expect. In any case he expressly states that his debt to any of the most famous writers on this subject was far less than it was to a 'nameless monk' who lived towards the end of the fifteenth century. On his margin he transcribes from this monk the names employed to describe the various stages through which those who aspire to reach the heights of meditation must pass; though he realizes that such terms as 'Tractation' and 'Dijudication' were alien to the English laity for whose benefit he wrote. In Hall's eyes the original rule of the Benedictines, which laid down that the monk must divide his day time into three equal parts: one devoted to prayer and meditation, one to manual labour and one to rest and recreation, was admirably designed. He had little liking for the purely Contemplative Orders; and felt that the ordinary layman who earned his living by working in the world, had a great advantage over the cloistered monk who devoted his whole time to contemplation.

In order to acquire the 'Art of Meditation' we must fulfil certain conditions. We must get rid of sin; for 'sin dimmeth and dazzleth the eye, that it cannot behold spiritual things'. (47) At the same time we must set the mind free from 'worldly thoughts'; for cares are a burden that prevent any man from climbing the steep hill of meditation. We must reduce meditation to a habit; no progress can be made if we only work 'in snatches'. Nor must we be dismayed by difficulty; for if we 'persist' we shall 'prevail'. At the same time we must recognize our limitations and when we feel that we have spent our strength and acquired as much benefit as we can carry away with us our strenuous labours should cease.

Success in meditation depends, to a considerable extent, on the conditions under which it is made. The mind must be at peace; and this can only be, if we enjoy silence and solitude. As for the time at which to meditate there is no definite rule. Each must choose the time that suits him best. Some prefer 'the golden hours of morning' when the mind is fresh and vigorous. Like Isaac, Hall found the best time to be the evening: he also found it easier to meditate when he walked than when he sat in his study or lay upon his bed.

The *theme* or subject on which we meditate must be chosen with care. Generally speaking it should be on some aspect of the Divine Nature as revealed in creation, providence, or redemption. Often it will deal with some incident in the life of Christ or with some activity of the Holy Spirit. In the present instance he deals with the 'Life and Glory of God's Saints', i.e. with Heaven. In the specimen which follows he deals with Death.

Every meditation must begin with prayer. We must ask for Divine guidance, for Divine power to avoid distraction, for Divine help to kindle our affections.

In the nature of things meditation must begin in the mind, for it is based on thought, but it must pass on to the heart. In other words it must evoke emotion. We must proceed in an *orderly* manner; but we need not concern ourselves unduly with attempts to make our thoughts move in a strictly logical sequence; for thought must be free, not bound. We must not rest content with *facts*; we must discover *causes*. Here Hall's Calvinism asserts itself; for him as for all other Calvinists there is, in the last resort, but *one* Cause – God.

> 'As he will not save thee without thy faith, so thou canst never have faith without his gift.' (59.)

The mention of *cause* leads to the thought of *effect*. In the present instance – *The Glory of the Saints* – the effect is unspeakable joy. In the New Jerusalem friend meets with friend; parent with child. There is perpetual vision of the Glorified Christ; unending communion with Him.

Yet to one who meditates on heaven with its unspeakable joy, thought instinctively turns by way of contrast to earth with its endless misery and to hell. All such thought must be reinforced by reference to the Bible. Throughout the meditation we must give heed to the testimony of Scripture.

> 'The most difficult and knotty part of meditation thus finished, there remaineth that, which is both more lively, and more easy unto a good heart, to be wrought altogether by the Affections; which if our discourses reach not unto, they prove vain and to no purpose. That, which followeth therefore, is the very soul of meditation; whereto all that is past serveth but as an instrument. A man is a man, by his understanding part; but he is a Christian, by his will and affections.'

We must *taste and see* how gracious the Lord is. We must lament our imperfections and express our fervent desire to possess the qualities we lack. We must acknowledge our utter inability to effect that which we desire and must pray earnestly for all we do not as yet possess. Having prayed in this way we must 'tread down our doubts' and display a *cheerful confidence*.

Every meditation must end with thanksgiving. We commend our 'souls and our ways' to God; and, if we are wise sing a versicle from one of David's divine psalms.

The exposition is followed by an epilogue. To every reader Hall says: If you have discovered a satisfactory method of meditation for yourself, do not abandon it for mine. If you have not, follow my method till you meet with a better.

Throughout this treatise the *theme* has been Life – the Joys of Heaven and the glory of the saints. In the meditation which follows, in which precisely the same method is adopted, the theme is Death.

(*c*) EARLY MEDITATIONS[1]

(A)

> *Meditations and Vows/ Divine and Moral/ Serving for directions on/ Christian and Civil Practice*. Three Centuries.

In this, as in most of his books, Hall begins with an apologia.

> 'Though the world is furnished with other writings, even to satiety and surfeit, yet of those which reduce Christianity to practice, there is at least scarce enough.'

He goes on to say that he had found these 'thoughts' 'comfortable and fruitful to himself' and that he regarded it as a duty to communicate them to others.

He gives a second reason for publishing the book. 'My body, which was ever weak, began to languish more.' If the worst should come to the worst and he were to die an untimely death (he was then 32) he was anxious to leave behind him 'a little monument of that great respect' which he 'deservedly bore' to Drury. The dedication of the first 'century' to Drury, with whom Hall was never on very cordial terms, reveals two unattractive features in its author. On the one hand flattery of the patron (a common vice in those days): on the other insincere self-depreciation. A sincere man who felt that his book was an 'unworthy scrowl' would not have published it.

The 300 'Meditations and Vows' are of varying length and excellence. One or two consist of a couple of sentences – less than twenty words in all: others are considerably longer; some even run to 400 words. The style throughout is characteristic: short sentences

[1] All references in this section are to Pratt, Vol. VI.

carefully formed; love of the sententious which reveals itself now in a clever epigram, now in a threadbare truism. As the main ideas reappear in the 'Holy Contemplations' there is no need to discuss them: we merely mention them.

(*a*) Throughout Hall's writings there is a strain of what may be termed Christian stoicism. The best example of this is to be found in Wotton's *Character of a Happy Life*, which may be regarded as a Christian version of the famous *Integer Vitae*.

But Hall was never the perfect stoic, nor even a good example of a Christian stoic. He was far too sensistive to the opinion formed of him by his fellow men.

> 'Next to the approbation of God and the testimony of mine own conscience, I will seek for a good reputation with men. . . . It is hard for me ever to do good, unless I be reputed good.' (P., VI 23, 99.)

His pessimistic outlook on life finds no echo in the author of *Integer Vitae*. 'I have not been in others' breasts; but, for my own part, I never tasted of delight.' (P., VI 19, 81.)

Youth knows the meaning of *Weltschmerz*. Let us hope that there were few Anglican vicars of 32, even in the seventeenth century, who, when the growing pains of adolescence were over, would have described life in the following terms: 'There is nothing below, but toiling, grieving, wishing, hoping, fearing; and weariness in all these.'

(*b*) Worldly wisdom made its appearance in Hall's earliest work, and remained with him almost until the end. Only after he had passed through the furnace of affliction and turned his aged eyes from earth to heaven, did he lose it. At times he seems to wear a 'knowing look' and to speak with a touch of cynicism.

> 'The rich man hath many friends; although, in truth, riches have them and not the man.'
>
> 'Great men's favours, friends' promises, and dead men's shoes I will esteem; but not trust in.'
>
> 'Friendship is brittle stuff. How know I, whether he, that now loves me, may not hate me hereafter?'

(*c*) Throughout his life Hall was intensely conservative.

> 'I will suspect a novel opinion, of untruth; and not entertain it, unless it may be deduced from ancient grounds.'

(*d*) He was all through life a firm believer in the need for diplomacy.

> 'Surely, he is not a fool, that hath unwise thoughts, but he, that utters them.'

(*e*) As we have already seen, there was one vice which he abhorred.

> 'Pride is the most dangerous of all sins.'

(*f*) One virtue which he admired in others and strove to cultivate in himself.

'Humility is ever the way to honour.' (*Contemplations*, I 253.)

(*g*) A certain kind of Christian whom at times he pitied; at times despised.

> 'He, that is but half a Christian, lives but miserably; for he neither enjoyeth God, nor the world.'

(*h*) One – the man of prayer – whom he wholeheartedly admired.

> 'Every good prayer knocketh at heaven, for a blessing: but an importunate prayer pierceth it, though as hard as brass; and makes way for itself, into the ears of the Almighty.'
> 'Good prayers, never come weeping home: I am sure I shall receive either what I ask, or what I should ask.'

(*i*) Many other ideas, with which we are already familiar, make their first appearance in these meditations. Hall felt that he lived in the closing years of the world's history. The world would soon pass away. The age in which he lived was of all ages 'the most boastful and least sound'.

(*j*) It was, of course, impossible to write such a book as Hall's *Meditations* without a good deal of self-reference: yet it is impossible to escape the feeling that in his early manhood Hall was far too self-conscious. The intense interest he took in himself was not entirely free from morbidness.

> 'I will endeavour, that my youth may be studious and flowered with the blossoms of learning and observation.'

(*k*) Long before the days of psycho-analysis he said:

> 'I will not lightly pass over my very dreams. They shall teach me somewhat; so neither night nor day shall be spent unprofitably: the night shall teach me what I am; the day, what I should be.'

(B)

Heaven upon Earth, or Of True Peace of Mind (1606).

Hall, says Fuller, was sometimes termed 'The English Seneca'. If this title were conferred on him before he was 31, it must have been a source of satisfaction to the recipient: for his admiration of Seneca was unbounded.

> 'Never any heathen wrote more divinely; never any philosopher more probably.'

This tract may be described as a Christianized version of Seneca's treatise on 'Tranquillity'. The result, as we shall see, was far from satisfactory. The tract was written when Hall was anything but a happy man. He was feeling the pinch of poverty and he was deeply grieved because his patron persisted in withholding a part of his stipend. As yet he was perhaps too young and had suffered too little to do justice to his subject. In any case the brochure smells of the lamp: it seems to emanate from the head rather than from the heart, and tells of what the author felt should be done rather than of what he had accomplished.

There are two 'universal enemies' of peace of mind. One is sin; the other affliction. So long as we are conscious of deliberate wrong-doing we can know no peace; for peace cannot be attained unless we are reconciled to God. We cannot be reconciled until sin has been remitted; and remission cannot come until satisfaction has been offered. Christ offered satisfaction and can give us peace; but only on condition that we put forth the hand of faith to receive the gift he offers.

Yet even when redeemed we are not exempt from temptation. Moral philosophers have given rules whereby reason can conquer passion; but no unregenerate man can profit by trying to obey them. He lacks power, and only Christ can give it.

The first obstacle to peace of mind is sin; the second the 'crosses' with which we meet on our way through life. Some of these are purely imaginary. For them our author prescribes the following remedy:

> 'Give thy body hellebore, thy mind good counsel, thine ear to thy friend; and these fantastic evils shall vanish away, like themselves.' (16.)

Trials, real trials, are sure to come and there are four ways in which we should prepare to meet them. In the first place, we must *expect* them; and as the soldier is trained to fight a foe he may never be called upon to face, so we must train ourselves to face whatever may befall. In the second place we must remember that these 'crosses' are sent by God; and it is useless to kick against the pricks. Then, too, we must bear in mind the *effect* which such trials have upon us.

> 'Crosses are the only medicine of sick minds.'

No doubt the medicine prescribed by the Great Physician is unpalatable; none the less it is efficacious. Finally we must call to mind the *issue* of all affliction. If rightly borne it delivers us from the sorrows of earth to the joys of heaven.

The *fear of death* is a source of disquietude to all. The only way in which to overcome it is to say to the grisly monster who seeks to terrify us, 'I shall conquer'. Christ is risen and I shall pass through the grim portal of the grave to the happiness of heaven.

Hall next proceeds to deal with what he calls the 'second rank of the enemies of peace'. In this section he seems to adopt the tone of a stoic philosopher rather than the attitude of a Christian minister.

The first of our enemies is wealth.

Surfeit, says our author, kills more than famine. Men covet

wealth as they covet social distinction: they fail to note that those who seem to have all that the heart of man can desire are rarely happy. Our only remedy against this temptation is to regard all external things as worthless. Wealth has never yet made man happy.

The second temptation is social eminence. Hall terms it honour. Even if we gain an exalted position we cannot transmit the qualities which gained it to our descendants. Even if we win the praise of our fellow men we cannot ensure its continuance. Indeed great prosperity exposes us to misery which may come from two very different quarters. God may withdraw it for our own good; man may destroy it out of jealousy and envy. 'He that is low need fear no fall.'

As for pleasure, she is the 'supreme sorceress'. Men seem to imagine that want of tranquillity means happiness. They are mistaken. Wise Solomon who sampled every form of pleasure came to regard it as 'vanity and vexation of spirit'. Like Delilah, pleasure is apt to rob men of their strength.

> 'Honours, Wealth, Pleasures, are casual, unstable, deceitful, imperfect, dangerous. We must learn to use them without trust, and to want them without grief.'

Passing on to what he calls 'the positive rules of our peace', Hall reiterates his belief in the impermanence of all earthly things; and insists that the permanent must be sought in God, where alone it is to be found.

Our only refuge from the storms of life is God. We may find Him even in prison or in exile. He will honour us when all despise us. As surely as the 'perfect fruition of fellowship with God is only to be found in Heaven'; so our 'inchoate conversing with him', which differs in degree but not in kind, from the former, makes of earth an imperfect heaven. There are two *subordinate rules* by which our *actions* are to be guided.

(1) 'We must refrain from all sin, and perform all duty.' The wavering heart in which conscience and pleasure are equally matched knows nothing but pain. It is because our Christianity is so often a half-hearted thing that we know no peace.

> 'It is a false slander raised on Christianity, that it maketh men dumpish and melancholic: for therefore are we heavy, because we are not enough Christians. We have religion enough, to mislike pleasures; not enough to overcome them.'

(2) 'We must do nothing doubtfully.' 'Resolution is the only mother of security.' So convinced is Hall of the necessity of 'Resolution' that he finds it hard to determine 'whether it be worse to do a lawful act with doubting or an evil with resolution'. '*Pecca fortiter*', said Luther. He tells us that he himself had been tempted to tamper with his belief that in all circumstances usury was a sin; that only

when he firmly refused to believe that anything could be said upon behalf of usury he found peace.

The discussion ends with 'Rules for Estate'. The first is to rely absolutely on the providence of God.

> 'Not that thou desirest shall come to pass, but that which God hath decreed.'
>
> 'Neither thy fears, nor thy hopes, nor vows shall either foreslow or alter it.'
>
> 'Strive or be still, thy destiny shall run on; and, what must be shall be.'
>
> 'That, which God hath decreed, is already done in heaven, and must be done on earth.'

Second, 'A persuasion of the goodness and fitness of it for us'. Our desires are insatiable: there is no living man who lacks a grievance but God knows best what is good for us. In any case we must submit.

> 'God willeth not things, because they are good; but they are good, because he wills them.'

In his 'Conclusion' Hall insists that tranquillity can be won only through strenuous effort. Men work hard in the pursuit of 'riches, preferment, learning, bodily pleasures'; why then should they not work equally hard to obtain peace of mind?

As a piece of devotional literature this essay cannot be regarded as a success. The views expressed may be true; they are not presented in an attractive form. They cannot have made many converts. Calvinism here assumes a form that is almost indistinguishable from fatalism, and the words with which the treatise ends are more in harmony with the spirit of a proud stoic than that of a humble Christian.

> 'Go now, ye vain and Idle Worldlings, and please yourselves in the large extent of your rich manors, or in the homage of those whom baseness of mind hath made slaves to your greatness, or in the price and fashions of your full wardrobe, or in the wanton varieties of your delicate gardens, or in your coffers full of red and white earth; or, if there be any other earthly things, more alluring, more precious, enjoy it, possess it, and let it possess you: let me have only my Peace; and let me never want it, till I envy you.'

(*d*) LATER MEDITATIONS

It would serve little purpose to examine in detail each of Hall's latest meditations. He was not a mystic: indeed his power of spiritual vision was but small. Two ideas occur over and over again. For the Christian – especially if he were an Anglican living in the time of the Commonwealth – earth was a desert drear: Heaven was his home. To imagine, as far as that is possible, the state of the faithful departed; and what is still more difficult to attempt to acquire a foretaste of their blessed estate is all that lies within the reach of the most devout.

So at least thought Joseph Hall. We therefore select three meditations and deal with them. No reader will miss much if he passes them by altogether. We end with an account of two booklets of much greater interest. One throws a good deal of light on Hall's character: the other gives us a good idea of the Elizabethan view of life in the world to come.

I

Sussurium Cum Deo/Soliloquies:/or,/Holy Self-Conferences of the Devout Soul, upon Sundry Choice Occasions;/with Humble Addresses/to the/Throne of Grace./By Joseph, Bishop of Norwich.

This is one of the most attractive pamphlets Hall ever wrote. The titles alone of the eighty pieces of which it is composed deserve attention; for they are most happily chosen and give an admirable description of the meditation which follows. False Joy, True Light, the Sure Refuge, True Wealth, Beneficial Want, the Sick Man's Vows, Unwearied Motion and Rest Eternal may serve as examples.

On the eve of Caesar's murder Shakespeare tells us that Casca was impressed by certain portents: a thunderstorm such as he had never seen before, the 'bird of night' sitting at noonday in the market place, the lion which he met over against the Capitol. Casca refused to accept a rationalistic explanation of such happenings. In this respect Hall and Casca were at one.

> 'Seldom ever do we read of any great mutation in Church or State, which is not ushered in with some strange prodigies: either raining of blood; or apparition of comets; or, airy armies fighting in the clouds . . . or, some such like uncouth premonitors; which the Great and Holy God sends purposely to awaken our security; and to prepare us either for expectation or prevention of judgments.'

'What are these?' says Banquo when he first meets the witches on the blasted heath,

> So wither'd and so wild in their attire;
> That look not like the inhabitants o' the earth,
> And yet are on't.

In one soliloquy entitled Satan's Prevalence, Hall finds one of the clearest proofs of Satanic influence in 'the marvellous multitude of witches abounding in all parts'.

> 'Once one of these clients of Hell, in a whole country, was hooted at as a strange monster; now, hundreds are discovered, in one shire. . . . What shall we say to all these over-pregnant proofs of the unusually prevailing power of Hell?'

We do not attach the same significance to portents as the Elizabethan did; nor do we believe in the existence of witches. In both respects Hall was a man of his time. Apart from these two instances, however, it would be difficult to find a single passage which might not have been written in the twentieth century. It is hard to name any other seventeenth-century bishop whose language so closely resembles that which a good writer would use today.

1

Hall writes as an old man with a wide experience of life. He finds three reasons for thankfulness.

(*a*) He had been reared in a good home.

> 'O God, it is Thy mercy, that Thou hast vouchsafed to allow me an early interest in Thee, even from my tender years.'

(*b*) Despite the fact that he had never been physically strong, he had never suffered intense pain. After telling us what many a better man had been called upon to endure: 'the painful girds of an unremovable stone, the amputation of a limb' (in days when anaesthetics were unknown) and so forth, he says:

> 'I cannot but acknowledge how just it might be in Thee, O God, to mix the same bitter cup for me; and how merciful it is, that, knowing my weakness, thou hast forborne hitherto to load me with so sad a burden.'

(*c*) All through life he had followed the *via media* in matters of devotion. He had never been a formalist who prayed by rote who could not dispense with a book of devotions forgetting 'that every beggar can, with sufficient eloquence, importune the passenger for his alms', and that we have to do with 'such a God as more esteems broken clauses made up with hearty sighs, than all the compliments of the most curious eloquence in the world'.

On the other hand, he had never been one of those who 'so abhorred all set forms and fixed hours of invocation, teaching, and so practising, that they may not pray, but when they feel strong impulsion of God's Spirit in that holy work', with the result, that 'at times whole days, yea weeks, have gone over their heads, unblessed by their prayers'.

2

Whether nature was originally 'red in tooth and claw', or whether the lower creation became cruel when man fell, Hall does not know. Nor does he greatly trouble; for he is far more concerned with the fact that 'Man's inhumanity to man makes countless thousands mourn'. A lifelong pacifist he now prays:

> 'O Thou, that art the Lord of Hosts and the God of Peace, restrain Thou the violent fury of those, which are called by Thy name; and compose these unhappy quarrels, amongst them, that should be brethren.'

3

In the late 1640s England seemed to Joseph Hall a very spiritual Bedlam. There had been Adamites as early as A.D. 194; and there were Anabaptists in Amsterdam in 1535. All through the centuries there had been heretics and atheists. Hall refuses to 'rake in the ashes of these old forgotten lunatics': he has enough to do with the 'prodigious phrensies of the present age; than which there were never, since the world began, either more or worse'.

> 'O Thou, that art the great and sovereign Physician of Souls; that, after seven years' brutality, restoredst the frantic Babylonian to his shape and senses; look down mercifully upon our Bedlam, and restore the distracted world to their right temper once again.'

4

Second only to Hall's concern about the spread of heresy was his concern about the low spiritual condition of many of the clergy. He quotes Maimonides to show how eager the ancient Jews were to have a priesthood void of physical defect. Thus it was, says Hall, that God trained men through 'external rites' and 'bodily perfections' to believe that what He really desired was 'inward purity of heart, and integrity of unspotted life'.

> 'Can we think the spiritual blemishes of Thine immediate servants under the Gospel, can be a less eyesore to God, than the external blemishes of the Priesthood under the law?'

5

Of almost every good man who lives to reach a ripe old age we may safely say that certain ideas, certain basic principles accompany him through life. We mention a few of these which occur in this meditation. Some as we shall see he derived from the Stoics; some from Christ.

(*a*) Hall lived and died a Calvinist. Like his great master he bowed in deepest reverence before the Majesty and Glory of God.

> 'If we could attain to settle in our thoughts a right apprehension of the Majesty of God, it would put us into the comfortable exercise of all the affections that belong to the soul.
>
> 'O God, let it be the main care of my life, to know Thee; and, whom Thou hast sent, Jesus Christ Thy Son, my Saviour, I cannot, through Thy mercy, fail of a heavenly disposition of soul, while I am here; and of a life of eternal glory, with Thee, hereafter.'

(*b*) Hall laid great stress on the part which conscience plays in the Christian life.

> 'Every man is a little world within himself; and, in this little world, there is a court of judicature erected, wherein, next under God, the conscience sits as the supreme judge, from whom there is no appeal.'

Yet conscience is not infallible.

> 'O my God . . . guide my conscience aright; and keep this great judge in my bosom, from corruption and error.'

(*c*) Hall strongly suspected the man who ever wore an unruffled brow.

> 'For spiritually there is never a perfect calm, but after a tempest; the wind, and earthquake, and fire make way for the soft voice.
>
> 'I desire nothing more in the world, than that this fire of Thine (i.e. the fire Christ brought) may flame up in the soul. . . . Set me at variance with myself that I may be at peace with Thee.'

(*d*) Man is here to *fight*.

> 'We are here in a perpetual warfare, and fight we must: surely, either fight or die.'

And to *work*.

> 'Labour is my destiny; and labour shall be my trade. Something I must always do, whose not unactive spirit abhors nothing more, than the torment of doing nothing.'
>
> 'Improvement gives a true value to all blessings. A penny in the purse is worth many pounds, yea talents, in an unknown mine. That is our good, which doth us good.'

(*e*) At a time when kindness to animals was less common in England that it is today, Hall was a lover of animals. If Coleridge is right in saying that 'He prayeth best who loveth best all things both great and small', Joseph Hall prayed well.

(*f*) In Hall's character there was a strongly ascetic element. Like his hero, the Apostle Paul, he strove to 'keep his body under'.

> 'Whom do we find more noted for holiness, than those, who have been most austere in the restraints of bodily pleasures and contentments? In the Mount of Tabor, who should meet with our Saviour in His Transfiguration, but those two Eminent Saints, which had fasted an equal number of days with Himself?'

(*g*) In conclusion, certain favourite ideas which occur over and over again are to be found here. Hall never escaped from Seneca, never entirely ceased to be a stoic.

> 'Friends may fail us.'
> 'All earthly pleasures have their drawbacks.'
> 'Want is beneficial.'
> 'All men are apt to be wise in their own conceit.'
> 'Wealth is "an internal state".'
>
> 'O God, give me to covet, that my mind may be rich in knowledge; that my soul may be rich in grace; that my heart may be rich in true contrition: as for the pelf of this world, let it make them miserable that admire it.'

II

The Breathings of The Devout Soul

Even though the title of this tract is not altogether a happy one (is it not better that others should describe us as 'devout' than that we should claim the title for ourselves?) this is one of the simplest and most beautiful of Hall's devotional works. To a large extent it is written in pure Saxon and contains an unusual number of monosyllabic words. It consists of forty-nine short meditations, all of which are virtually prayers; some indeed, are actually written in the form of prayers. Some are so personal that they seem to have little reference to other people: yet even these may be read with profit. Others, of a more general character, might yield material of value to any one who desired to compile a book of private devotions for his own personal use.

First then, let us consider those prayers which are almost purely personal; which spring, so to speak, from experience and characteristics peculiar to Joseph Hall.

(*a*) In early manhood he did not expect to enjoy a long life. Now he is old and this is his prayer.

> 'Crown my decayed age with such fruits, as may be pleasing to Thee, and available to the good of many.'

(*b*) To one so sensitive to public opinion his downfall was a bitter blow. After his ejection from his bishopric he found that:

> 'Some pitied my condition, others praised his patience; one favoured him out of the opinion of some good, that he thinks he sees in me; another dislikes me for some imagined evil.'

At long last he has reached the conclusion which many a lesser man reaches earlier in life.

> 'All, is in what terms I stand with Thee, my God.'

(*c*) No one who knew him would ever have described Joseph Hall as a happy man. He was, by nature, a pessimist, who found it difficult to take a cheerful view of life. He knew his weakness, knew that he was guilty of the sin of *acidie*.

> 'O my God, I am conscious of my own infirmity: I know I am naturally subject to a dull and heavy dumpishness, under whatsoever affliction.
>
> 'I confess, O Lord, how much I am wanting to myself, in not stirring up this holy fire of spiritual joy; but suffering it to be raked up, under the dead ashes of a sad neglect.'

(*d*) In these 'Breathings' Hall deals with himself more faithfully than he does in any other of his writings. He knew that he was prone to pride.

> 'O Lord God, how subject is this wretched heart of mine to repining and discontentment! If it may not have what it would, how ready it is, like a froward child, to throw away what it hath! I know and feel this to be out of that natural pride, which is so deep-rooted in me; for could I be sensible enough of my own unworthiness, I should think everything too good, everything too much for me. . . . Lord let me find my own Nothingness: so shall I be thankful for a little, and, in my very want, bless Thee.'

It was a great change to leave a palace to live in a 'cottage', to exchange affluence for poverty. Like many another Hall found that it is 'the small attritions which wear us down'.

> 'Alas, my Lord God, how small matters trouble me! Every petty occurrence is ready to rob me of my peace; so as, methinks, I am some little cock-boat in a rough sea, which every billow topples up and down, and threats to sink.
>
> 'Let my heart be taken up with Thee; and then, what care I, whether the world smile or frown?'

This was one way in which Hall sought to conquer the impatience which petty cares and annoyance aroused in him: but there was another. Wherever he looked, at the close of the Civil War, he saw men maimed, 'plundered of estate', bereaved and so forth. In such a mood he cried:

> 'Who am I, Lord, that, for the present, I enjoy an immunity from all these sorrows?'

(*e*) In his great work on the subject, Rithscl has described Pietism as the recrudescence of medieval asceticism on Protestant soil. In his eyes Hall would have been undoubtedly regarded as a Pietist.

> 'I wander here, in a strange country; what wonder is it, if I meet with foreigners' fare, hard usage and neglect? Why do I intermeddle with the affairs of a nation, that is not mine? Why do I clog myself, in my way, with the base and heavy lumber of the world? Why are not my affections homeward? Why do I not long to see and enjoy my Father's house? O my God, Thou that hast put me into the state of a pilgrim, give me a pilgrim's heart; set me off from this wretched world, wherein I am: let me hate to think of dwelling here: let it be my only care, how to pass through this miserable wilderness, to the promised land of a blessed eternity.'

(*f*) There can be little doubt that Puritanism is at once more virile, more noble and inspiring than any form of Pietism. In one respect at least Hall was a thorough Puritan. He tried to live and work 'as ever in the Great Taskmaster's eye'. Until his Captain gave the signal for release he wished neither 'to cease from mental strife', nor to let his sword 'sleep in his hand'.

> 'O my God, I perceive my night hastening on apace: my sun draws low: and the air begins to darken. Let me bestir myself, for the time: let me lose none of my few hours: let me work hard, awhile; Because I shall soon rest everlastingly.'

(*g*) Let us turn in closing to consider those beliefs which meant so much to Hall that he wished to persuade others to accept them.

(1) Man, however much he may desire to do so, is unable in his own strength to do the will of God.

> 'Lord, work me to what Thou requirest; and then, require what Thou wilt.'

D

(2) When we offer thanks to God for all His goodness, we much remember the evils we have escaped as well as the good we have received.

(3) In Elizabethan England, as in every country affected by the Renaissance, men had a passionate desire to be remembered after they were dead. *Non omnis moriar*. Hall shared this feeling.

> 'Every man, Lord, is unwilling that his name should die: we are all naturally ambitious, of being thought on when we are gone.'

In view of this he prays:

> 'O God, let it be my care and ambition, whatever become of my memory here below, that my name may be recorded in heaven.'

(4) God has given Hall (and many another man) one talent: he is at a loss to know whether to pray for more power or to ask for grace to use the little power he has to better purpose.

> 'Here I am before Thee, to await Thy pleasure: Thou knowest whether it be better to give me more ability, or to accept of that poor ability Thou hast given me; but since when Thou hast given me most, I shall still and ever stand in need of Thy forgiveness; let my humble suit be to Thee always, rather for pardon of my defects, than for a supply of Thy graces.'

(5) In his tract on Chilianism, Hall deals with the errors of those who believed that Christ was about to reign on earth for a thousand years. There he argued: here he prays.

> 'O my Saviour, while others weary themselves with the disquisition of Thy personal reign here upon earth for a thousand years, let it be the whole bent and study of my soul, to make sure of my personal reign with Thee in heaven to all eternity.'

(6) Whilst God has been good to Joseph Hall, has loaded him with benefits, he has made a poor return for all this kindness. Therefore he prays:

> 'O Thou, that has been so bountiful in heaping Thy rich mercies upon me, vouchsafe to grant me yet one gift more: give grace and power, to improve all Thy gifts to the glory of the Giver.'

III

Select Thoughts (1647–48)

In these 105 'Select Thoughts' Hall gives a summary of ideas he had often expressed.

(1) As against those whose motto seems to be *nil admirari* he is determined to admire *everything* in God's marvellous creation.

(2) As against those who turn the object of their love into an idol, as David did with Absolom, he is resolved to love none however dear save 'in God'.

(3) Unlike the worldling who judges all by sense, the Christian 'looks not on the things which are seen'. He lives by faith, 'that heroical Virtue, which makes a man, with a holy contempt to overlook all the pleasing baits of the world'.

(4) 'Sooner or later we grow weary of all we have or do; only in heaven is there no satiety. . . . Since my heart can be sometimes in heaven, why should it not be always there.'

(5) The wise man does not worry about the future of the world. That is in God's hands. The Christian's business is 'quietly to take his part in the present'.

(6) Man passes through three stages: childhood, youth, age. So does the world. Once man lived in a state of nature; then came the law: when the true 'Sun of Righteousness shone forth in person, it was high noon'. Now we live in the 'evening of the world, and a summer's evening is a winter's day'. Time is drawing to a close; soon the Saviour will reappear.

(7) To Calvinism Hall owed one virtue: he was entirely free from sentimentalism. He never wearied of impressing on his readers that in the presence of God – at once Father and Judge – man must be filled with holy awe.

> 'It is our honour and his favour, that we are allowed to love God: it is our duty to fear Him. We may be too familiar, in our love: we cannot be too awful in our fear.'

(8) Hall never cared for money; never admired those whose chief claim to distinction was wealth. The man whom he esteemed was one who was 'fraught with knowledge, eminent in goodness, and truly gracious'.

(9) He was sensitive, perhaps too sensitive, to the good opinion of others; and by no means blind to the influence of environment.

> 'Good like evil is contagious: next to being good, is, to consort with the virtuous.' (XX.)

(10) When things go badly, all men are apt to blame others rather than themselves. Adam tried to blame his wife for his sin.

> 'Yea, rather than we will want shifts, our very stars shall be blamed; which are no more accessory to our harms, than our eyes are to the eclipse of their most eminent lights.' (XX.)

(11) Affliction is blessing in disguise.

> 'Every man can say he thanks God for ease: for me I bless God for my troubles.' (XXI.)

(12) 'It is not hard to observe, that the more holy any person is, the more he is afflicted with others' sin.' (XXXVIII.)

(13) Over and over again Hall emphasizes the great truth that God can, and does turn our sin to our advantage. (XXXIX.)

(14) Here, as in many other places, Hall tells us that he is dismayed at the sight of 'ignorant and unlearned men presuming to interpret the most obscure Scriptures'. (There was plenty of that sort of thing when he wrote.)

> 'In the waters of life, the Divine Scriptures, there are shallows, and there are deeps: shallows, where the lamb may wade; and deeps, where the elephant may swim.'

Exegesis is like every other art.

> 'In the Tailor's trade, every man can stitch a seam; but every man cannot cut out a garment: in the Sailor's art, every one may be able to pull at a cable; but every one cannot guide the helm.'

So it is in medicine: so it ought to be, but is not, in Biblical exposition. (XLIV.)

(15) Man is half angel and half beast. He cannot remain where he is.

> 'Either he must degenerate into a beast, or be advanced to an angel.'

Hall's aim was 'to come as near to the angel, as this clog of my flesh will permit'. (LXII.)

(16) God does not suffer a divided affection. There are many 'double-hearted' men: but a man with two hearts is as much of a monster as a man with two heads. (LXII.)

(17) Few thoughts occur more frequently in the writings of Hall (and in those of many of his contemporaries) than that the world is soon to come to an end.

> 'We are fallen upon the old age of the world; the last times, and therefore, the nearest to dissolution.
>
> 'There is ice in our spiritual veins. Our age is more wickedly miserable than all its predecessors. Ours has the common fault of age, loquacity. No age was ever so guilty of tongue and pen. Every man thinks what he lists, and speaks what he thinks, and writes what he speaks, and prints what he writes. Neither would the world talk so much, did it not make account it cannot talk long.'

(18) 'God, though he be free of his entertainments, yet is curious of his guests.' (Col. iii. 9, 10.) (LXXVI.)

(19) 'He who fights and runs away lives to fight another day' is a maxim in which Hall firmly believed.

> 'In the carriage of our holy profession, God can neither abide us cowardly nor indiscreet. . . . True Christian wisdom and not carnal fear, is that, wherein we must consult for advice, when to stand to it, and when to give back.' (LXXXIV.)

(20) Only the man who has learned to 'Contemplate' can bear to be alone.

> 'Men of barren and unexercised hearts can no more live without company than fish out of water.' (LXXXV.)

(21) Occasionally, if infrequently, our author sheds light on his own character. He tells us he was ambitious. Speaking of Christ's Ascension he says:

> 'Even nature is ambitious; and we do all affect to mount higher as to come down is death.' (XCIX.)

(22) Occasionally we are given a side-light on the England of that day.

> 'I blush and grieve, to see how far we are exceeded by Turks and Infidels; whom mere nature hath taught more tenderness to the poor brute creatures, than we have learned from the holier rules of charitable Christianity.' (C.)

(23) In all that Hall wrote after the overthrow of episcopacy he is careful to leave the subject entirely alone. He devoted the whole of his attention to the advocacy of something which he had always believed in his heart of hearts to be of far greater moment than the particular form of Church Government which this or that Christian Community had seen fit to adopt.

> 'Pious thoughts, heavenly affections, fervent love, reverential fear, spiritual joy, holy desires, divine ravishments of spirit, strict obediences, assiduous devotions, faithful affiances, gracious engagements, firm resolutions, and effectual endeavours of good, and whatsoever might work a dearness of respect betwixt the soul and the God of Spirits.'

From a purely literary standpoint Hall never wrote anything less pleasing in the whole course of his long life. And yet perhaps in this attempt to crush into the shortest possible space all the elements of the devout life, as he understood it, he was never more successful. This is his testimony: the last of those 'Select Thoughts' by which he hoped to serve his fellow men and to be held by them in grateful remembrance when he could write no more.

IV

The Holy Order, or Fraternity of The Mourners in Sion

Richard Baxter was forty years younger than Hall. Like Hall he was a prolific writer. Nearly two hundred books, it is said, stand to his credit. His wife maintained that he had written far too much and no doubt she was right. Like Hall he knew by experience the meaning of sickness and sorrow. But in one respect he differed from the Bishop. He was in spite of all his sufferings a cheerful man. When he was nearing his end Hall wrote *The Holy Order, or Fraternity of Mourners in Sion*: in the same year Baxter published his book *Right*

Method for a Settled Peace of Conscience. On the ninth page of this book the following words occur:

> 'Keep company with the more cheerful sort of the Godly; *there is no mirth like the mirth of believers.* . . . Converse with men of the strongest faith, that have this heavenly mirth.'

Undoubtedly Hall had good reason to feel despondent. After forty-four years of married life he had lost his wife. He was poor and lonely. The Church in which he had once occupied a prominent position and to which he was passionately attached lay in what seemed to be final ruin. Heresy of every kind abounded, morals were lax, the end of a wicked world was close at hand.

In this lamentable state of affairs what was he to say or do? The only explanation he had to offer of the evils by which he was encompassed including the Civil War with its aftermath of suffering and unsettlement, was that England had sinned and was therefore being chastised by God. His only remedy was repentance and amendment of individual lives. To this end he suggested that all who agreed with him should bind themselves into an Order which was a curious blend of a Roman Catholic fraternity and the bands of Jews one sees in Jerusalem beating their heads against the Wailing Wall.

It is hard to determine whether Hall hoped that those who agreed with him would eventually form a visible society: probably not. It is obvious that he desired to stimulate certain feelings in his readers and to direct these feelings into a specific channel. One cannot say that he desired like the German Pietists of the following century to create an *ecclesiola in ecclesia*, for in his eyes the English Ecclesia had for the time being no formal existence. Yet the truth remains that in this tract he comes nearer to German Pietism than he does in any other; and that the pietism to which he approached was not so much the energetic beneficent kind with which we meet in Francke: but the 'other-worldly' type which we find in Spener.

For the purpose of this Holy Order of Mourners, Hall thought it meet 'to tie ourselves, by our secret and silent vows, to these rules following'. They are fifteen in number and are set out in some twelve hundred words.

The backbone of the order was to consist, it would seem, of (dispossessed) clergymen. The fourteenth rule runs as follows:

> 'That, whensoever we shall be called to deliver the message of God to His people in public auditories, we shall not fail to lay open and bewail the sins of the time: to rouse up our hearers, with all zealous exhortations, to a lively sense of just sorrow, for the universal overflowings of wickedness; and to a vehement and godly striving against the stream thereof by their prayers and utmost endeavours.'

It was hoped, however, that as many as possible of the laity would join the Order, even though they were so busy that they could not carry out all its rules.

Once a week the Order was to devote a whole day to fasting and prayer. The members were to live an austere life in which they reduced pleasure to a minimum and eschewed every kind of convivial gathering. The badge of membership was to be an abundant flow of tears.

> 'We, that are Sion's Mourners, shall not need to be distinguished, as other Orders are wont, by colours, devices, habiliments, our qualifications will be easily discerned, by our sad faces, wet eyes, deep sighs, mortified carriage, willing neglect of those vanities wherewith others are transported, our holy retiredness, assiduous devotions, and strict professions of godliness.'

Two of the rules deserve attention. The Brethren are to be filled with ardent love for one another; and, in bewailing sin they are to 'spend our main censures upon ourselves: not being apt to fly out upon the weaknesses and defects of our brethren' (i.e. of those who do not belong to the Order).

And since the sole object of the Order is to bring peace and welfare to God's Church, its members must 'carefully avoid all such ways and means, which may in any sort, endanger the widening of the unhappy breaches, and multiplying of the many and miserable distractions thereof'.

This then was the mood in which Hall left the world. No wonder he speaks with enthusiasm of the felicity which awaits him in heaven. We do not propose to quote from such passages at length. They are too conventional to afford much enlightenment.

Calamy tells us that Baxter 'talked in the pulpit with great freedom about another life, *like one that had been there*, and was come back as a sort of express from thence to make a report concerning it'. In this respect, it seems to us, Baxter was superior to Hall. Therefore instead of presenting a number of pious aspirations we shall end by giving some account of Hall's idea of heaven.

V

The Invisible World

As we have already seen there is a marked difference in style between Hall's sermons and his meditations. In the former he speaks as the mouthpiece of the Church and relies to a large extent on external authority: in the latter he speaks as a private Christian and expresses opinions, which, though based on the Bible reflect his own personal experience and the view of life to which personal experience gave rise.

His scholarship was less extensive than that of Usher, his learning less profound than that of Lancelot Andrewes – 'the miracle of our times'. None the less he could always lay his hand on an apposite quotation from the Fathers when he desired to do so. Like those of his contemporaries, his sermons were studded with quotations from patristic works, at that time regarded as at once the bulwark and the hall-mark of orthodox opinion. But Hall did not confine quotation to the writings of the Fathers. His innate conservatism, his firm belief that every novel opinion was certainly dangerous and probably erroneous, led him to seek support for his opinions in the writings of others, who, though regarded as less authoritative than the Fathers were yet held in high esteem. There was probably no man of his generation who drew upon this source of support so freely as Joseph Hall: and just as no preacher of his time presents us with a more vivid picture of contemporary society: so there is no preacher who by means of apt quotation brings to us so many statements of views then almost universally accepted but now obsolete and almost utterly forgotten; yet for that very reason of not a little historic interest.

Hall's 'meditation' on the invisible world, is not so much a devotional work – though it contains many devotional passages – as a treatise on angelology, as understood in Elizabethan times. If it does nothing else, it serves to remind us who live after eighteenth-century rationalism and nineteenth-century biblical criticism have done their work, after the views of twentieth-century scientists in regard to the nature and constitution of the universe have revolutionized the cosmic outlook of all educated men, how far removed the Elizabethan world is from our own, how near in spite of Reformation and Renaissance were many of its philosophical and theological views to those of the Middle Ages.

The Invisible World began as a devotional tract, and developed into a theological treatise in which the views of a typical Elizabethan in regard to the nature of angels and the state of the soul after death are expressed. To this it owes its interest to any student of the Elizabethan Age. From it as from no other of Hall's writings do we realize how deep is the cleavage which separates that most marvellous age in English history from our own.

In the opening section there is a characteristic statement which gives us a clear picture of the views of our forefathers in regard to the part which angels play in the life of the universe.

> 'Surely, all, that know they have souls, must needs believe a world of spirits, which they see not; if from no other grounds, yet out of that analogy, which they cannot but find betwixt this lesser and that greater world. For, as this little world, Man, consists of an outward visible body; and an inward spiritual soul, which gives life and motion to that organical frame, so possessing all parts, that it is wholly in all, and in each part wholly; so must it also be

> in this great universe, the sensible and material part whereof hath being and moving from those spiritual powers, both supreme and subordinate, which dwell in it, and fill and actuate it.'

That, then, is the Elizabethan view of the relation between the spiritual and the material world.

> 'The material world is surrounded by the spiritual: yet this is not a mere involution only, but a spiritual permeation and inexistence; yet without confusion.' (Par. 2.)

The angels play a part in the management of our world.

> 'The God of Order hath given them their own separate essences, offices, operations; as for the managing of their spiritual commonwealth within themselves, so for the disposing, governing, and moving of this sensible world.'

He quotes with approval 'the great word' of Aquinas. 'One angel is of such power, that he were able to govern all the corporeal creatures of the world': and expresses his own view in these words: 'If we say that it pleases God by their ministration to sway and order the marvellous affairs of this great universe, we shall not, I suppose, vary from truth.' (Par. 4.)

Hall laments the fact that he has often forgotten God; so, though we are guarded by *millions* of angels he has often forgotten their existence to say nothing of their presence.

> 'O Blessed Spirits, ye are ever by me, ever with me, ever about me: I do as good as see you; for I know you to be here; I reverence your glorious persons; I bless God for you; I walk awfully, because I am ever in your eyes; I walk confidently, because I am ever in your hands.'

Having discussed the existence and the presence of angels Hall proceeds to discourse on their *power*. He recalls the fact that one angel destroyed all the first-born in Egypt, another Sennacherib's army. But if angels are used to destroy they are also used to preserve; and therein lies our safety.

Angels excel in strength; they also excel in knowledge. True, the 'closet of man's heart is locked up from them; as reserved solely to their Maker'; but even here there are 'insensible chinks' through which they look. That, however, is their only limitation.

> 'All other things, whether secrets of nature, or closest counsels or events, are as open to their sight, as the most visible objects are to ours.'

Yet their knowledge is even more profound than this. 'They do not only know things as they are in themselves, and in their inward and immediate causes; but do clearly see the First and Universal Cause of all things, and that in his glorious essence. . . .'

The next point discussed is the way in which angels are employed. Whilst millions of angels attend God's throne and sing endless

Hallelujahs, others are busy with the affairs of this world. Many references are made to stories of angelic activity recorded in the Old Testament. Such activity, Hall maintains, still persists. 'Have we been raised up from deadly sicknesses, when all natural helps have given us up?' Hall quotes with approval a passage from a sermon which his beloved Gerson once preached on angels;

> 'Whence is it, that little children are conserved from so many perils of their infancy; fire, water, falls, suffocations, but by the agency of angels?'

The angels are responsible for 'unusually violent hurricanes, earthquakes and the like. . . .' Nothing hinders, but that the Almighty, for the manifestation of his power and justice, may set spirits, whether good or evil, on work to do the same things sometimes with more state and magnificence of horror. When in a great storm 'huge massy stones and irons of the churches are transported above the possibility of natural distance, together with the strange preservation of the persons assembled, with other accidents sensibly accompanying those astonishing works of God, still fresh in the minds of many, shewed them plainly to be wrought by a stronger hand than nature's'. Hall gives a list of inexplicable occurrences, e.g. a man is warned in a dream to leave his house and in this way saves his life and asks a question, 'Whence can this be, but by the suggestion of spirits?'

The question of degree and order occupied almost as prominent a place in Elizabethan thought as it did in the Middle Ages. Hence we are not surprised to find that our author transfers ideas derived from purely human experience to the angels. Amongst them, too, he is convinced, there must be degrees and orders.

> 'Heaven hath nothing in it, but perfection: but even perfection itself hath degrees. Equality hath no place, either in earth or in hell: we have no reason to seek it in heaven.'

Hence it is that the angelic host is divided into 'Thrones, Dominions, Principalities' and so forth. If there are angels there are also archangels. In dealing with this mysterious subject Hall gives evidence of his native shrewdness and common sense. He is indignant with a certain ecclesiastic, Forner by name, who solemnly assured mankind that God was a king who kept a celestial court in which the Seraphim were lords of the chamber, the Cherubim lords of the cabinet-council; whilst Thrones were 'the entire favourites, in whom the Almighty placeth His rest'. Not content with these very questionable statements Forner goes on to insist that Archangels are ten times as beautiful as Angels: Principalities twenty times as beautiful as Archangels; Powers forty times more splendid than Principalities, and so on through elaborate calculation which ends with the statement that the Seraphim are ninety times more glorious than the Cherubim. Of Forner's spiritual mathematics and of similar speculations from other sources to which he refers, Hall says:

> 'For me, I must crave leave to wonder at this boldness; and profess myself as far to seek, whence this learning should come, as how to believe it. I do verily believe, there are divers orders of celestial spirits: I believe, they are not to be believed, that dare to determine them; especially when I see him that was wrapt into the third heaven, varying the order of their places in the several mentions of them.' (Cf. Eph. i. 21 with Col. i. 21.)

Yet, Hall continues, all such knowledge of angels – their number, power, knowledge, glory – would be of little value to us unless we knew that they appeared to men. In other words, he firmly believed in angelic apparitions. He admitted, of course, that many such stories were spurious. He did not believe, for instance, in the 'Genius' of Socrates, which the old philosopher maintained 'was wont to check him, when he went about any unmeet enterprise; and to forward him in good'. Then too there were many Roman Catholic stories of angelic ministration which he dismissed with contempt. But though there were many false stories there were many true. 'This we know, that so sure as we see men, so sure we are that Holy men have seen angels.' He accepts, without question, every story of angelic appearance recorded in the Bible. He also believed that angels appeared to members of the primitive church. . . . 'I doubt not, but the holy Virgins, Theophila, Agnes, Lucia, Cecilia, and others, saw the good angels protectors of their chastity.'

Confessing that he was one who had learned to take 'the mid way betwixt distrust and credulity' he was ready to grant 'that those retired saints of the prime ages of the Church had sometimes such heavenly companions, for the consolation of their forced solitude'. As the Church grew older angelic apparitions became less needful and therefore more infrequent. In his own day, Hall felt that they had almost ceased. Almost but not entirely. There are still authentic instances of angelic apparitions in modern times. Such a one, says Hall, was that which Melancthon – 'that worthy divine' – records in his commentary on Daniel. Grynaeus, a distinguished scholar of Heidelberg, came to hear a celebrated preacher in Speyer. Displeased with certain passages in the sermon, he interviewed the preacher, and pointed out parts of his doctrine in which he was at fault. Incensed at this, the Papal authorities determined to punish him. He was dining with Melancthon and one or two other friends, when 'a grave old man of a goodly countenance, seemly and richly attired' knocked at the door. In a friendly way he warned Grynaeus that he was to be arrested and imprisoned within the hour. Grynaeus made his escape. His enemies sought him in vain. In telling the story, Melancthon 'acknowledged God's fatherly providence in sending this angel of his for the rescue of his faithful servant'.

A few such instances are recorded by 'Simon Goulartius, in his collection of admirable and memorable histories of our time'. To this book 'for brevity sake' Hall refers his readers.

Hall, however, was convinced that he had no need to turn to books for examples of angelic activity. In his last visitation of the Diocese of Exeter he took 'a strict and personal examination' into the cure of a cripple who being thrice admonished to wash in a well at St Maderne's (St Maternus) in Cornwall, was completely cured. And after all, this was but one case out of many.

> 'How many have we known, that have fallen from very high towers, and into deep pits, past the natural possibilities of hope, who yet have been preserved not from death only, but from hurt. ''Whence'', he continues, ''could these things be, but by the secret aid of those invisible helpers?'' '

Yet though the blessed angels do minister to our bodily needs, their main concern is with our souls. They fill the mind 'with good motions, enlighten the understanding, repel temptation, comfort our sorrows, quicken our dullness and encourage our weakness'.

Last of all 'after they have carefully attended us here below', they 'convey our souls to their glory, and present them to the hands of their faithful Creator'.

> 'It is hard to believe that there have been occular witnesses of these happy convoys. Who lists may believe such stories. But Lazarus, whose soul was conveyed to Abraham's Bosom, was no exception to the general rule. As the souls of all God's saints land in one common harbour of blessedness, so they all participate of one *happy* means of portage.'

Finally Hall asks the question, 'How are we to regard angels, how behave towards them?' Here he reveals himself as a stout Protestant. He calls to mind that the Angel of the Apocalypse said to the writer of that mysterious book when he sought to worship him, 'See thou do it not, I am thy fellow servant'. He remembers that St Paul forbade 'a voluntary humility in worshipping of angels'. He even refuses to go as far as Bernard who said that we owe the angels 'reverence for their presence, devotion for their glory, and trust for their custody'.

We must not, then, give too much honour to angels; at the same time we must not rob them of the honour that is their due:

> 'A high and venerable conceit of their wonderful majesty, glory and greatness; an awful acknowledgment and reverential awe of their presence; a holy joy and confident assurance of their care and protection: and finally a fear to do ought, that might cause them to turn away their faces, in dislike from us.'

VI

The Souls of Men

Between his treatment of the holy angels and the fallen angels, Hall introduces us to his view of the soul.

Despite the fact that many learned men have denied the soul's existence, he finds it impossible to believe that man is purely material. It would be interesting, he says, to discuss the nature, origin, faculties, occupations of the soul as we meet with it when 'clogged with flesh'. But he must leave this to others; for his purpose is to consider the soul when 'Divested of this Earthly Case, and clothed with an eternity' either of bliss or woe.

It will be remembered that in dealing with the first section of this tract, we found that what was originally intended to be a devout meditation insensibly changed into a theological treatise. So here: the writer begins by referring to Socrates, Plato, Aristotle and other heathen thinkers who firmly believed in the immortality of the soul. He then proceeds to outline in a simple way what a modern might term his doctrine of sense-perception. But since the tract is neither an apologia nor a philosophical treatise, the discussion is of a very rudimentary character. 'The body can do nothing at all without the help of the soul: but the soul hath actions of its own.' Such is the germ of his theory.

> 'We walk, move, speak, see, feel, and do other human acts; the power, that doth them, is from the soul; the means or instrument, whereby they are done, is the body: no man will say the soul walks or sees, but the body by it; but we can no more say that the soul understands or thinks by the aid of the body, than we can say the body thinks or understands by means of the soul. These, therefore, being distinct and proper actions, do necessarily evince an independing and self-subsisting agent. . . . O my soul,' he concludes, 'thou couldst not be thyself, unless thou knewest thine original, heavenly; thine essence, separable; thy continuance, eviternal.'

It might be argued that in all this we find in a very rudimentary and inchoate form, ideas to be met with in two such different writers as Locke and Kant. Yet as the psychology is so crude and the reasoning so unconvincing, it is mentioned only to show how, despite their knowledge of Plato and Aristotle, English divines reasoned before modern psychology came into existence, before philosophy had undergone that 'Copernican change' which it owes to Kant.

In justice to Hall, however, we must remember that he attached little value to reasoning of this kind. It was on revelation, not on ratiocination that his beliefs were based. 'But, what do we call in reason and nature to this parle, where faith, by which Christianity teacheth us to be regulated, finds so full and pregnant demonstrations.'

It is to such sayings in the Bible as 'Father, into thy hands I commend my spirit', and to the passages in the Apostles' Creed, which deal with death and resurrection, that Hall turns for confirmation of his belief in the soul's immortality.

> 'If then he may be a man, certainly a Christian he cannot be, who is more assured, that he hath a soul in his body, than that his soul shall once have a being without his body.'

In this life, most men misunderstand the soul: 'entertain but dull and gloomy thoughts concerning it; as if it were no less void of light and activity, than it is of materiality and shape; not apprehending the spiritual agility and clearly-lightsome nature of that, whereby they are enlived.'

God has set a 'shining lamp' in each man's breast, whereby he may 'sufficiently discern natural and moral truths, the principles and conclusions whether of nature or art'. In those in whom this 'natural light' has given place to the spiritual, 'the soul can attain here and now, to see him that is invisible, and in his light to see light'. (Ps. xxxvi. 9.)

Now, it is true the soul is 'over-shaded with the interposition of this earth'; but 'as soon as this veil of wretched mortality is done away, it straightway enjoys a clear heaven for ever, and sees as it is seen'.

Hall refers with warm approval to a favourite saying of his beloved friend the late Earl of Norwich, that the moment the soul leaves the body it enjoys the vision of God and immediately 'passes into a condition like the angels'. He also believes that as the soul passed through degrees of grace in its earthly life; so it passes through degrees of bliss in the life after death. He approves the belief of Lancelot Andrewes that the angels receive 'an augmentation of happiness at the day of the last judgment, when they shall be freed from all charge and employments' and enter into that rest in which the perfection of their blessedness consists.

The next subject which Hall discusses he calls 'the soul's perpetual vigilancy, and fruition of God'. He condemns those, including Pope John XXII, who believed that the disembodied soul sleeps until the resurrection: and regrets that this heresy has reappeared in his own day, since it is entirely at variance with the promise made to the dying thief, 'This day shalt thou be with me in Paradise': with the Lord's words (John xviii. 24) and with the teaching of St Paul 'For now we see through a glass darkly: but then face to face'. 'Away then,' he cries, 'with that impious frenzy of the soul's, whether mortality or sleep in death. No, my soul, thou dost then begin to live: thou dost not begin to live, thou dost not awake, till then.' What sort of knowledge is that which the faithful departed possess?

For an adequate answer to this question, says Hall, we must wait until after death. 'Meanwhile,' he says, 'we may feel certain that we know much less of the thoughts of the departed than they can know of ours.' For they are like angels, whose knowledge comes from vision; not from sense and ratiocination. They receive supernatural light when they enter upon their glorified state.

We cannot say that they know the 'particular occurrences which we meet with here below': they certainly possess clear knowledge 'of all those things, which do any way appertain to their estate of blessedness'. Angels know each other. They take 'special notice of those souls, which they have guarded here, and conducted to their glory. If this be so, if the knowledge of our beatified souls shall be like theirs', it follows that we shall know our friends in heaven.

There was a time when Hall refused to draw such conclusions; now he can say:

> 'Surely our dissolution shall abate nothing of our natural faculties; our glory shall advance them, so as what we once knew we shall know better: and if our souls can then perfectly know themselves, why should they be denied the knowledge of others.'

We said at the outset, that this tract is rather of the nature of a theological treatise than a simple meditation. That is true; yet the devotional element, in some places more pronounced than in others is never entirely absent. Here, for instance, is the way in which Hall ends his discussion of the possibility of friends recognizing each other after death.

> 'How often have I measured a long and foul journey, to see some good friend; and digested the tediousness of the way, with the expectation of a kind entertainment, and the thought of that complacency which I should take in so dear a presence and yet, perhaps, when I arrived, I found the house disordered, one sick, another disquieted, myself indisposed: with what cheerful resolution should I undertake this my last voyage, where I shall meet with my best friends, and find them perfectly happy, and myself with them.'

As may be imagined, his account of 'the Glory of heaven enjoyed by blessed souls' based entirely on passages of Scripture is still more lyrical. It reminds us of the *O quanta qualia* of Abelard: of the *Urbs beata* of 'Bernard'.

Hall next proceeds to discuss the question of how the blessed spend 'not their time, but their eternity'. His answer is short and simple. 'In the exercise of the perpetual acts of their blessedness; Vision, Adhesion, Fruition.'

Each of these corresponds to one of the Christian virtues. On earth we have Faith; in heaven, Vision. Our eyes see God and this makes us blessed. That which was once Hope, is now Adhesion; we *possess* that which we once longed for. Charity has become Delight –

delight in the thing possessed – (Fruition). Thus instead of Faith, Hope, Charity we have and have for ever Sight, Possession, Enjoyment.

Two other points remain to be discussed. (1) On what terms do the departed stand to us? (2) What is the relation between the disembodied spirit and the body it has left behind?

(1) In leaving earth the saints leave certain graces behind them. They have no further need of Faith or Hope or Patience. But Charity 'can never be out of date' – charity both to God and man. Therefore the saints sue to God for us that we may be delivered out of the miseries and temptations which beset us in this earthly life, and for 'our society with them in their blessedness'. 'Other terms of communion we know none.' Hall lived and died a consistent Protestant. 'Where God is silent', he said, 'let us be willingly ignorant.' He rejects all Roman Catholic stories about saints revisiting this earth: believes in fact that such manifestations are produced by devils. He refuses to discuss what happened to Lazarus, the widow's son, Jairus' daughter when restored to earthly life. Of this we neither know nor can know anything. So in conclusion he turns to a point of far greater interest, (2) What is the relation between the disembodied spirit and the body it left behind? He firmly believed in the resurrection of the body: probably though he does not say so *in resurrectionem carnis*. The resurrection body, however, whatever it is must be 'of a clear brightness, without all earthly opacity: with agility, without all dullness; with subtlety, without grossness; with impassibility, without the reach of annoyance or corruption'.

He sums up his views on the future life in these simple and touching words:

> 'There, and then, shalt thou, O my soul, looking through clarified eyes, see, and rejoice to see, that glorious body of thy dear God and Saviour, which he assumed here below; and wherein he wrought out the great work of thy Redemption. There, shalt thou see the radiant bodies of all those eminent Saints whose graces thou hast wont to wonder at, and weakly wish to imitate. There shall I meet with the visible partners of the same unspeakable glory; my once dear partners, children, friends: and, if there can be room for any more joy in the soul that is taken up with God, shall both communicate and appropriate our mutual joys. There shall we, indissolubly, with all the choir of heaven pass our eviternity of bliss, in lauding and praising the incomprehensibly-glorious Majesty of our Creator, Redeemer, Sanctifier; in perpetual Hallelujahs to him that sits upon the throne.'

There are those unmoved by the picture of a golden city, whose hearts are touched with the picture of a heaven so much more homely if not so splendid and magnificent given in the lovely hymn 'There is a land of pure delight'. So there are many to whom endless hallelujahs are less attractive than a life of endless service and unwearied activity. For there are more Marthas than Marys (at least among English folk). Hall was a scholar, a man who had that almost insatiable curiosity which marked so many of the Elizabethans. He loved truth and longed to possess it, to know even as he was known. This is at once his strength and his weakness, for all men possess the defects of their qualities. In the last resort each man must form his own conception of heaven and his conception is likely to be far removed from the unspeakable truth. '*Eye hath not seen, nor ear heard, neither have entered the heart of man, the things which God hath prepared for them that love Him.*'

Yet there is no reason why brother should not reveal his dream to brother; for with dreams and nothing but dreams must we be content until the day dawns and the shadows flee away.

THE FALLEN ANGELS

The tract ends with an account of the Fallen Angels; for if it behoves us to think of the Good Angels for our comfort, we must consider the Evil Angels 'for our terror, caution and resistance'.

As one might expect, Hall begins his discussion with an attempt to answer the old, old question 'How was it possible for evil to enter God's creation?': How, to use his own expression, 'Should the good that He made, produce the evil, which He hates?' At their creation angels were endowed with 'perfection of understanding and freedom of will'. Unfortunately, however,

> 'those free inclinations of some of them swayed them away from that highest end, which they should have solely aimed at; to a faulty respect, unto oblique ends of their own.
>
> 'Hence was the beginning of sin. The revolting angels did not order their own particular, supposed, good, to the supreme and utmost end; but suffered their will to dwell in an end of their own: and, by this means, did put themselves into the place of God: not regulating their wills by another superior, but making their will the rule of their own desires; which was, in effect, to affect an equality with the Highest.'

Further than this, Hall, who regards all discussion as to what the first sin committed by the Fallen Angels really was, as futile, refuses to go.

Number

Of the number of the fallen angels Hall speaks with more confidence. If, he says, the evil spirits who 'possessed' one poor demoniac could be described as 'legion', i.e. 1,225, it is obvious that their total number must run into many millions. He agrees with Tertullian that no mortal man escapes their unwelcome attentions from his cradle to his death-bed.

Power

Of their power, Hall speaks with even greater confidence. He approves the statement of Aquinas, 'One angel is of such power, that he were able to govern all the corporeal creatures of the world'. In spite of this, however, we need not be afraid, nay more, we may feel perfectly secure; for their power is limited, is curbed by God and 'our protection is infinite'.

Knowledge

Their knowledge is equal to their power. Though fallen, they retain the knowledge they originally possessed. They know 'the natures and constitutions of the creatures': they understand 'our tempers, dispositions, inclinations, faculties; our wants and weakness'. Thus 'they can make shrewd conjectures in regard to our thoughts and purposes'. Then too, they have learned to improve their tactics through experience acquired during thousands and thousands of years.

Malice

Their power and knowledge is equalled, perhaps exceeded by their malice. When asked why God does not destroy them Hall replies with a statement which we have met with in other words over and over again:

> 'God knows how to fetch more honour to Himself by drawing good out of evil, than by the amotion and prevention of evil.'

We do not know the secret thoughts of our fellow men, how then can we expect to understand the crafty devices of the Devil? We do not know the particular designs of the Evil One; yet we have learnt by bitter experience something of their nature. For an adequate account of this Hall tells us that 'he is not unwilling to learn and borrow of that great Master of Meditation, Gerson'. Those who are interested in the matter, will find in Section V of the tract, a passage of some 1,200 words in which Gerson's views as expressed in his *de variis tentationibus*, are summarized and presented.

Apparitions

As there have been apparitions of good angels, there have been apparitions of bad ones. Volumes have been written on this subject and Hall is unwilling to add to their number. Discounting many such tales as purely legendary, he is convinced that many are substantially true.

'I should hate', he said, 'to be guilty of so much incredulity, as to charge so many grave judges, and credible historians with lies.'

He accepts as authentic records of examinations and confessions of witches and sorcerers in several regions of the world to be found in such a work as Bodin's *Daemonomania ubique* 'agreeing in the truth of their horrible pacts with Satan, of their set meetings with evil spirits, their beastly homages and conversations'. One famous story Hall cannot 'forbear to relate'. It is of Magdalen de la Croix, born in Cordova in 1545. When 12 or 13 she received a visit from the Devil disguised as a 'blackamoor'. He asked her to marry him and, for dowry, promised that she would have such fame and honour on account of her sanctity that she would be the wonder of all Spain, Whilst Magdalen yielded to the solicitations of the Devil in her cell, her place in choir was taken by another fiend who assumed her form. In due course she became an Abbess consulted by Popes, Emperors and all the grandees of Spain. At last, however, she grew weary of a life of hypocrisy and deception, confessed her sins and received absolution from the Pope. (So Goulartius in his *Histoires admirables: Casside Reney en ses relations: Zuinger Theatre de vie humaine.*)

The apparitions of good angels – as we learned in the first section of this tract – grew fewer and fewer as the Church increased in age: so it is with the apparitions of fallen angels.

> 'As for these visible devils, they are in these days, very rare; and, where they have appeared, have wont to work more affright, than spiritual prejudice. Evil spirits are commonly most pernicious to the soul, when they are least seen; not caring so much for our terror, as our seduction.'

The most vehement attacks of evil spirits are most likely to be made in *articulo mortis*, either because the soul is about to pass beyond the reach of the powers of evil; or because man, at the point of death, is at his weakest. Hence in former times the dying saint was fortified for his last conflict by the Viaticum, 'the strongest spiritual cordial of the Blessed Eucharist'. Throughout his life Hall viewed with profound suspicion all Roman practices and it is not easy to determine his exact attitude to the Viaticum. In any case he does not urge its use: contents himself with saying that he is perfectly prepared to leave it entirely to God 'whether to restrain the fiend, or to give his dying saints the strength they need to resist him'.

Our Attitude to Evil Spirits

How are we to behave to evil spirits? How are we to prevail against them? Some, Hall says, rely on charms, spells, amulets and so forth. He scorns their use; regards their power, which he admits, as due to diabolic agency. Every one admits, he says, that by means of charms 'diseases have been remedied, wounds healed, blood stanched, serpents stupified, winds procured'. Any one who doubts facts so notorious, would 'make himself a wonder of incredulity'. But, he goes on to ask 'By what power do we think these things done?' 'Natural it cannot be: supernatural it must be.' It cannot be of God, who has given no warrant for such practices. Therefore 'it must be by devilish operation'.

His own resolution in the matter is perfectly clear.

> 'Let those, that have given to Satan their souls, take favour of him for their bodies: let us, that defy the author, abhor the courtesy. . . . Let me die, rather than owe my life to my Maker's Enemy.'

The Roman Church believes in exorcism – a practice 'so disrelished by us, that we ordinarily place conjurers in the same rank of sorcerers and professors of the black and damned arts'.

Yet in Hall's opinion the views held by the Anglicans of his day utterly opposed as they were to every kind of exorcism were almost as far removed from truth as those of the typical Roman Catholic. In spite of Romish superstition and abuse Hall felt certain that there was a place for exorcism when practised by the spiritual expert. He reminds his readers that the Apostles and their 'primitive successors' ejected devils. He claims himself to have seen exorcism successfully practised in Nottingham and Lancashire by a 'Mr Dayrel, a godly and zealous preacher'. But, he continues, the use of exorcism must be restricted to 'the most learned and eminently holy doctors'. It was not every man, nay more, it was not every clergyman however devout, who was a Dayrel. As for the rest:

> 'all that we have to do concerning malignant spirits, is, to repay them with hatred; to persuade our hearts of their continued dogging of us for mischief; to arm ourselves with constant resolutions of resistance; diligently to watch the ways of their temptations; to keep the strongest guard upon our weakest parts; to fortify ourselves, by our faithful prayers; and, by the virtue of our faith, to make Him ours, who is able to strengthen us, and to make us more than conquerors.'

THE WOEFUL ESTATE OF THE SOULS OF THE DAMNED

'Every evil spirit carries his own hell about with him: yet, doubtless, there are degrees of their torture.' Reprobate souls are at once 'partners of their pain and objects of their fury'. On this dark subject, Hall throws little, if any light. He is a man of his age and his age is not ours.

> 'But, if I could conceive of a body frying a whole day in a continuous flame, Lord, how should I be affected with the sad compassion of that intolerable torment, and burn inwardly with the sense of another's pain but, to think of a whole year's broiling in such a fire, how can it but turn our bowels within us! What then, Oh, what is it, to conceive of lying in a fire more intense than nature can kindle, for hundreds, thousands, millions, yea millions of millions of years; yea, further beyond these, than these are beyond

> a minute of time to all eternity: where, besides the endurance, everything, that makes toward the mitigation of other pains adds to these!'

The one thing that can be said in favour of this ghastly picture is that it is free from the horrible doctrine, attributed by many good scholars to Aquinas, that the blessedness of the redeemed is increased by the sight of the sufferings of the lost. Hall pities the lost and that is something in his favour. Yet his pity is not unmingled with a touch of scornful contempt. 'Surely, if infidelity had not robbed men of their wits, they could not resolve to purchase the momentary pleasures of sin, with so dreadful and eternal damnation.'

But the tract does not end here. No doubt Hall did really mean this work to be his swan song: but, as we have said before, as long as life lasted he was bound to wield his pen. Other pamphlets were to follow. In spite of that, however, he ends this tract, with a solemn (and somewhat rhetorical) farewell to the world he was so soon to leave. It was a truly Elizabethan gesture.

He bids, as he puts it, a *willing* farewell to this visible world: to earthly honours, ever fickle; to wealth, always deceitful; to pleasure – he is as puritanical in his eighties as he had been in his twenties – which had 'more sting than honey', 'which debauched and emasculated the mind'. The last farewell is to his friends. We quote his words because they show us how much the Old Adam remained in Joseph Hall to the very end: how bitterly he resented the loss of the high ecclesiastical position he once held, the esteem or at least the pretended esteem of those who admired him when he was a bishop but forgot him when all bishoprics were done away.

> 'Farewell, friends, some of whose unsteadiness and unfaithfulness hath helped to add to my load, which the fidelity of others had not power to ease; whose love might be apt to condole my shipwreck, but could not spare me a plank to swim to the shore; shortly, whose common misery may be more ready to receive, than give comfort.'

Lastly he turns from the past to the future; tells us that the only honour he now seeks is the crown of righteousness; the crown of glory; the only wealth, the treasure laid up in heaven; the only pleasure, the fullness of joy at the right hand of the Almighty for evermore.

The closing words are these:

> 'The friends that I ambitiously sue for, are those, that shall receive me into everlasting habitations. Lastly, farewell, vanishing life; and welcome, blessed eternity: even so Lord Jesus, come quickly.'

Hall was a boy of 14 when the Armada set sail for England. Nearly seventy years had come and gone since then. There had been great changes and all, or almost all, of these changes had been, in Hall's opinion, for the worse. No wonder he took a pessimistic view of the future of his country and the world. He was almost the last of the Elizabethans; and though in all his writings he could throw no fresh light either on angels or on the future life of the redeemed, he is at least able to tell us how men thought of these things when Elizabeth was queen.

V – MISCELLANY

We now turn to consider some miscellaneous works by Hall.

(1) *A/Paraphrase/upon the/Hard Texts/of/ the Whole Divine Scripture*

The first few years of Hall's episcopate were the most miserable he had hitherto known. Laud's spies discovered that he was showing too much indulgence to Puritans and on three separate occasions he was summoned to the royal presence to give an account of his conduct. By 1634, however, he had received from Laud a clean bill of health; by 1632 it is possible that in the eyes of the king and the archbishop he had begun to mend his ways. In any case this lengthy work of 1,100 pages is dedicted to the king. 'My meanness hath boldly endeavoured this great work.' To whom could he dedicate it more fitly than to his 'sovereign Master, eminent no less in goodness and piety, than in greatness and power; the great pattern of devotion, twice every day, even in public view, constantly busied in this book of God'?

In an age in which so many persisted in reading their own private fancies into the sacred text, it was indeed desirable that men should be able to refer to some standard work, in which they could find the consensus of the best exegetical opinion. Others had attempted to do this for various parts of the Bible: Hall claimed to do it for the whole. His efforts were doomed to failure. No such consensus exists. But even if it did Hall was the last person who was qualified to present it. For by nature he was an advocate rather than a judge; he always found it wellnigh impossible to take an unbiased view of one who differed from him. It is possible that Hall conceived the plan of this book when he learnt what Dutch Divines had done. After Dort the Dutch published an authoritative exposition (in the spirit of the decrees of the Council) of certain parts of Holy Scripture. Eleven years after Hall's work was published a volume appeared in England: *Annotations on all the books of the Old and New Testaments. The joint labour of certain learned divines.*

Even a cursory study of Hall's work reveals two facts. The first that the 'hard passages' are chosen in the most arbitrary manner: the second that the paraphrase is exceedingly poor. Of this and the work which we next mention, a not too generous description might be Love's Labour Lost. In any case to the modern student the work is at once unreadable and worthless.

(2) *Solomon's Divine Arts*

This work which is now entirely obsolete was published in December 1607 and was dedicated to the young Earl of Essex, son of Elizabeth's favourite, who had just returned from his foreign travels. (See Epistle 7 in Epp decade I.) In the dedication Hall expressly says that the 'matter was all Solomon's; the method and that alone, his own'. He 'merely endeavoured to be the commonplace book of that great king; and to refer his divine rules to their heads, for more ease of finding, for better memory, for readier use'.

Here is the title: *Solomon's Divine Arts/of/*1. *Ethics,/*2. *Politics/* 3. *Economics./that is/The Government/of* 1. *Behaviour/*2. *Common-wealth/*3. *Family./Drawn into Method out of his Proverbs and Ecclesiasties.*

And here is a specimen of how the subject is developed:
Solomon's/Ethics, or Morals/in four books/The 1. *Of Felicity/*2. *Of Prudence/*3. *Of Justice?/*4. *Of Temperance/Fortitude.*

Few nowadays would accept the hypothesis that Solomon was the sole author of the Book of Proverbs; fewer still that he wrote Ecclesiastes; none but a handful of obscurantists that in what he wrote 'he could not err'.

(3) *How to Become Devout*

Here we have three tracts, each dealing with the same subject, and giving much the same advice in slightly different words.

(*a*) *Holy decency in the worship of God*

In this short tract Hall calls attention to some of the imperfections in the worship of the Anglican Church of his time. He disliked popish superstition: he equally disliked Protestant slovenliness. In their revolt against Rome with its magnificent cathedrals and its elaborate pageantry many Protestants went to the opposite extreme. In their eyes stately temples were the dwelling-place of the scarlet woman; costly vestments the symbols of idolatry. They seemed to take little interest in keeping their churches in good repair. 'Clay and sticks', said Hall, 'please them better than marble and cedars.' They wore no 'Sunday clothes' and their manners in Church left much to be desired.

> 'They stumble into God's house without all care or show of reverence; and sit down at his table, like his fellows with their hats on their heads: they make no difference of coming with full paunches to that heavenly banquet; and that the very dogs are allowed free access and leave, to take up their legs, at those holy tables, where we partake of the Son of God.'

(b) The remedy of profaneness

The tract with which we have been dealing (written no doubt under Laud's influence) is chiefly concerned with external behaviour; is an expression of the sort of criticism that Laud might have passed, and no doubt *did* pass on many a congregation. His diary reveals the fact that he was a sincerely religious man. Of this, however, the outside world knew little or nothing till after his death. To the average Englishman he was a martinet who resembled an inquisitive government inspector or a fussy schoolmaster rather than a Father in God. With the help of his numerous spies he made it his business to see that the clergy had clean surplices and that they wore them (*vide* Carlyle), that churches were kept clean and in good repair; that bishops did their duty by repressing what was wrong and by promoting what was good for the Church in the eyes of their Metropolitan; and that the clergy were dutiful and obedient to the will of their civil and spiritual overlords. Laud assumed, or seemed to assume, that if this were done God's kingdom would surely come.

Hall's whole training and experience made him regard the matter in a very different light. Despite his readiness to fall in with the desires (and to some extent, the views) of his Metropolitan, he felt that Laud's diagnosis of the disease which afflicted the Church, was totally inadequate. In some cases his remedy might serve as a prophylactic; it could never serve as a cure. In this tract, therefore, he sets himself to discover the root cause of the 'profaneness' so widely deplored, and to offer an adequate remedy.

The cause of profaneness, he says, is that men have an utterly false conception of God. If they really knew God in all His might and majesty, they could not think of Him as they did. Where profound awe and filial fear are lacking men do not know the true God. Only as their eyes are opened to spiritual *reality* can they be cured.

That is the burden of this tract. But Hall was a man of his time. In an age when the vast majority of Englishmen believed in the Calvinistic doctrines of election and justification by faith, he develops his view at considerable length, and expressed it in the idiom (now largely obsolete or at least obsolescent) of the day.

(c) The Devout Soul/or/Rules of Heavenly Devotion (1643)

In the first of these tracts Hall described the disease: in the second he professed to offer a better diagnosis than Laud: in the last he goes on to suggest how the disease should be treated.

According to Hall there are two kinds of devotion. (1) On the one hand there is a 'General Kind of Devotion', that 'goes through the renewed heart and life of a Christian'. This he terms 'Habitual and Virtual'. (2) On the other hand there is a 'Special and Fixed

Exercise of Devotion'. This he calls 'Actual'. Devotion of either kind, he maintains, involves two things (*a*) a right apprehension of God as he really is; (*b*) a constant sense of God's nearness. Lest either kind should 'cool with intermission', the devout heart 'takes all occasions both to think of God and to speak to him'. (1) Habitual devotion. All nature speaks of the marvellous works of the Creator. We are intended to learn from 'these silent documents' to ascribe glory to God.

Our praise must be vocal. For the most part it must consist 'a hundred times a day' of 'pious and heavenly ejaculations'. In this however we must maintain the Golden Mean. We must not resemble those who use such ejaculations so infrequently that their hearts 'grow strange and hard to God'. Yet we must be *unlike* the Papists, who use them so frequently and so carelessly that in course of time they become meaningless.

(2) Actual devotion consists of three parts: prayer, reading and hearing the word, reception of the Sacraments.

On each of these subjects Hall has a good deal to say. But as we have heard it all before there is no need to repeat it now.

(4) *Christian Moderation*

As we have said this is one of the most interesting of Hall's tracts; in certain ways it is amongst the most attractive. It is interesting because it reveals his wide reading and his ability to lay his hand on apt quotations whenever he wants to do so. There are upwards of 250 allusions to other writers and many of these are worth making. Then, too, there is a mellowness of spirit, an absence of the scorn and bitterness revealed only too often in some of Hall's other works. One might even say there is a touch of genial benevolence which is rare with him. Nor is this altogether unexpected. In favour with his king and his metropolitan, Hall had won the affection and esteem of the more serious members of the public. He now looks on his fellow men with greater kindliness and tolerance than he has ever done before or will ever do again. He has climbed the ladder of success to its topmost rung; he is, for the moment, the most popular, the most highly respected bishop in England. A career of great distinction seems to be drawing to a splendid close. The sun is sinking like a crimson ball of fire; the sky is bathed in splendour. But night is near, a long night of a dozen years, and night is to bring with it nothing but disaster and suffering to Joseph Hall.

Taking the idea of the *Golden Mean* from Greek philosophy, Hall here seeks to apply it to the Christian life. God is not opposed to pleasure. On the contrary he has provided man with rich variety of meat and drink for his enjoyment. In eating and drinking we must avoid excess; for 'many have dug their graves with their teeth', and the number of drunkards in England is a fact which all deplore. In spite of this, however, man has a palate and it is only natural and right that the consumption of meat and drink should afford him pleasure. So it is with sexual desire. Virginity is for the chosen few; marriage for the many. The physical pleasures involved in marriage are not frowned upon by God. Far from it.

The limits set by moderation in all these things are determined by the fact that we must take God with us into our enjoyments. We receive our pleasures *from* God; we enjoy them *in* God, and we direct them *to* God as their 'end and scope'.

The *kind* of pleasure it is open to us to enjoy is determined by our position in society. Most men, for instance, may act a part in an historical drama with impunity; but a 'professed divine' should not appear upon the stage: it is 'unmeet'.

In regard to the *quality* of our pleasures 'reason and religion require that we should not be wanton and over-delicate in our contentments: that our pleasures should be like ourselves, masculine and temperate'.

> 'Happy are we, if we know how to use our blessings; and have learned so to order our appetite, as that we make it neither a slave nor a wanton.'

As for *quantity*, pleasure is honey. *Eat not too much honey*, saith Solomon: 'that is to be tasted on the finger; not to be scooped up with the whole hand.' This holds good of every form of pleasure, whether 'of the board, or of the bed, or of the field'.

What has been said of our delights applies with equal force to our desires. We must adopt a right attitude to 'wealth and honour'; for as Augustine says: 'Every soul is either Christ's spouse or the Devil's harlot.' Like Christ and His Apostles we must 'earn what we have, and have what is sufficient'.

'Oh, the infinite avarice and ambition of men! The sea hath both bottom and bounds; the heart of man hath neither.'

If we must be moderate in our desires, we must be equally moderate in our passions. Sorrow, whether worldly or spiritual, must be strictly controlled. As for worldly crosses, 'if we turn them round and view them on all sides: we shall find that if their face be sour and grisly, their back is comely and beautiful'.

Then, too, we must moderate our fears, especially the fear of death.

> 'Death is not an enemy; he is a friend; if his visage be sour and hard, he is no other than the grim Porter of Paradise, which shall let thee in to glory.'

As to anger. There is, as the Apostle says, a sinless anger: but even here there must be moderation. 'The cause may be just: the quantity may offend.'

In the second book Hall deals with what he terms 'moderation in matter of judgment'. He lays down twelve rules for guidance. The chief are these. Whilst we dare not be lukewarm in religion, our zeal must be tempered with discretion and charity. We must learn to distinguish between a heretic and a herseiarch: between vital truths and truths of secondary importance. We must avoid 'curiosity in the disquisition of Truths'. The old Greek was right when he said: 'Wisdom consists not in the knowledge of many things, but of things profitable.' Whilst we must rest in fundamental truths revealed in Scripture, we should not stress too much unimportant verities, or censure too severely those who do not agree with us in regard to them. Another rule which we must take heed to follow is this. We must not attribute an adversary's opinion to sin.

> 'God forbid that either Church or man should be tried and judged by his adversary.'

Nor must we judge an opponent's statement by the logical consequences which *we* think it involves. Again, if a prominent churchman expresses an opinion which we intensely dislike we cannot assume that the Church to which he belongs endorses it. Knox for instance and some others with him, expressed regrettable views in regard to monarchy. That however does not imply that all the members of the Reformed Church share his opinions.

In every instance in which a matter that is not absolutely vital is discussed adversaries should draw as closely as they can to one another. Wherever differences exist in regard to religious matters we *must* 'refrain from all railing terms and spiteful provocations'. Finally our supreme aim must be 'unity and peace' however much opinions differ in regard to 'lesser verities'.

That then is what Joseph Hall has to say in his exposition of Christian ethics. In one sense it is his final utterance. Here for almost the last time he addresses men and women as creatures of flesh and blood who have to live in the world of sense and time. In future he will direct his thoughts chiefly to heaven. Earth and the things of earth mean less and save when he deals with casuistry or opposes a heresy, he speaks of the life to come. But between this tract and its successors there is an interlude.

Christian Moderation was licensed for printing in October 1639. A month previously Hall learned that the General Assembly of the Church of Scotland had met and decided that episcopacy must be overthrown. Straightway he enters into correspondence with Laud. The result of this correspondence, as we shall presently see, was *Episcopacy by Divine Right*. In this treatise, still more in the correspondence which preceded it, Hall reveals himself in a very different character. Each of the precepts included in the second book of *Christian Moderation* seems to be utterly forgotten. Hall expressly says that he has dropped gall into his ink. He attacks with vigour, at times with venom. There is no moderation in what he says. And later when he slanders or allows his son to slander the moral character of John Milton he throws aside every trace of 'moderation', every sign of charity, every attempt to reach the truth.

The Old Adam dies hard in all of us: it died hard in Joseph Hall. Only after he had suffered the loss of almost all that he held dear, one is sometimes tempted to think, did he see God. Like the patriarch Job he had heard of God by the hearing of the ear and in countless pages had recorded what he had heard. Only perhaps in extreme old age did he pass from hearsay to vision. In any case like most other men, he found it easier to describe ideals than to reach them; to show the path of salvation to others than to walk along it himself with feet which did not falter, with eyes that never wandered from the far-distant goal.

(5) *The Christian*

Hall is living in retirement near Norwich, and has plenty of leisure to observe his fellow men. He is distressed at what he sees: for whilst every man or almost every man professes to be a Christian, many, perhaps most, are Christian merely in name. He feels how different a place the world would be, 'if all, that are willing to wear the livery, were as ready to do the service'.

> 'If words and forms might carry it, Christ would have clients enough: but if holiness of disposition and uprightness of carriage must be the proof, woe is me!'

Forty years previously Hall had introduced the 'Character-Sketch' (based on the work of Theophrastus) into English literature. Now he adopts very much the same method as he proceeds to write a 'character-sketch' of a genuine Christian. His hand has not lost its cunning; his literary touch is as sure, his economy in the use of words as pronounced, his ability to write graceful English as evident as ever. In short this is a charming tract. Of course he has nothing new to say: in thousands of pages he had told men all that he knew about the way in which Christians ought to live. None the less the tract is well worth reading.

This is how it begins:

> 'The Christian is a man, and more; an earthly saint; an angel clothed in flesh; the only lawful image of his Maker and Redeemer; the abstract of God's Church on earth; a model of heaven, made up in clay; the living temple of the Holy Ghost.'

In twelve short chapters we are told how the Christian spends his day. We see him at work, at leisure, at table and in bed. We are told how he behaves to his fellow men, what he thinks of religion, how he meets suffering and conflict, and how he faces death. In our opinion it is all well done; that others may judge for themselves we quote a short excerpt.

> 'He is not apt to spend himself in censures; but, as for revilings and cursed speakings against God or men, those his soul abhorreth.
>
> 'He knows to reserve his thoughts, by locking them up in his bosom, under a safe silence: and, when he must speak, dares not be too free of his tongue; as well knowing, that, *in the multitude of words, there wanteth not sin.*
>
> 'His speeches are no other than seasonable; and well fitted both to the person and occasion. Jiggs at a funeral, lamentations at a feast, holy counsel to scorners, discouragements to the dejected, and applauses to the profane, are hateful to him.
>
> 'He meddles not with other men's matters, much less with affairs of state: but keeps himself wisely within his own compass; not thinking his breath well spent, where he doth not either teach or learn.'

This is no picture of a young Christian filled with divine ardour: it is the portrait of an elderly man who has learnt much as he made his way through life. In fact it is a portrait self-painted of Joseph Hall, when he had retired from public life and was preparing as best he could to leave this world for another.

(6) *Hall as Peacemaker*

No account of Hall's many interests and activities would be complete without some reference to his efforts to produce peace. If he admired James I because he regarded him as the wisest man who had sat upon a throne since the days of Solomon, he admired him even more because he believed that James had justly earned the title which flatterers had conferred upon him, 'The Peacemaker'.[1]

If Hall's intense hatred of the Church of Rome was mainly due to her manifold errors and corruptions, it was largely inspired by the fact that she claimed to be the one ark of salvation outside of which it was impossible to be saved. If he hated sectaries he hated them not so much because their views on liturgy and episcopacy were mistaken, as because their very existence threatened the homogeneity, and therefore the peace, of the Church of England.

> 'Those that fly from a true established Church, and run ways of their own, raising and fomenting sects and schisms amongst God's people, let them receive their doom; not from me, but from the blessed Apostle.' (Romans xvi. 17, 18.)

[1] 'The invincible aversion he had to war.' (Bishop Burnet.)

It may be that he did not altogether approve the Lutheran formula *cuius regio, eius religio*; none the less he was firmly convinced that every Reformed Church should be *national.* In his desire to obtain unity Hall was prepared to allow considerable latitude in the form of organization which a national church chose to assume; and he was firmly convinced that if each church were to lay the main, still better the entire emphasis, on those few essentials – the supreme authority of Scripture, the Ten Commandments, the Apostles' Creed, the two sacraments, Baptism and the Lord's Supper – on which all were agreed, peace would immediately ensue. On minor matters theologians had always differed; and they might safely be left to continue to differ so long as they did not introduce their discussions to the notice of simple believers or attempt to embody them in the *fides communis* of the Catholic Church. These views are put forward in a number of pamphlets. Amongst the most important are *Columba Noae* (1624), *De pace inter evangelicos procuranda,* and two other tracts, one in Latin and one in English of which we must now say a word.

(*a*) '*Pax Terris*' (*1647*)

Pax terris was dedicated to Thomas Morton, at one time Bishop of Durham. In the palmy days of episcopacy he had won fame as a controversialist, had 'made Rome groan', to use Hall's expression. Now, however, the great enemy of the Church had shifted his ground. Old heresies, such as Arianism and Socinianism, which once seemed dead, were waking to vigorous life. The Church was split into a number of warring fragments; the most urgent task was to allay the bitterness of contending sects (*innumerarum sectarum*) and, if possible, to reunite the scattered parts into one whole.

Hall introduces himself to his readers in these words: '*Ecce me, nuncium pacis Evangelicae*'; the burden of his message is, '*Deponite arma, Christiani*'.

With most of the ideas in this tract we are already familiar, for Hall's lifelong motto was *Non nova sed nove.*

If ever we are to get reunion we must bear in mind the fact that in the primitive Church the articles of belief were few and simple. Most of the troubles, which began early, and were never more acute than in the seventeenth century, were due to the fact that men persisted in drawing deductions – many of them false – from the original *fidei capita.*

If only we could get an Oecumenical Council which would officially determine what the *fidei capita* were, if private Christians would content themselves with this and leave all theological discussion to the professional theologians, the world would soon be a happier and better place. To bring this desirable state of things about the private Christian must refuse to have 'itching ears', avid for novelty. This does not imply however, that he should be fed on 'milk' throughout his life. Far from it. Let him have as much meat as he feels he can digest; but let him keep his private opinions to himself. Above all let him steadily refuse to censure those who differ from him. Hall quotes with approval the words of Augustine: '*Potest mihi aliquid videri, alteri aliud: sed neque ego, quod dixere, praescribo alteri; nec ille mihi.*' (Aug. in Ps. xvi.) Hall's own summary is a paraphrase of the Apostles' Creed; the Bible regarded as *ipsissimum Dei verbum*: the two Sacraments: Prayer to God through Christ; the Divine Law (i.e. the Ten Commandments); justice and charity to man. 'These suffice. *Quisquis, inquam, ista arcte tenuerit, quicquid sit de reliquis, hic mihi Christaianus erit.*' (Par. VIII.)

Christ set us an example in this respect by refusing to take sides in the Jewish controversies of His time. St Paul, Polycarp, Cyprian and others allowed latitude of opinion in regard to secondary truths. Theodosius laid such stress on peace that he said to a bishop: '*Si tu pacem fugis, ego te ab Ecclesia fugere iubeo.*' In all ages, says Hall, the usage (*mos*) of the Christian Church has been '*libertatem hanc de rebus parum gravibus quidlibet operandi*'. He condemns the Dominicans '*superciliosi orbis magistri*' for insisting that those who did not agree with them *must* be in the wrong; agrees with Gerson, whom he greatly admired, '*In omnibus aliis, praeterquam in materiis quae sunt pure de fide, Ecclesia fallit, et fallitur, servata caritate*'.

There were far too many 'novelties' in the seventeenth century to please Joseph Hall. To him men seemed to be following wandering fires. As we should expect, he insists that long-established custom (e.g. episcopacy) should receive consideration; but he now admits that each Church has a perfect right to make its own laws and to adopt the mode of church government best fitted to meet its own peculiar needs. For doing this, he says, no one has any right to blame them.

In the interpretation of Scripture all must seek to reach agreement. This can only be done if men are willing to accept what philosophers of the Scottish school were wont to call the *sensus communis* – '*communem Doctorum Ecclesiae sensum suo semper praeferandum*'. Even when agreement cannot be reached men can still love each other; and so long as there is charity mere difference of opinion will not prove fatal to peace. On the other hand, party names are as evil in the seventeenth century as they were in the first. We know how St Paul addressed those who wore party badges and said, I am of Paul, I of Apollos; I of Cephas.

'Damnentur,' says Hall, 'ad imum usque barathrum, illa nominum opprobria, Lutheranorum, Calvinianorum, Arminianorum, Puritanorum, Prelaticorum, Presbuterianorum, Indepentium; quas fidei eiusdem professoribus vulgo obiectari solent. Christiani et audiamus, et vere simus: non magis fidei unitate, quam caritatis vinculo coniunctissimi.'

Now, if ever, is the accepted time for men to sue for 'Evangelical ɜace'; to beat their swords into ploughshares, their spears into ·uning hooks. Yet when we speak of peace there are those who cry ıt for truth and justice. Admittedly there can be no peace in the ›sence of truth and justice; none the less peace and truth, truth and stice not only *may* but *must* kiss each other.

Once more Hall proclaims his belief that a 'heretic' and a 'herearch' are two very different people. The Church must indeed deal ith the anti-social man who refuses to unite with his brethren '*non* ·*m ore gladii, quam gladio oris*'. The sword of the magistrate and ıe sword of the Church should assist each other to *preserve* the ›uls of men. Arians and Socinians – and these alone – should ·ceive drastic treatment at the hands of the State; for the safety f the people is the supreme law.

'We are they', says Hall in conclusion, 'who have lived to see hrist's prophecy fulfilled: The Judge is standing at the door.' ⁄Iatt. xxiv. 6, 7, 8.)

'At his first advent the whole world enjoyed the "Augustan peace". t his second advent he will find a world both troubled and turbulent. herefore we wait for him and are ready to welcome the "Prince of ɜace, the Vindicator of Truth, and Justice, the Rewarder of Patience, ıe Consoler of the Church".'

·) *The Peacemaker*

his lengthy tract was addressed to the Clergy of the Diocese of ·orwich by their 'faithful and loving fellow-labourer Joseph Nor-ich'. It is virtually a repetition of the one with which we have ɜen dealing. Here he insists once more that the prime cause of ·vision is the emphasis laid on purely secondary matters. He goes on · name another cause of strife: it is 'Temper'. If we could conquer ·ide, self-love, envy, covetousness; and replace them by meekness, illingness to obey our spiritual guides, readiness to place a charit-›le interpretation on the words and deeds of our brethren; if, ıally, we were to manifest a conciliatory spirit, we should be well ı the way to peace.

All this may be done and must be done by private individuals. At ıe same time the Government must play its part. Spiritual dissension ıust be nipped in the bud. Those who broach novel opinions must ɜ gently reclaimed. Heresy must be repressed and heretics placed in quarantine. The Press must be controlled. Catechization must b universally employed and a panel of orthodox divines, skilled i polemics, released from all other work to devote their entire tim and attention to presenting the case for orthodoxy.

(7) *Hall's Views of the Millennium*

Over and over again Hall tells us that the end of the world is nea that already – to use his own words – 'The Judge is at the door'. I the seventeenth century many shared his belief. In his early thirtie Milton not only believed that Christ's second coming was close a hand: in a sublime prayer he entreated the Divine Prince to leave hi royal chambers and come to earth for the deliverance of the faithfu But neither Milton nor Hall professed to know exactly what woul happen on Christ's return. With others it was different. Hence th tract.

The/Revelation Unrevealed/concerning the/Thousand Years' Reign/of the/Saints with Christ upon Earth./Laying forth/ The Weak Grounds and Strange Consequences,/of that Plausible and Too Much Received Opinion.

In his preface to this brochure of some 23,000 words, Hall cal attention to two facts which are familiar to every student of the Bibl (1) The Apocalypse has proved a stumbling block to all expositor In every generation, the wisest and most learned among them hav confessed that they could find no satisfactory explanation of some c the many obscure passages with which this book is filled. (2) In spit of this, perhaps even because of it, many Christians in all ages hav been fascinated by this mysterious work.

One passage in particular has engaged attention and stimulate speculation. Chapter XX, vv. 4–10 in which we read of the 'Mi lennium'. On the strength of this statement myriads of Christiar have been persuaded that one day in the future near or far Christ wi descend from heaven and rule over his saints, on earth, in bodil form, for a thousand years.

In the early Church, those who cherished this dream, whose wa of life was coloured by this strange belief, were known as Chiliast As time went on the majority of their fellow-Christians came t regard their fantastic dreams with such disfavour, that after 'th time of Jerome and Augustine' – to use Hall's phrase – Chilias disappeared. Little if anything was heard of it until the time of th Reformation. But when the Bible was placed in the hands of the lai and they were urged to read it in their native tongue, some laid suc stress on the right of private judgment that they refused the aid c professional exegetes and trusted almost entirely to that spiritual enlightenment, which, they maintained had come to them from Christ. Small wonder, then, that when such simple-minded Christians studied the Apocalypse, the old chiliastic dreams revived. Throughout the seventeenth century in general, and during the early days of the Cromwellian period in particular, there were many Chiliasts in England. In 1643 a typical specimen of chiliastic literature, *Personal Reign of Christ on Earth*, was published by the Rev John Archer. This is the book which Hall examined and sought to confute.

To begin with he refuses to admit that certain passages in the Old Testament, e.g. Daniel xii. 11, 12, on which Chiliasts laid great stress, were relevant to the discussion. In Hall's opinion nearly all Old Testament prophecies referred to Israel as she was before and during the Exile. Many, perhaps most of these prophecies, says Hall, were fulfilled at the return from the Exile: others refer 'in an analogical (allegorical) way to the Christian Church'. Chiliasts in all ages have been keenly interested in the fate of 'The Lost Ten Tribes'. Hall, who was not devoid of a definitely anti-Semitic bias, dismisses this subject with contempt and confines his argument to the passage in the Apocalypse (Chapter XX) to which we have referred.

He begins with a fair and lucid analysis of Archer's book and goes on to give an account of primitive chiliasm. He then proceeds to point out the flaws in Archer's argument; refers to (1) the 'universal strain and ground of error' running throughout the book; (2) 'The chief of those bold paradoxal and unwarrantable assertions' such as the two Days of Judgment with an interval of 1,000 years between them; the three advents of Christ, the twofold resurrection of the dead; the threefold ascension of Christ, which Archer's theories involve. The extraordinary picture of the life of the saints, free from pain and sorrow, their children sinless, without Sacrament and Ordinance at once mortal and sinless, and so forth, is, says Hall, incredible. (3) Hall has no difficulty in showing that Chiliasts differ in their views. In opposition to Archer, 'Alstedius' maintained that none but martyrs were to have any part in the 'First Resurrection'. In order to get over the difficulties involved in St Paul's statement that the dead (all the holy dead) shall rise; that those 'which sleep in Jesus will God bring with him', this ingenious commentator suggests that the words 'which sleep in Jesus' really mean 'which sleep *for the sake of* Jesus'; in other words the martyrs. (4) Finally Hall gives his own (orthodox) exposition. First he gives a paraphrase of the passage from the Apocalypse; but paraphrasing was never Hall's forte and this paraphrase is a poor one. He concludes with four statements (which of course are developed at some length).

(1) Christ has no kingdom save one which is spiritual.

(2) On earth men have never known, on earth they will *never* know freedom from sin and affliction.
(3) The wise Christian will neither 'put the Last Day' far from him it will come speedily, though its precise date cannot be determined
(4) The one and only message addressed to Christians on this matter the one and only course they are asked to pursue, may be expressed in five words: 'Take care to be ready'.

From what has been said it is obvious that this tract is now fo most men of purely academic interest. The doctrine of litera inspiration has been abandoned by all save a handful of obscurantists The whole subject of Apocalypse has been studied by men lik Charles, with the result that whilst Christians will always cherish th wonderful picture of the New Jerusalem which the author of th 'Revelation of St John' has bequeathed us, his 'prophecies', if suc they may be termed, in regard to the 'End of the World' leave u entirely unmoved and unconcerned. In this tract Joseph Hal expresses in the idiom of his age, as against Archer and all Mil lenarians, the reasoned judgment of the Christian Church.

(8) *Casuistry*

To many, perhaps to most, the word *casuistry* suggests the Jesuit and their influence on the Church of Rome, or the *Provincial Letter* of Pascal, in which that form of casuistry is held up to scorn an ridicule. Throughout the seventeenth century, however, a series c books was published, partly by Anglicans, partly by Puritans, i which a very different kind of casuistry was presented to the world Never, indeed, before or since, was so much attention given to thi subject in England.

In his brilliant chapter on the English Casuists of the seventeent century,[1] Hensley Henson has pointed out that in the Roman Churc books on casuistry were written for the benefit of priests who deal with penitents in the confessional: their theme is moral pollution. I the Reformed Churches, on the other hand, books on casuistry wer written primarily, as Richard Baxter said in his preface, to hel 'Junior Ministers' to deal with scruples of conscience, moral per plexities arising in the minds of various members of their congrega tions. At the same time they had in view 'Masters of Families' an 'the more judicious amongst private Christians'.

The Father of English Casuists is William Perkins (1558–160 who, when Fellow of Christ's College, Cambridge, preached celebrated sermon on Isaiah l. 50.

> 'The Lord God hath given me a tongue of the learned, that I shou know, to minister a word in due season, to him that is weary.'

[1] *English Religion in the Seventeenth Century* (London, 1903).

> 'I gladly call to mind', says William Ames in the preface to his *Cases of Conscience*, 'when being young, I heard worthy Master Perkins, so preach in a great assembly of students, that he instructed them soundly in the truth, stirred them up effectually to seek after godliness, made them fit for the Kingdom of God; and by his own example showed them what things they should chiefly intend, that they might promote true religion, in the power of it unto God's glory and others' salvation:
> And amongst other things which he preached profitably, he began at length to teach, How with the tongue of the Learned one might speak a word in due season to him that is weary, out of Esai. 50, 4 by untying and explaining diligently Cases of Conscience (as they are called).'

The book into which this famous sermon was expanded is called *Cases of Conscience*. It deals with the 'nature and differences of sin', the nature of conscience, the various temptations by which man is beset, and the different virtues he is expected to possess. It treats of man, in the first instance, in his personal relation to God: it goes on to discuss how one should act in relation to his fellow men.

Perkins died at the very beginning of the century; towards its close Richard Baxter, when prohibited from preaching (1664–65), produced a huge volume of 1,000 pages. It was published in 1673 under the title *A Christian Directory or a Sum of Practical Theology and Cases of Conscience*. It was divided into four parts, Christian Ethics (private duties), Christian Economics (family duties), Christian Ecclesiastics (Church duties), Christian Politics (duties to rulers and neighbours). Despite the work done by his predecessors, in particular by Perkins, Ames, Jeremy Taylor, Baxter said that the demand for books on casuistry seemed to be inexhaustible. Apart from Perkins, two works of major importance were produced. One was written by a Puritan the other by an Anglican. Like many another Puritan Ames or Amesius,[1] as he was known on the Continent, at one time Fellow of Christ's had fled to Holland in order to enjoy liberty of thought and expression denied to him by King James. For several years he was Professor of Theology at Franeker, acted as private secretary to the President of the Synod of Dort, produced his clebrated *Medulla* (translated into English by order of the Long Parliament), and a book on casuistry. As the *Medulla* is perhaps the best and briefest summary of Calvinistic doctrine ever given to the world, so, we venture to think this treatise on conscience is probably the ablest produced in any branch of the Reformed Church.

To Ames theology was *doctrina Deo vivendi*: ethics *ars Deo vivendi.* As John Newton could not find in Livy or Horace 'a word about Jesus'; so Ames believed that no treatise on philosophical

[1] The best short account of Ames will be found in *Die Vorbereitung des Pietismus* by Wilhelm Goeters, pages 61–79 (Leipzig, 1911).

ethics could afford any reliable guidance to the Christian who sought to live unto God. On the contrary, just because the life of the Christian is a supernatural life, every rule of conduct could be and ought to be, deduced from Holy Scripture.

On the other hand, Jeremy Taylor who, like all his predecessors, regarded Jesuit casuistry as 'poison', considered his *Ductor Dubitantium* to be his most important work, his chief claim to be remembered by future generations, based his casuistry on 'Holy Scripture, right reason, and universal testimonies'. His work was intended to be a systematic treatise on Moral Theology, which dealt not so much with particular instances of perplexity, as with the nature and work of conscience, which when rightly understood, would almost automatically give adequate guidance in all. He knows the work of his predecessors, including Hall 'the late eloquent and reverend Bishop of Norwich' and yet feels in 1660 that 'for any public provisions of books of casuistical theology, we were almost wholly unprovided'. Like every member of the English School he 'studiously avoided all questions that are curious and unprofitable': unlike all others he 'took his pattern from Trebonianus the lawyer who out of the laws of the old Romans collected some choice rules which give answer to very many cases that happen'.

In this group of able and eminent men Joseph Hall has a place. He belongs to the school of Jeremy Taylor rather than to the school of Amesius. Indeed he deliberately ignores Amesius whom he met and heard at Dort. He remembered no doubt that his hero James – that crowned Dillitantetheolog, as Goeters calls him – had used his influence to prevent Amesius from obtaining a professor's chair at Leyden. He was well read in Jesuit casuistry and was perhaps the only English casuist of the time who had met Jesuits face to face and entered into argument with them. His *Cases of Conscience* was published late in life when he felt unable to produce a systematic treatise on casuistry on which he said so much that was good had been already written. He divides his work into four sections (decades, as he termed them). The first deals with economics, 'Profit and Traffic' as it is called; the second with cases of 'Life and Liberty'; the third with 'Cases of Piety and Religion', the last with 'Cases matrimonial'.

(1) Living as he did at a time when the medieval theory of Usury was giving place to the modern theory of Interest and Investment, he has little real guidance to offer those who were confronted by economic problems. Men, he says, should strive to live by the Golden Rule; the animating principle of their lives should be Christian charity. 'Too much charge is robbery.' 'Conscience must be the clerk of the market.'

(2) In his day there was no adequate police force; men had to depend on themselves for protection from assault. The main question with which Hall is concerned is, 'Is it ever lawful for a man to kill another?' Duelling and abortion (at that time prevalent) are strongly condemned.

(3) Like others of his generation Hall believed firmly in the active agency of evil spirits. On their assaults he has much to say. Another topic which receives attention is the nature of vows and the extent to which they are binding.

(4) Finally he deals with marriage. He does not object to second marriages, but he feels that it is deplorable that men often rush into a second marriage before their former wives are cold. He believes that the innocent party may remarry. He allows though he regrets the marriage of first cousins.

This brief outline does less than justice to Hall though it must suggest that Hensley Henson overrates his importance as a casuist.

> 'Bishop Hall enjoyed among his contemporaries a reputation as a preacher, divine, and devotional writer which has thrown into obscurity his character as a casuist, but that he was no mean proficient in this respect also will be at once apparent to the student of his Resolutions.'[1]

But after all this brief treatise (The Resolution of Cases of Conscience) gives a very imperfect view of Hall's activity and ability as a casuist. Like all Calvinistic preachers he was faced with a great problem. As the result of the Doctrine of Election which he so constantly and so fervently proclaimed he found that some men fell into one error some into another. Again and again he speaks of those who give way to presumption: again and again he addresses those who were tempted to despair. Can man know that he is in 'a state of grace' that he is saved?

Once a man whose life was far from blameless said to Hall, 'If I were told that every man in the world would be lost, that only one would be saved; I should answer "That man am I".' Surely 'presumption could go no farther'. On the other hand Hall, as a boy, had seen his mother tormented by 'scruples of conscience', had seen these scruples removed by Antony Gilby. When his own father lay on his death-bed he wrote to Hall to let him know that he was greatly troubled. The reply sent is still preserved and may be read today. The fact of the matter is that those who broke away from Rome, who were told that they could no longer cast their burdens on an infallible church, but had to shoulder responsibility, live and give answer for the deeds done in the body to God and to God alone, were often perplexed; for the Bible is not an easy book to understand

[1] Op. cit., page 191.

and the lengthy doctrinal sermons delivered from every pulpit in the Reformed Church seemed often to darken counsel by words.

When a doctor deals with a sick man, he does not deliver an abstruse lecture on anatomy or physiology in the hope that the patient may apply the knowledge thus acquired to his recovery; he devotes the knowledge he has acquired to a specific case.

The ordinary teaching given from the pulpit in the Reformed Church if it were to be effective *had* to be supplemented by personal contact between parson and people: yet whilst Romanists flocked to the confessional, Anglican and Puritan alike seemed loath to consult a minister. Like Perkins and Jeremy Taylor, Hall again and again bewailed the fact that men not only refused to confess their sins to a minister or at least to some 'discreet' person; they refused to take advantage of his superior knowledge when faced with spiritual problems. Perhaps that is one reason why so many books on casuistry were written. In any case Hall wrote and wrote. As Fuller put it he might almost be said to have died with pen in hand. Again and again he wrote of spiritual problems as for instance in *Satan's Fiery Darts quenched* in the effort to give spiritual guidance: again and again he wrote as in his *Balm of Gilead* to comfort and console. In all such writings he reveals the tact and the desire to help which is the hall-mark of the writings of every casuist who belonged to what we have called the English School. Unlike the Pharisees whom we meet with in the pages of the New Testament who sought through casuistry to minimize the demands God makes of men; our English casuists made it their business to quicken conscience, and to convince their readers that God's demands are absolute.

VI – CONTROVERSIES

In old age, when his energies were almost entirely devoted to the production of devotional literature, Hall said that he regarded his controversial writings as mere digressions from his main business in life. Here as elsewhere he reveals the fact that he had never prayed with the poet that he might receive the gift of seeing himself as others saw him; or that if such prayer were ever offered, it remained unanswered. It is easy therefore to over-simplify his character. This is what it seems to us that a recent American writer[1] has done. In a short sketch of a few epigrammatic and somewhat supercilious pages, he has attempted to give a picture of Hall's life and work. 'He warmed easily', says our author, 'to a choleric righteousness which quickly boiled over in a rush of words, well-chosen and neatly phrased. Though generally muddled in his ideas, he thought himself open-minded. . . .' There are few Lytton Stracheys in this world; smaller men are well advised to leave impressionism severely alone, and to content themselves with a duller presentation of objective facts. It is not easy for us who live in an age in which indifference to religion has produced an atmosphere of easy tolerance, to realize the passion with which Protestant and Catholic fought in the sixteenth and seventeenth centuries, or to see the fluctuating course of events through their eyes.

(*a*) Writing about 1610 Hall said, 'The brood of that lame Loyola shall have this miserable honour, without our envy: that if they had not been, Rome had not been'. At one time it seemed as though, through Luther's fierce onslaught, the fate of the Roman Church was sealed. Writing in 1540, Melancthon said, 'Whole libraries (of Lutheran literature) have been carried from the recent Leipzig Fair to Italy'. About the same time Caraffa (afterwards Paul IV) wrote to Paul III, 'The whole of Italy is infected with the Lutheran heresy, which has been extensively embraced by both statesmen and ecclesiastics'. 'As late as 1555', says a Jesuit writer,[2] 'that rock of a man St Peter Canisius used sometimes to despair as he watched the Protestant flood with its silt of moral corruption rise everywhere higher.'

The rapid advance of Protestant ideas was not destined to continue. Rome rallied her forces and met attack with counter-attack. At the Council of Trent (1545–63) the Roman Church as it was known in

[1] William Haller, *The Rise of Puritanism*, page 327 ff. (N.Y., Columbia University Press, 1938.)
[2] *The Origin of the Jesuits*, James Broderick, page 213. (S.J., Longmans, 1940.)

the period with which the Middle Ages closed, came to an end; the Roman Church as she is known today, came into existence. Henceforth there were to be no more Borgias and no more Bembos. The virus of scepticism which came in with the Renaissance, especially in Italy, was driven forth; the laxity which had obtained so long replaced by boundless energy. Inspired to a large extent by the Jesuits, doctrine was clarified, that which was once fluid became rigid, obvious evils were removed; the Church, as if reborn, went forth conquering and to conquer. Devoted missionaries set out for Asia and America, whilst desperate efforts were put forth to regain territory in Europe which had been lost.

At once hated and feared, brilliant controversialists like Bellarmine sought to present the Catholic faith in its most attractive aspect and to show how far the heretic had strayed from the straight and narrow path; whilst men, less able but not less devoted, went forth to face, and often to suffer, a painful death as they persisted in offering the forbidden sacrifice of the Mass, whilst they laboured in season and out of season to overthrow heresy, to regain the lost and to win fresh converts to their faith.

It is against *this* background and not in view of a tolerant age like ours in which indifference to religion is so pronounced, that we must read the pulpit diatribes, the anti-Roman tracts and treatises of men like Joseph Hall.

(*b*) Whilst Protestants were agreed in their hatred of Rome, which they often identified with the Scarlet Woman of the Apocalypse; whilst they were unwearied in their denunciation of the superstition alike in ritual and doctrine with which, in their view, she abounded, they could not agree among themselves. In the very country, for instance, in which the Reformation began, Lutheran and Reformed differed, as well as on many minor matters, in their doctrine of the Sacrament of the Altar. Every attempt to reconcile their conflicting views ended in failure.

The Tridentine Church was like an army which gladly rendered implicit obedience to one supreme commander; whereas the Protestant Churches resembled a group of allied armies fighting under various generals each of whom had a different plan of campaign. This, no doubt, was one of the main causes which led to the remarkable success of the Counter-Reformation.

(*c*) In England the position was even more complex than it was abroad.[1] Whilst it would be unfair to suggest that the English Reformation was due rather to political causes than to any change

[1] 'As to the Anglican Church, the English could never explain to me its essence or its nature.' George Buchanan when examined by the Portuguese Inquisition, 1547–52. Quoted from Rose Macaulay, *They went to Portugal*, page 69.

in religious conviction, in no other country do we find a sovereign who claimed to be the Defender of the Faith, described himself as Supreme Governor of the Church (under God) and prescribed to his subjects what they were to believe and how they were to worship. In any case the Anglican Church was from the outset steeped in Erastianism: and despite Elizabeth's personal popularity, at least during the earlier part of her reign, the Elizabethan Church never commanded the affection and respect of a united nation. Apart from the adherents of the 'Old Religion', in whose eyes it was entirely heretical, there was a large minority who disliked its constitution and its ritual. These men were divided into two groups. Each felt that the monarch had usurped the place of Christ and claimed obedience where obedience was not due. But whilst one – known later as Independents and Baptists – asked only to be allowed to secede from a Church in whose ritual and doctrine they did not believe, and to be allowed to worship God in various conventicles, in the only way their conscience approved; the other, whose members believed as firmly as the Anglicans in a national all-inclusive Church, and showed equal intolerance to seceders, maintained that the reformation in the English Church was incomplete, that she retained too many Roman forms and practices, and desired that she should conform in all respects to the type of Protestant worship to be met with in Scotland and on the Continent where it was technically described as 'Reformed'.

Hence the Anglican establishment, as it was in the days of Elizabeth and her successor, was attacked from three quarters: from adherents of the 'Old Religion', from Sectaries, and from those who wished to see the Anglican become a Presbyterian Church. To each of these opponents the Anglican Apologists and Controversialists directed their attack. Of such controversialists none was more active than Joseph Hall.

(*a*) HALL VERSUS THE CHURCH OF ROME

To the Roman gibe 'Where was your Church before Luther?' Hall replied: For centuries there was one undivided Church. From this Church we derive the three creeds (Apostles', Nicene, Athanasian) and the decisions of the four great Oecumenical Councils at which all vital points of Christology were settled. That once united Church is now divided. Rome herself forms part of it, a very corrupt part, but still a part: all other truly Christian Churches belong to it. The Church of England, therefore, is not the erring daughter of the Church of Rome: she is her sister long dominated by her and by her misled into the most grievous error. Now, thanks to the Reformation, she has been purged of wrong belief and superstitious practices; she is at last entirely free from all the errors and accretions which had gradually crept into the Roman Church – errors entirely opposed to the teaching of all the primitive Fathers. The Church of England was not founded by the Roman monk, Augustine; she existed in a purer form than any he ever knew, before he set foot on our island. No Church in all the world so closely resembles the Primitive, and indeed the Apostolic Church, as ours which derives in unbroken descent from bishops who received their commissions from the Apostles as they in turn received theirs from Christ himself. The English Church, preserving as she does the form of Church government instituted by the Apostles under God's Spirit, and the three great Catholic creeds; accepting as she does the decrees of the four general councils of the undivided Church, and the exposition of Christian doctrine to be found in the writings of the Fathers, so far from being heretical is divine. On the contrary, the Church of Rome is corrupted by grievous error and marred by the grossest superstition. She holds by the three creeds, it is true, none the less she is opposed in many ways to Scripture and the Primitive Fathers. Of an infallible Pope the Fathers know nothing. The view of justification, which, thanks to Jesuit influence, gained the day at Trent, is entirely false. The Scriptures plainly teach that man is justified by faith and by faith alone; not by any good works that he can do.

'To be imputed therefore', says Hall, 'and to be inherent differ no less than God and man, Trent and Heaven'. Of purgatory and indulgences the Scriptures are entirely ignorant; just as in Scripture there is no distinction drawn between 'venial and mortal' sin. The Fathers taught that Scripture is set over the Church, *not* that the Church is set over Scripture. The Fathers 'did not hang all the authority of Scripture on the sleeve of the Church'. 'All necessary determinations of faith are to be fetched from the voice of God' i.e. from the Bible. As for compulsory vows of celibacy, Scripture is entirely opposed to them. The Primitive Church had no knowledge of them; they came in about the time of Hildebrand, and since the Roman Church adopted them the morality of monks has been deplorable. 'Our strumpet', said Jewel, 'is their Penelope.' 'The heroical spirit of Luther, for I cannot be flouted out of that word,' says Hall, 'hated the brothelry of their cloisters; and chose rather, which galls them to the heart, to be an honest husband than a fornicating friar.' As for transubstantiation, the sacrifice of the Mass, invocation of Saints; these are unhestitatingly condemned. At Holy Communion Christ's Presence is of a spiritual not a corporal kind.

> 'In remembrance of Christ's death, we take and feed upon the body of Christ by our faith. And what is this feeding upon Christ but a

> comfortable application of Christ and his benefits to our souls? Corporally to eat, if it were possible the flesh of Christ, as it could, in our Saviour's own word, profit nothing (John. vi. 63): so it could be no other, than a kind of religious cannibalism.' (P., IX 372.)

Such then, in brief outline, are the views which Hall put forward at great length. Before we leave the subject, however, it may be worth while to ask what effect they had on those who first studied them, what importance is attached to them at the present day.

Of a great contemporary we are told, that he succeeded in converting between forty and fifty thousand Protestants to the Roman Catholic Faith. 'I', said a cardinal, himself a famous controversialist, 'can confute the Calvinists; but to persuade and convert them you must carry them to Francis de Sales.' We know how Joseph Hall sought to confute his adversaries; with what success he met in the much more arduous task of 'persuading and converting' them, we cannot tell.

There is no record of conversions; but there is evidence to show that Hall's attack on Rome did not meet with approval in certain sections of the Anglican Church. 'How', they asked, 'can the Synagogue of Satan be regarded as a Church in anything but name?' In conceding that Rome though corrupt was still in some sense a branch of the One Catholic Church, Hall's critics – and they were both numerous and vocal – felt that he had gone too far. Ever sensitive to popular opinion he asked certain eminent divines, whose sturdy Protestantism was unquestioned, to support his contention. They did, and those who care to do so may still read what they said. It only remains to ask, 'What value has Hall's apologia for Anglicanism at the present day?' Every apologia, of course, is primarily addressed to readers who lived at a certain date, deals with conditions which obtained at a specific time and at that alone. The interest of most works of this character, therefore, is purely historical: yet there are some which, because they reach down beneath temporary conditions to eternal principles, will endure for ever. The greatest apologia in the English language is Hooker's Ecclesiastical Polity. Hall's apologia is not of that order: it is a period piece; for even as he wrote many, perhaps most Anglicans, were beginning to drift away from the position he sought to maintain.

In spite of Newman's sophistry the Anglican articles are Protestant. Hardwicke has shown that they are largely Lutheran in origin. To begin with, they were most certainly read in a Calvinistic sense. For a whole generation, one might even say for two generations, the theology taught in the two English universities was almost exclusively Calvinist.

This state of things, however, did not continue; for the average

Englishman has never been profoundly interested in philosophy or theology. For one man who studied the articles there were at least five hundred who used and loved the devotional parts of the Prayer Book. And though the 'articles' are Protestant much of the Liturgy can be, and was intended by some (Elizabeth for instance) to be understood in a 'Catholic' sense. 'The Anglican Prayer Book', says Newman, 'consists largely of Catholic prayers, even though these, in the translation, have passed through heretical intellects.'

More and more, then, the 'protestantism' of the articles fell into the background of men's minds and the influence of the 'catholicism' implicit in the Prayer Book increased. Gradually the Elizabethan Church forgot her debt to the continental reformers and when in difficulty turned for support and guidance to the Fathers. She tried to make the best of both worlds, to take what she could from Reformation and Renaissance and to combine that with the teaching of the earlier and more reputable Fathers. England has a genius for compromise; and in the political sphere this has served her well. Whether in such an absolute matter as religion eclecticism is desirable or compromise possible is open to dispute. In any case one has only to read through the list which we have given of Roman beliefs and practices which Hall so unhesitatingly condemned, which have found re-entrance into hundreds of Anglican Churches to realize that apart from his unblushing Erastianism now so generally deplored, he cannot be regarded as an adequate exponent of Anglicanism as it exists today.

A word must be said, though there is no space for adequate discussion, on Hall's view of Episcopacy.

Over and over again we have called attention to the fact that he lived in an age before Biblical criticism and the doctrine of development had revolutionized men's view of Scripture. Hence he made two assumptions, neither of which would today be granted:

(*a*) The authenticity of the Pastoral Epistles, which Hall, like his opponents, took for granted, on which so much of his theory depended, is now denied by many scholars.[1]

(*b*) His view of the episcopate was static not dynamic. He assumed that apart from differences in wealth, social position, political influence and the like, the *episkopoi* of whom we read in the New Testament were identical (in function) with the bishops of his own time. One has only to read the conclusions reached by scholars like

[1] No one denies that there is genuinely Pauline material in the Pastorals. Of recent books, see *The Problem of the Pastoral Epistles*, P. N. Harrison, D.D.; *The Primitive Church*, B. H. Streeter, page 153; and, above all, *The Pastoral Epistles*, Sir Robert Falconer (1937).

Gwatkin,[1] Weizsaecker[2] and Harnack[3] to realize how greatly he was mistaken.

No one denies that as a form of Church government there is much to be said in favour of episcopacy (just as there is not a little to be said against it).[4] In any case it has withstood the stress and strain of centuries better than any other. If one could hope that new light would be forthcoming on the sub-Apostolic Church – concerning which we are so abysmally ignorant – agreement as to the origin and functions of episcopacy might be reached. That hope however seems destined to remain unrealized. Meanwhile opinion is deeply divided. There are those who believe, though they cannot prove, that Episcopacy is, if not of Christ's appointment, at least in harmony with His will and purpose. There are those, on the other hand, who find it impossible to believe that the Apostles who were one and all convinced of the immediacy of their Lord's return, spent their time in devising an elaborate scheme of Church government for the perpetuation of a society whose days on earth were numbered. Others again, in their dislike of 'Catholic' views, would go so far as to agree with the sentiments of the most brilliant member of the Anglican Episcopate during the opening half of the twentieth century:

> 'Two historically disproved assumptions have been the roots of limitless evils in the long and strangely tangled record of the Christian religion – the Apostolic succession of Bishops and the Roman Popedom of St Peter.' – H. Hensley Henson, *Retrospect of an Unimportant Life*, Vol. II, page 90.

(*b*) JOSEPH HALL AND THE SECTARIES

Whilst Hall was at Emmanuel College, a man – John Robinson by name – was at Corpus Christi. He became a Fellow of his college and later held a curacy at Norwich. In course of time, however, he was attracted to Puritanism and joined a congregation which worshipped at Gainsborough. In 1606 this little 'Independent', or, to use the term applied to such bodies in later days, this Congregationalist Church was divided into two. One part remained at Gainsborough; the other settled in the neighbouring village of Scrooby. Of this little congregation, John Robinson became minister. He was at once a good man and an able man. Robert Baillie, Professor of Divinity in Glasgow University, who had little love for 'Independents', described him as 'the most learned, polished and modest spirit that ever that sect enjoyed'. A later writer says that he was 'a man of

[1] H. M. Gwatkin in Hasting's *Dictionary of the Bible*, Vol. I, page 441.
[2] Weizsaecker, *Apostolic Age*, Vol. III, page 291 (English translation).
[3] Harnack, *Expansion of Christianity*, Vol. III, page 57 (English translation).
[4] Cf. Section 9 (Church Organization) in Falconer's *The Pastoral Epistles*.

uncommon gifts of intellect as well as rare virtues of character, a learned theologian, and an accomplished writer'.[1]

The Scrooby congregation, desperately harassed by government agents, determined to leave England and made their way, with the utmost difficulty, in small detachments to Amsterdam. There they remained for a year: but, finding the spiritual atmosphere of the city uncongenial, moved to Leyden. Here the congregation increased from one to three hundred and the Dutch Presbyterians thought so highly of the English preacher that they invited him to state the Calvinist case against Episcopius, one of the most distinguished exponents of Arminian views. In course of time, however, Robinson and his congregation came to feel that it would be difficult to maintain their existence as a Church and to retain their children, if they remained in Holland; so, in 1620 part of the congregation sailed for America. These were the Pilgrim Fathers. Robinson hoped to follow the first party of emigrants with the remainder of his flock; but before he could do so, he died (1625). Yet when the Pilgrim Fathers sailed, Robinson delivered an address which those who love liberty in general and religious liberty in particular, will not willingly let die.

In this address he pointed out that the Reformed Churches had apparently come to the conclusion that it was neither necessary nor possible to advance beyond the positions which Luther and Calvin had reached. For his own part he regarded it as incredible 'that the Christian world should come so lately out of such thick Antichristian darkness, and that full perfection of knowledge should break forth at once'. He was convinced that in due course further light would break out of God's word; and urged his hearers to expect and welcome it.

Soon after Robinson left Scrooby for Amsterdam (1608) Hall took upon himself to address a letter to 'Mr Smith and Mr Robinson, Ringleaders of the Late Separation' in which he set forth 'their Injury done to the Church, the Injustice of their Cause, and Fearfulness of their Offence' in which, moreover, he 'censured and advised them'. This epistle he dedicated, along with certain others to his patron (by this time he was one of Prince Henry's chaplains) 'the High and Mighty Prince, Henry to whom His Highness's unworthy servant humbly prostrated himself'.

In this letter, which adopts a somewhat patronizing air, Hall maintains that 'no man can do a greater injury than to flee from his mother'. The Church of England, he insists, has been thoroughly reformed: there is no trace of popery left in it. The ceremonies to which some object are unimportant.

[1] G. P. Fisher, *History of the Church*, page 462.

> 'These ritual observations are not so much tile and reed; rather like to some fane upon the roof; for ornament, more than use: not parts of the building; but non-necessary appendances.'
>
> 'It had been a thousand times better to swallow a Ceremony, than to rend a Church': for 'even whoredoms and murders shall abide an easier answer than separation.'

Robinson straightway replied in his *Answer to a Censorious Epistle*. It is obvious that if this 'answer' had been written a few years later – for Robinson increased in tolerance with age – certain complaints against the Church of England which were good targets for Hall, and entirely unneeded to support the validity of Robinson's position, would probably have been omitted. Be that as it may, Hall received Robinson's 'answer' and proceeded to reply to it. This he did in a pamphlet, *A Common Apology for the Church of England against the unjust challenges of the over-just sect commonly called Brownists*. The dedication runs as follows: 'To our gracious and blessed mother, the Church of England: the meanest of her children' (here, as so often, Hall adopts the language of Uriah Heep) 'dedicates this her apology and wisheth all happiness and peace.'

There is no need to repeat what we have already said of Hall's picture of the Apostolic Church. In the opinion of many, perhaps of most modern scholars it is quite inaccurate. All we need do, therefore, is to point out the main issues on which the combatants were engaged. Yet before doing this we may call attention to two points.

(1) Here, as elsewhere in his controversial writings, Hall shows himself to be entirely destitute of imaginative insight and compassion. The Scrooby congregation did not leave England out of mere wilfulness: they left England with heavy hearts. It was no light matter for a band of English peasants to settle down in a country whose language they did not understand in order to earn a hard living in ways to which they were unaccustomed. For the feelings in their hearts when they felt they *had* to leave their native land if they were to worship God in the way their consciences directed; for the feelings in their hearts when they felt called upon to forsake civilized Europe for the barbarous coasts of America, Hall had neither understanding nor sympathy. He did not, he could not conceive, that a time was to come when a great nation would regard these humble peasants as heroes, would speak of their achievements with admiration and boast that the noblest in their country were proud to claim descent from these heroic men and these humble women long after Joseph Hall had ceased to interest any but a little band of historians and antiquaries.[1]

(2) Thirty years later Hall was to sneer at Milton; to suggest that

[1] In *Saints and Strangers* (Heinemann, 1945) G. F. Willison gives a 'realistic' as opposed to an over-sentimental picture of the Pilgrim Fathers.

he gave up his original intention of becoming a minister in the established Church because he realized that in that Church he would meet with no promotion. So now he sneers at John Robinson, in the eyes of posterity a far greater figure than himself. Of him he said that he would never have turned Separatist but for the fact that he was disappointed in not securing an appointment in Norwich on which he had set his heart. By such ungenerous and malicious statements it is difficult to advance a cause however good.

There were three main reasons why the early Separatists objected to the Anglican Church as it existed in their time.

(1) They felt that no earthly king had the right to impose forms of belief and modes of worship on his subjects. In a true Church, they said, Christ is king. In any Church therefore, as distinguished from the State, there is no king but Christ. In his epistle, Hall had said that a Separatist was worse than a whoremonger and a murderer. To this the Separatist replied:

> 'The terrible threat you utter against us, that "even whoredoms and murders shall abide an easier answer than separation", would certainly fall heavy upon us, if this answer were to be made in your Consistory Courts or before any of your Ecclesiastical Judges: but, because we know, that, not Antichrist, but Christ shall be our Judge, we are bold, upon the warrant of his Word and Testament, which being sealed with his blood may not be altered, to proclaim to all the world, Separation from whatever riseth up rebelliously against the Sceptre of his Kingdom, as we are undoubtedly persuaded, the Communion, Government, and Worship of the Church of England do.' (P., 479.)

To this Hall replies (page 413) that even if it be granted that there are abuses in the Church of England, these abuses cannot be remedied by private persons. It is for the private Christian to accept without question what the king provides: it is for the king and the king alone to introduce change of any kind. Hence no toleration of any kind can be allowed to Romanist or Puritan. King James had often been 'importunately solicited for a Toleration of Religions'. 'His Christian heart' held such toleration to be 'unchristian and intolerable'.

(2) The Anglican clergy were very far from satisfactory. (*a*) Many were 'Pluralists'; that is to say they held several livings and were often absent from their flocks. 'The hungry sheep look up and are not fed.' (*b*) The mental, moral and spiritual qualities of many, many parsons was extremely low, whilst (*c*) many of the 'godly' men who had both the desire and the ability to preach were 'silenced' by the bishops. When reminded by Robinson that when forbidden to preach the Apostles replied 'We ought to obey God rather than men', Hall made answer:

> 'Your headstrong conceit is, that it is a sin to be silenced. Men must preach, even when they may not.
>
> 'All times, before you, would have wondered at this paradox: for, however the Apostles, which had not their calling from men, would not be silenced by men; yet we find that all their successors held that these hands, which were laid upon their heads, might be laid upon their mouths. . . .'

According to the law of England every man *had* to attend Church whether he liked it or not, unless he were prepared to pay a heavy fine. Human nature being what it is, the chances are that the spiritual level of the average Elizabethan congregation was not very high. Lecky has told how in the eighteenth century sceptics who made mock of the Christian faith periodically attended Church and received the sacrament in order to fulfil the conditions of the Test Act. This sort of thing which is bound to obtain, where religious observance is compulsory yet undesired, grieved the Separatist who felt that only those whose lives were Christian should participate in the most solemn service of the Christian Church.

In reply Hall says one sensible thing. Try as you will you cannot get a 'pure church'. You have no right to assume that those who accepted the religious settlement imposed by Elizabeth did not welcome it. No man can read the secrets of another's heart. But then *more suo* he has a gibe at the Puritans:

> 'How scornfully do you turn over our poor rude multitude, as if they were beasts, not men; or, if men, not rude but savage! This contempt needed not. These sons of the earth may go, before you, into heaven.'

(3) The Separatist objected to many of the Anglican 'ceremonies'. Now there were few Anglican divines who attached so little importance to ceremonies as did Joseph Hall. All through life he attached far greater importance to soundness of doctrine than to meticulous attention to ritual. Obviously he honestly felt that Puritans made much to do about nothing. But for once Puritan and Laud were agreed. In his efforts to deprotestantize the Anglican Church Laud attached enormous weight to ritual observance. Without knowing anything of modern psychology he divined by instinct, that ritual acts unconsciously mould belief. The Puritan felt the same.

The whole of Hall's argument may best be summed up in his own words, 'Christians cannot do what they ought not. Contrary to the laws of your prince and country, you have fled, not only from us, but from our communion. Either is disobedience no sin, or might you do this evil that good may come of it?' (Page 415.)

The insolent way in which he addressed a man who was quite as well educated as himself may best be gathered from the following passage:

> 'If you come back we'll ride out on horse-back to meet you. If not these not solid reasons, these petty pamphlets, these formal flourishes shall one day be fearful and material evidences against you, before that Awful Judge, which hath already said, that Judgments are prepared for the scorners, and stripes for the backs of fools.' (Proverbs, xix. 29.)

(c) HALL AND THE SCOTTISH PRESBYTERIANS

In England popular discontent with the policy of the Government could find expression in Parliament: in Scotland it was otherwise. There, Parliament modelled more or less on French lines carried little weight. Power rested almost entirely in the hands of the king and privy council; and the only public forum in which popular opinion could be expressed was the Church. Hence it was that the Scottish clergy, who maintained that they had the right, nay, more the duty, of rebuking sin whether in prince or peasant frequently referred to national affairs; in other words they criticized the conduct of the king. Over and over again their remarks were so pointed that James (VI and I) strongly resented them. Nor need we wonder when we remember that many ministers spoke as plainly as did a well-known Edinburgh preacher, who said in the course of a sermon delivered in St Giles Cathedral in 1594: 'I look not for any great good thing at his (Majesty's) hand till he repent him of his sins. Unless he does so he must go from evil to worse till he be destroyed.' Between 1590 and 1596, there were many instances of such plain speaking. Calderwood's *History of the Kirk of Scotland* is full of stories of heated interviews between a stubborn minister and an angry king.

In August 1590 the General Assembly of the Church of Scotland met in Edinburgh. At its eighth session the Assembly asked the king to 'grant three articles: to ratify the liberties of the Church; to purge the land of Jesuits and to provide adequate endowments for the ministers'.

> 'In all Parliaments,' the King replied, 'the Liberties of the Kirk were first ratified.' He then went on to praise God 'that he was born in the time of the light of the Gospel in such a Kirk, the sincerest Kirk in the world'. He then continued, 'the Kirk of Geneva keepeth Pasche and Yuille; what have they for them? As for our neighbour Kirk of England, it is an evil said Mass in English wanting nothing but the Liftings (i.e. Elevation of the Host). I charge you my good people . . . to stand by your purity and to exhort the people to do the same: and I forsooth so long as I bruike my life and crown, shall maintain the same.'[1]

Despite this solemn promise to safeguard the liberties of the Church, to provide for the maintenance of her ministers and to

[1] Calderwood, *History of the Kirk of Scotland*, Vol. V, pages 105–6.

uphold the Presbyterian system, James had definitely determined by the end of 1596 to overthrow Presbyterianism altogether and to replace it by some form of episcopacy. Thus only, he had come to feel, would it be possible to secure that absolute control over Church and State without which he could not be king in reality as well as in name.

Fate played into his hands. In December 1596 there were disturbances in Edinburgh the whole blame for which James – quite wrongfully – laid on the shoulders of the leading ministers in the city. These were removed.

No one has ever been able to explain the mystery of the Gowrie Affair. Did Gowrie try to kill the king, or did the king plan to murder Gowrie? No man knows. In any case when James gave orders that the clergy were to preach appropriate sermons and that the citizens were to show their delight at the preservation of the king, by bonfires and other modes of public rejoicing, he learned with anger and dismay that the clergy were not prepared to accept his version of the story until it had been confirmed from other quarters. He had intended that his deliverance from the hands of his enemy should be commemorated every year by solemn sermons and popular rejoicing as was later done when he escaped unscathed from the Gunpowder Plot. Their scepticism cost the clergy dear both in cash and credit. They were denied their salaries and denounced, if not as traitors, at least as warm supporters of a would-be regicide.

This was the first way in which James attempted to undermine the Presbyterian Church. One by one most of her leaders were banished on this or that charge either to remote parts of the Kingdom (where they could do little harm, or beyond the sea where they could do even less). The king's main objective however was not a group of individuals however distinguished, but the General Assembly itself. This he contrived to overthrow in two ways. In the first place he changed, without warning and in the most arbitrary way, the Assembly's appointed time and place of meeting. By this means he gradually forced the General Assembly to surrender its powers to a body of commissioners – largely nominated by himself – who assumed its functions and acted as its substitute.

The second means which James employed was of a very different character. In the old Catholic days fifty-one bishops, archbishops, abbots and priors had represented the Church in Parliament. James now suggested that this 'Third Estate' should be restored. It was unworthy of her dignity, he said, that the Church should have to approach Parliament as a suppliant: whereas if she had her own representatives in Parliament as a constituent part, her position would be greatly improved. To allay misgivings he gave his solemn assurance that he had no intention of creating a body of prelates on the English model. In spite of this however – such was the dislike of bishops in Presbyterian Scotland – it was with the utmost difficulty and by the narrow majority of fifty-one votes to forty-eight that the king's proposal was carried. Even then the powers vested in these church representatives were strictly limited.

(1) They were not elected as James desired *ad vitam aut ad culpam*, but *annuatim*.

(2) They were not allowed to introduce any matter to Parliament save one which directly concerned the affairs of the Church.

(3) They had to submit a report of their actions in Parliament, to the General Assembly every year.

(4) The king and not the Church had to pay their expenses.

(5) In addition to their parliamentary duties they were to continue to do the work of an ordinary parish minister and, like every other minister were to be subject to the control of the Presbytery of which they happened to be members.

(6) They were to possess *no jurisdiction whatsoever over their brother Presbyters.*

This may seem a rather unpromising beginning. Yet James was at once cautious and firm of purpose. He lived to provide the Church of Scotland with a 'Bench of Bishops'.

John Knox had said 'Except the tree be cut down bough and branch, the crow will have its nest again'. And there were men who saw clearly that the parliamentary representative of the Church was a bishop in embryo. 'Busk, busk, busk him as bonilie as ye can, and bring him as fairly as ye will, we see him well enough, we see *the hornes of his mytre*.' So said John Davidson in the Synod of Fife.[1] At the same synod – at which the king was present – Melville addressed him in these terms, 'Sir, you are to remember that you sit not here as Imperator but as a Christian *ades ut intersis non ut praeses*'.

Basilicon Doron – the king's advice to his son – was printed secretly in 1599. One of the seven copies was shown to Melville who copied out certain extracts. These he communicated to his friends. Two of them run as follows: (7) 'Parity amongst the ministers cannot agree with monarchy.' (9) 'Without Bishops, the Three Estates in Parliament cannot be established; therefore Bishops must be and parity banished and put away'.[2]

In due course the gloomy vision of Calderwood was realized.

> 'This year (1596) is a remarkable year of the Kirk of Scotland, both for the beginning and the end of it. The Kirk of Scotland was now

[1] Ref. Calderwood, V, 681.
[2] Records of Scottish Privy Council, VI, 35. Note by Masson.

> come to her Perfection, and the greatest purity that ever she attained unto in doctrine and discipline, so that her beauty was admirable to forraine Kirks . . . the end of this year began that doleful decay and declining of this church, which has continued to this hour proceeding from bad to worse; so that now we see such corruption that we thought not to have seen in our days.'

James had still a long way to go before he reached his goal. But by 1602 there were three or four ministers who bore the title of bishop – the Scots called them 'Tulchan Bishops'. They were regarded by the majority of their ministerial brethren merely as ordinary parish ministers 'with honorary diocesan designations'. Yet, as Masson points out[1]

> 'the Presbyterian party had been undermined, and something like power, as well as dignity, had begun to gather round the name of Bishop. . . . The old Presbyterian spirit had subsided. The majority of the clergy in all parts of the country had accommodated themselves to the King's Ecclesiastical Polity and were prepared to accept, whether willingly or with gradually decreasing reluctance, the extension of that moderate Episcopacy which already existed in a small and tentative scale.'

It is doubtful, however, if James could have succeeded in transforming his three or four titular bishops into real bishops (and filled up their number) but for the fact that he succeeded to the English throne. 'It was from England', says Masson[2] 'that he struck his blows against Presbyterianism.' The king issued orders: the Privy Council carried them out. Space does not permit us to tell the story of these blows: many of them were cunning, some base and treacherous. Suffice it to say that when James died episcopacy was apparently the form of Church government established in Scotland. How far appearance differed from reality was clearly revealed when Charles I sought to impose the Laudian liturgy upon his Scottish subjects. Clarendon said that if Charles had introduced the liturgy in 1634 when he went to be crowned in Edinburgh it would have met with a very different reception. In this he is almost certainly mistaken. He neither liked nor understood the Scots and even a superficial study of the records of kirk sessions shows how little this enforced episcopacy affected the mode of worship and even the form of government of the Scottish Church. One might even venture to say that the only men who took these Scottish bishops seriously were the bishops themselves. Scotland tolerated James's bishops and to a very considerable extent ignored them: it was a very different matter when the dean began to recite the prayers of the Laudian liturgy in St Giles' Cathedral. The service was not suffered to go on: the congregation would have none of it. What followed is too familiar to need repetition.

[1] Register of the Privy Council of Scotland, Vol. VI, page xxxvi.
[2] Records of the Privy Council of Scotland, Vol. VII, page xliv.

The National Covenant was drawn up and signed – men say it was sometimes signed with blood – peer and peasant took a solemn oath to root out episcopacy and to restore the Presbyterian polity which the great mass of the people undoubtedly preferred. An army was raised and Charles was not strong enough to resist it. In 1638 the first free General Assembly was held at Glasgow. Every previous Assembly since 1596 was declared invalid: its acts null and void. Bishops were expelled – some found refuge in Holy Isle. Once more the Presbyterian system was restored in Scotland. A year later another General Assembly met in Edinburgh. At the eighth session of this Assembly a somewhat dramatic incident took place.

> 'On the 17th of August, a paper dated Feb. 11th was given in, signed by George Graham, styling himself "sometime pretended Bishop of Orkney", in which he formally disclaimed and abjured all episcopal power and jurisdiction, with the whole corruptions thereof, condemned by the Negative Confession, promising that he would never directly or indirectly exercise the same, or even approve thereof in private discourse.'[1]

It is at this stage of the proceedings that Joseph Hall comes upon the scene. The result of his entry was a bulky volume entitled *Episcopacy by Divine Right*. The contents of this book need not detain us: they are already familiar. The work consists of fifteen *postulata* or axioms. These are developed at considerable length and, as some have said with not a little skill. The *postulata* may be reduced to two. The Apostles acting under the guidance of Divine inspiration created and introduced the episcopal system. We have already seen on what flimsy evidence this claim is based. The episcopal system thus introduced was universally accepted and remained unquestioned throughout Christendom until the Reformation. Those of the reformers who rejected episcopacy, i.e. almost every Protestant Church but the Church of England – though some of these Hall said, desired it and would have obtained it but for the fact that in the disturbed state of Europe this was impossible – were guilty of grievous error if not of schism: 'for truths which are new and unheard of in all the ages of the Church in main and essential points are well worthy to be suspected' and 'to depart from the practice of the Apostles' times, and to betake ourselves voluntarily to a new form lately taken up, cannot but be odious and highly scandalous.' (Hall to Laud, October 28th, 1639.)

All this we have heard before from Hall in his controversies with Romanist and Sectary. Except that throughout it expresses 'higher' claims on behalf of episcopacy than he had previously made, it would be hard to find a single new idea in the book. Those of its readers who accept Hall's interpretation of the pastoral epistles

[1] Grub, *Ecclesiastical History of Scotland*, Vol. III, page 62.

Correspondence re Episcopacy by Divine Right to be found in C.P.S.D. 1639 ff.

and the sub-Apostolic Age will be confirmed in their beliefs. Those who accept the conclusions of modern criticism in regard to each will dismiss Hall's claims on behalf of his Church, with the impatience they deserve.

The importance of this book lies not in any contribution it makes to the understanding of episcopacy – that, in view of Hall's previous volumes is almost negligible – it depends entirely on the light it throws on its author's character.

We have already pointed out in our sketch of Hall's life that in the beginning of his episcopate he was so unpopular with Laud and the king, that he was sorely tempted to resign his bishopric. We have also shown that from 1634 to 1638 (a year before *Episcopacy by Divine Right* was written) a great change had taken place. Charles and Laud were now completely satisfied. The fleece of the wandering sheep, once so black, was white as the driven snow. Of this the general public, which admired Hall as a Calvinist and as the author of a long series of devotional books in which there is no reference to High Church doctrine, knew nothing. Hence their amazement when the book appeared.

Masson rightly says that Hall must have been one of the first men in England to obtain a copy of the Acts of the General Assembly held at Edinburgh in August 1639. Straightway, on September 28th he writes a letter to Laud. It begins as follows:

> 'Yesternight I had the view of the Acts of the late Scottish Assembly which I could not read without much indignation, in seeing the only true and ancient government of the church so despitefully trod upon, by ignorant factionists; upon the perusal whereof, I began to think it were pity and shame they should carry it away so, and that so public an insolence could admit of none but a more public remedy.'

He then proceeds, with many expressions of humble deference, to suggest a scheme. As it is impossible in present circumstances 'to right the Church by the Sword', a synod should be convened. It should consist of bishops from England, Scotland and Ireland together with 'the chief of the learned and dignified clergy and the professors, and some other doctors of all the Universities. Thus it might be seasonable, safe and happy to employ the spiritual sword'. In this way 'the schismatic Scots might be convinced of their absurd errors' or at least 'censured and condemned publicly before all the world'. The Scots 'heady and ignorant opposers of government and good order would certainly be confounded and the rest of the world seeing the errors of these men would hiss them out of countenance'.

As this scheme did not commend itself to Laud and the king, Hall next suggested that certain learned bishops should draw up a short statement in which the 'Action of the Edinburgh Assembly' should be condemned and the true doctrine of Church government set forth. Once more Laud rejects the suggestion. The best way in which to deal with the matter, he said, was for Hall himself to write a book on the subject. Even then, however, Laud and the king did not trust Hall sufficiently to allow him a free hand. Every paragraph, as it was written, was to be sent to the archbishop for criticism and amendment. To this Hall willingly consented.

In the course of the somewhat lengthy correspondence which ensued, Hall lets words escape which we suggest shed a not altogether pleasing light on his character. Over and over again in his innumerable pages he had extolled the virtue of Christian charity, had proclaimed the necessity of gently shepherding wandering sheep into the fold. Now (October 16th) he tells Laud that he 'did not aim in any way at the reclamation of those stiff spirits'; his sole purpose was 'their conviction and shaming, together with the satisfaction and settling of any wavering minds at home or abroad'.

In a letter written on October 28th he explains the plan of his book 'humbly yielding it to your censure or better advice'. He proposes 'wherein I do somewhat please myself, if you be so pleased', to begin with the eighth session of the Assembly at which the letter from George Graham, formerly Bishop of Orkney, was read 'renouncing his episcopal title and pretended powers'. Hall promised to 'take this Master George to task and somewhat warmly to expostulate the matter with him'. He did. This is how the book begins:

> 'Good God what is this that I have lived to hear? That a Bishop, in a Christian Assembly, should renounce his Episcopal Function, and cry mercy for his now-abandoned calling.
>
> 'The world never heard of such a penance: you cannot blame us if we had much better to have remained unborn, than to live to give so heinous a scandal to God's Church, and so deep a wound to his holy truth and ordinance. . . .'

Laud graciously permitted Hall to let off his fireworks; but suggested that he must bear in mind the dignity of his office and the seriousness of the matter with which he had to deal.

Unlike Hall, he made no pretension to be a wit.

> 'I leave you free to work on George Graham's baseness and ignorance as you please, assuring myself that you will not depart from the gravity of yourself or the cause therein.'

There is to be no more of that witty satire which Hall had employed so constantly in his fight with Rome. On the other hand he was told not to seek to curry favour with foreign divines and churches by suggesting as he had so often done that lack of episcopacy was their misfortune rather than their fault. Laud made his views on this matter abundantly clear. In a letter to Hall (November 11th) he says: 'The Christian Faith was never yet planted anywhere, but the very first feature of the body of a church was by or with episcopacy.' 'Never yet', he continues, 'was there any church where it (episcopacy) has not obtained.'

He took great pains to instruct Hall in regard to the *via media* of true Anglicanism and showed him how to steer his bark between what he called the 'Rock of Rome' and the 'Great Rock in the Lake of Geneva'. Thus Hall was forced – no doubt unwillingly – to take a step which hitherto the great majority of Anglican divines had refused to take, to deny to foreign Protestants the right to regard themselves as part of Christ's One Catholic Church.

In seeking to justify the passage in his book to which Laud took exception Hall slyly suggested that his words were carefully chosen to conceal his true meaning. In regard to foreign churches and divines he says:

> 'I have held it best not to be sparing of good words, though in reality of the tenet (i.e. the Laudian view of Episcopacy) I have gone further than most others. . . . Those authors,' he continues, 'whom I mention with so fair respect, are in those things for which I cite them our friends, but if you find any phrase too high or unseasonable, it is but a dash of your chaplain's pen, to whom I beseech you to give absolute freedom in this behalf.'

As for 'Sabbatarians' – once he had been almost one himself – 'I have put a drop or two of vinegar into my ink in two several places'. Thus then, *Episcopacy by Divine Right* is the work of a very different man from the Joseph Hall who had incurred Laud's severe displeasure a dozen years before. Then he had 'favoured' Puritans: now he had become if not Laud's tool at least his mouthpiece. Small wonder that when Puritans and Presbyterians read this book they were amazed. The Anglo-Catholic king, whose favour Hall had once so nearly lost, the king whose frown had nearly driven him to 'throw up his rochet' he now addresses in terms as fulsome as those he once used when speaking of his father and his elder brother. He now breaks forth into paeans of praise for 'the invaluable blessing of our peace – this when the Scots had taken up arms – and the happy freedom of his Gospel which we do comfortably enjoy under his Majesty's sweet and religious government'.

'The chief glory of our holy profession', says the obsequious bishop, 'it has hitherto always been to render us still loyal and obedient and in this regard to triumph over the false religion of our "opposites".'

Hall was no statesman. He either could not or would not realize the strength of those forces which were already gathering: forces destined to destroy the king and the archbishop who had so often misled him. Hall saw everything merely from the standpoint of the court and the episcopate. For this lack of insight it is easier to find excuse than it is to overlook the lack of candour which *Episcopacy by Divine Right* displays. Within a year he was to produce a pamphlet – 'a poor thing though the King admires it' – a little more in harmony with his original, perhaps his real, opinions. Throughout a long life, as we have more than once suggested, Hall was never completely ingenuous. Of this, *Episcopacy by Divine Right* is a convincing proof.

(*d*) HALL AND THE ENGLISH PRESBYTERIANS

Parliament was summoned to meet in February 1641; and it was known that the chief subject of debate would be the reform of the Church. Already a great petition had been prepared, signed it was said by no fewer than 15,000 London citizens, in which the petitioners humbly craved that the Anglican hierarchy be abolished. It was also known that there was an active and resolute party in Parliament itself who shared the views of the petitioners and were determined that the Church should be reformed in 'Root and Branch'.

In view of this Hall published a pamphlet or rather a booklet five weeks before Parliament met. It was entitled *An humble remonstrance to the High Court of parliament by a dutiful son of the Church.* Though this *Humble Remonstrance* covered much the same ground as its predecessor, *Episcopacy by Divine Right*, it differed from it as might be expected in form and spirit. The tone is much more urbane – in a sense the tract is an apologia – and the claims made on behalf of episcopacy are somewhat modified. Hall now explains what he said or intended to say in *Episcopacy by Divine Right* in the following terms:

> 'First, our position is only affirmative; implying the justifiableness and holiness of an Episcopal calling, without any further implication. Next, when we speak of Divine Right, we mean not an express law of God, requiring it upon the absolute necessity of the being of a Church, what hindrance soever may interpose; but a Divine institution, warranting it where it is, and requiring it where it may be had.'

Of the continental Churches (Lutheran and Reformed) he now says – as in his 'pre-Laudian days' he had so often said before:

> 'We love and honour those Sister-Churches, as the dear Spouse of Christ. . . . Those particular Churches, to whom the power and faculty (i.e. Episcopacy) is denied, lose nothing of the true essence of a Church, though they miss something of their glory and perfection, whereof they are barred by the necessity of their condition. . . .'

Hall was never ingenuous. His admirers are forced to admit that in his desire for peace he was too apt to be swayed by what he termed 'authority', that is to say by a king or an archbishop. His enemies regard him as a time-server prepared to set his sails in any direction which promised to yield a favouring breeze. In regard to Laud's position there is no room for doubt. In plain, unambiguous terms he stated his belief: 'No Bishop, no Church'. Read in the light of the correspondence that took place between Hall and Laud *Episcopacy by Divine Right* makes it abundantly clear that in 1640 Hall professed to accept the Laudian view according to which the continental Churches which lacked episcopacy were Churches merely in name. The question inevitably arises therefore, 'Did Hall really change his views within a few months?' Did he feel that in *Episcopacy by Divine Right* he had yielded too much to Laud and on further reflection determine to revert to his own earlier position which he held consistently throughout his life? It is hard to say; for it is difficult to determine what Hall really meant when he said, as he so often did, that the Reformed Churches on the Continent would have become episcopal if this had lain within their power. That it was at once untruthful and disingenuous is hard to believe. The only solution of the problem therefore seems to lie in the fact that he was the victim of 'wishful thinking'. In any case the view which he so often states that the lack of bishops in continental Churches was their misfortune and not their fault is certainly mistaken. For granted that Hall could refer to a few books in which reference is made to the undoubted fact that at various times and for divers reasons certain Reformed Churches had toyed with the idea of appointing 'superintendents' possessed of quasi-episcopal powers, the fact remains that these men were never meant to develop into a special order. In the sense that Roman Catholics and Anglicans use the word they were never meant to become *bishops*.

In this very tract Hall tells us that whilst the king gives a bishopric it is God who makes a bishop. He could distinguish clearly between a Laudian prelate to whom the king assigned large revenues, the rank of a peer and political influence, and a bishop who enjoyed no such pleasures. These were accidental – suitable and agreeable, no doubt – but *not* essential. The fact that no continental ruler had offered to treat any reformed minister in this way had no bearing on his religious status. But Hall knew his Luther: he must have heard of the view attributed to the greatest of all the Reformers: 'When a man is made a bishop, ten devils enter into him.' He knew some distinguished Huguenots, ministers of that Church to which he referred as our dear sister Church of France: but in all his writings he does not quote a single instance of a French, Belgian or Dutch minister who either sought episcopal ordination when he became a Presbyter or expressed a desire to be made a bishop. Had any of these men really desired it episcopacy could have been had for the asking and amongst the very first who would have been delighted to take part in the act of 'consecration' would have been Joseph Hall himself. Already certain of James's Scottish 'bishops' had received episcopal consecration at the hands of English bishops. If Scotsmen, why not Dutchmen, Frenchmen, Swiss?

The fact of the matter was that the Presbyterian Clergy in every Reformed Church maintained that *their* view and not that of Roman Catholics and Anglicans was *God's* view of the way in which a Church should be organized and governed. Mistaken they may have been: intolerant no doubt they were. Yet this as they would have been the first to proclaim, and not Hall's version, is the true account of their theological and ecclesiastical position. In a word Hall's view of continental Presbyterians is at once (though perhaps he did not know it) illogical and completely untrue to fact. To complete the picture we need only add that in this *Humble Remonstrance* which its author described as 'meek and gall-less', which its enemies said was neither humble nor a remonstrance, of which Baillie said, 'The King likes it well, but all else pities it as a most poor piece', Hall reaffirms two lifelong convictions. One – the Pope is the Man of Sin – well-calculated to please the great majority of the members of Parliament. The other – James settled the whole matter of liturgy and episcopacy once and for all at the Hampton Court Conference – which could hardly fail to arouse hostility in the minds of those who refused to believe either in the Divine Right of Kings or in the immutability of Royal Decrees.

Hall further admits 'with a bleeding heart' the 'manifold scandals of the inferior clergy' and, as against Laud and the Anglo-Catholics, insists that ritual is a matter of secondary importance. To him, he said, it was incomprehensible that those who were agreed 'in all other doctrinal points of religion' should seek to 'rend the seamless coat of Christ'. 'Is it a title,' he asks, 'or a retinue, or a ceremony, a garment, or a colour, or an organ-pipe that can make us a different church, while we preach and profess the same saving truth?'

To this pamphlet (and at the same time to *Episcopacy by Divine Right*) a group of five Presbyterian ministers replied. They called themselves *Smectymnuus*.[1]

They had no difficulty in finding passages in the Fathers which contradicted the Anglican claims. Commenting on Titus, for instance, Jerome says: 'A Presbyter and a Bishop is the same.' According to the same authority, 'a Bishop as it is a superior order to a Presbyter, is a human presumption: not a divine ordinance'.

In regard to Hall's claim that Anglican bishops were virtually

[1] A composite name for five Presbyterian Ministers, Stephen Marshal, Edmund Calamy, Thomas Young, Matthew Newcomen and William Spurstow.

identical with the 'bishops' of the Primitive Church the Smectymnuans said:

> 'He knows but little of Antiquity, that knows not, that there is so vast a difference between our Bishops and those that were in the first 400 years that Episcopacy is like the *Argo* so often repaired that nothing was left of its first material, but bore the same name.'

They quote the well-known words of Jerome: 'When they had wooden chalices they had golden priests: when the chalices were golden, the priests were wooden.' After Constantine had enriched the Church, says Chrysostom in his eighty-sixth homily on St Matthew, 'religion brought forth riches and the daughter devoured the mother and then a voice of angels was heard from heaven *Hodie venenum in Ecclesiam Christi cecidit*'. Our bishops, they continue, execute their 'judicatory power' in a way unknown to antiquity. Ambrose had no 'vicar': Augustine no 'chancellor'. No primitive bishop extracted an *ex officio oath*, or sat in a Court of High Commission. As for alteration of the liturgy King James's declaration was not, like the Laws of the Medes and Persians, unalterable. It is absurd to claim that the English Prayer Book resembles the service book of any Reformed continental Church. It was deliberately framed, not to express the devotions of a Reformed congregation: but 'to bring the Papists to our Churches'. In this respect it has been a signal failure. Not till A.D. 416 were set forms of prayer compulsorily imposed. The early English reformers wished the litany to be a help to those who could not lead a congregation in prayer. No other Reformed Church is *tied* to a service book: for 'ability to offer up the people's wants to God in prayer is part of the ministerial office'. The prayer book as now used prevents this. They end by calling attention to the fact, that if ceremonies are so unimportant, it is strange that Laud has insisted on introducing so many novelties, each of a Romish character: that terms such as 'host' are now used in Anglican services which were unheard of in the time of James.

The answer to the *Humble Remonstrance* was published in March; a month later Hall issued his reply: *A Defence of an Humble Remonstrance*. In June the Smectymnuans reply to Hall's reply; in July or August, he gives his final answer to his opponents.

We have no space to deal with this controversy in detail; nor is there need to do so, for each of the combatants firmly maintained his ground and used over and over again the arguments which he employed when first he entered the fray. Neither side did or could convince the other; since each based his arguments on very different premises. In debating power there was little to choose between the opponents. On the whole, it has been said, the Smectymnuans were more logical: certainly Hall was more rhetorical. Yet throughout the controversy Hall revealed that flaw in his moral character which led him to assume, consistently, that all his opponents were at once intellectually blind and morally wrong. For instance, he describes his defence as being directed against '*the frivolous and false exceptions*' of Smectymnuus; claims to vindicate the *right of liturgy and episcopacy* against the '*vain cavils and challenges*' of their foes. In dedicating the work to the king, he says that the 'quarrel has been insolently managed' by his 'impotent assailants', and concludes the *defence* with the following words:

> 'Thus, I hope, you have a sufficient answer to your bold and unjust demands; and to those vain cavils, which you have raised against the *Humble Remonstrance*. God give you wisdom to see the truth, and grace to follow it!'

To the work however a postscript is attached: it runs as follows:

> 'In the mean time, I beseech the God of Heaven to humble you, in the sight and sense of your grievous uncharitableness; and to put, at last, into your hearts and tongues, the Counsels of Peace.'

His final pamphlet *A Short Answer to the Tedious Vindication of Smectymnuus* ends thus:

> 'Shortly, then, since I see that our Smectymnuans have vowed, like as some impetuous scolds are wont to do, to have the last word; and have set up a resolution, by taking advantage of their multitude, to tire out their better employed Adversary, with mere length of discourse; and to do that by bulk of body, which by clean strength they cannot; I have determined to take off my hand from this remaining controversy . . . with this yet for a conclusion, that if, in this their wordy and wearisome volume, they shall meet with any one argument, which they dare avow for new, they shall expect their answer by the next post.'

Thus did our good bishop, with wonted self-complacency, feel that the battle had been won: that he left the field with his habitual gravity and dignity, bearing in his arms the spoils of victory. In this, however, he was sadly mistaken.

MILTON'S ANIMADVERSIONS

Since Masson wrote his great work, many fresh studies of Milton have appeared. Nowhere, perhaps, has the research on which such studies are based been more diligently pursued than in America. Amongst those who have dealt in some detail with the Milton-Hall controversy is Professor William Riley Parker.[1]

Amongst other statements which he makes are these:

(*a*) 'It was his (Milton's) first attempt at flippancy and wholesale sarcasm, and, though somewhat heavy handed, it was effective.'

[1] Columbus University. The Ohio University Press, 1940.

(Op. cit., 266.) As will presently appear, this statement is far too mild.

(*b*) Masson had suggested that the composition in which Milton's moral character was traduced, was either the work of Joseph Hall himself or Joseph Hall with the assistance of his son Robert, or, most probably, the work of Robert with the help of his father. Parker says that Masson had no right to assume that Robert was the author: it might have been another of Hall's sons. To us it matters little which of Hall's sons was responsible, especially as Parker admits that Milton was right 'in his personal suspicion that Hall assisted or advised in the composition'.

(*c*) In reference to Milton's claim that he 'brought timely succour to those ministers (Smectymnuans) who had some difficulty in maintaining their ground against the bishops' (Usher and Hall) eloquence', Roper[1] says 'his opponents can hardly have taken his role in the controversy so seriously as some of his biographers'.

Of Usher's opinion we know nothing, of Hall's feeling there can be no doubt. Milton stung him as no other opponent ever did. Masson well says that when Hall read Milton's tract he was 'stunned'. He was, indeed.

Milton knew himself to be a dedicated spirit; everything that he had hitherto done, intense study, severe self-discipline, foreign travel was intended to fit him for the performance of his self-chosen, nay, rather his God-given task of writing a great, perhaps an immortal, poem. He knew himself to be a genius: the noblest poets like Dante, the loftiest thinkers like Plato he regarded as his peers. In their society and only in such society did he feel entirely at home. To use his own simile, he was 'like an eagle mewing her mighty youth, purging and unscaling her undazzled eyes in the full light of the midday sun'. Of *l'homme moyen sensuel*, he knew nothing; of the average Presbyterian minister and the average Presbyterian congregation, he knew little more. He was apt to take for granted that the men in whose cause he fought were as noble as himself. 'He assumed', as Tillyard says, 'that every ruffian who cried out "Down with the bishops!" was inspired by motives as lofty as his own'. For if he were in one sense a Puritan who loved righteousness and hated iniquity, he was at the same time the noblest humanist of his age and reverenced the greatness of man. If there were one thing he desired beyond all others it was liberty, freedom to lead his own life in his own way: if there was a body of men who seemed to hate liberty, to fear liberty, to aim at the destruction of liberty, it was the bench of bishops. There could, he felt, be no hope of the establishment of liberty in England till bishops were dethroned. Who

[1] Roper, *Milton's Contemporary Reputation*. An essay, page 16.

were to succeed them, what form of government the Church was to assume after their expulsion was a matter of purely secondary consideration. His immediate task, the task of all true Englishmen was to get rid of bishops. 'I resolved,' he said, 'though I was then meditating certain other matters, to transfer into this struggle all my genius and all the strength of my industry.'

Before dealing with the substance of Milton's tracts, we must say a word in regard to his method. He was not a born debater. As we have said elsewhere, his favourite weapon was the bludgeon and not the rapier. He identified the cause to which he was opposed with one of its representatives, attacked this man with every means in his power under the impression that by confounding his opponent he thereby overthrew the cause he represented. After Laud, Hall was the most prominent bishop in England. Therefore it was Hall, a man whom he regarded as altogether unworthy of the great reputation he enjoyed, that Milton selected as his victim. Selecting those earlier writings of a satirical character, which their author fondly hoped had been completely forgotten, Milton poured out the vials of his wrath and denounced the unhappy satirist in no measured terms. Hall had once said that there were certain things that a layman might do which a clergyman could not do. He gave as an example the stage whereon no clergyman should appear though a layman might do so with a clear conscience. Milton had no difficulty in showing that the whole tone of *Mundus alter et idem* was entirely unfitting in one who regarded himself and was regarded by others as a grave divine. Throughout the argument however Milton showed that like many others he had two sides to his character. He was at once Jekyll and Hyde. On the one hand he was the most highly cultured man in Europe; on the other he could pour out the most vulgar abuse like a common fish-wife. Even the 'idolatrous Masson', as Haller calls him, can find no excuse for some of the expressions used by Milton in his savage attack on Joseph Hall. None who reads them can fail to regret that one so great as John Milton should have used such words. But on the other hand, these same tracts contain some of the most magnificent passages ever written in English. It is not only Masson who sings their praise. Tillyard speaks of Milton's 'gorgeous prose' and Bowra says and says truly, 'It may even be doubted whether the grand style can be grander than Milton's or the heroic temper more sublime than his'. Even if this be written of his verse, it is almost as true of the most splendid passages of his matchless prose. Then too, we must remember, that when Milton wrote the tracts with which we are concerned, he was convinced that Christ was about to return to earth in order to lead his Englishmen by a new Exodus out of Egyptian darkness into an era of light and liberty such as men had never known; and that when exultant saints sang forth his praise they were to make use of the words of John Milton.

Bacon once said: 'As far as real knowledge is concerned we are the classics ourselves, having surpassed the ancients by wider experience and profounder thinking.' This is precisely the attitude which Milton adopts to the whole of Christian antiquity on which his opponent so heavily relied. To him Hall stood for the old order; he himself stood for the new. Save when he deals with the many shortcomings of the Anglican clergy, Milton writes less as a Puritan who demands reform of morals, than as a man of the Renaissance who hated the barbarous Latin and the ignorance of the Middle Ages.

He knew the weakness of so many of the Anglican clergy of his time, their lascivious youth, their studies in

> 'unprofitable questions and barbarous sophistry, their middle age in ambition and idleness, their old age in avarice and diseases. . . . In the Greek tongue most of them unlettered. In the Hebrew text, which is so necessary to be understood, except it be some few of them, their lips are utterly uncircumcised.'

For the ordination and maintenance of these men it was the bishops who must be held responsible; and amongst those bishops was Joseph Hall.

Having spoken as a Puritan, Milton goes on to speak as a son of the Renaissance.

(*a*) First he deals with the Fathers to whom Hall so persistently appealed, whom Hall and other Anglicans regarded with a reverence to which the Fathers had no claim. The Fathers belonged to the ages of darkness from which men were slowly being delivered. They were ignorant and their doctrines do not agree.

> 'These doctors, who had scarce one-half the light we enjoy, who all except two or three were ignorant of the Hebrew tongue and many of the Greek. . . . Who is ignorant of the foul errors, the ridiculous wresting of Scripture, the heresies, the vanities thick sown through the volumes of Justin Martyr, Clemens, Tertullian, and others of eldest time?'

(*b*) With even greater confidence did Anglicans trust, with even greater reverence did they regard the Councils. Milton's study of Church history led to very different conclusions. After speaking of the 'ambition, corruption, contention, combustion' by which these councils were marked, he goes on to say:

> 'Finding, therefore, that the most of their actions in single to be weak, and yet turbulent; full of strife and flat of spirit; and the sum of their best councils there collected, to be most commonly in

F*

> questions either trivial and vain, or else of short and easy decision, without that great bustle which they made; I concluded that if their single ambition was such, then certainly united in a council it would be much more; and if the compendious recital of what they there did was so tedious and unprofitable, then surely to set out the whole extent of their tattle in a dozen volumes would be a loss of time irrecoverable.'

For these views he found support in Gregory of Nazianzen who said to Procopius that

> 'of any council or meeting of Bishops he never saw good end; nor any remedy of evil in the Church but rather increase of evil. For their contentions and desire of lording no tongue is able to express.'

(*c*) Of bishops Milton said in his own way what many others had said before him. He was convinced that there was little resemblance between a primitive and a caroline bishop.

> 'But he that will mould the modern bishop into a primitive, must yield him to be elected by the popular voice, undiocesed, unrevenued, unlorded, and leave him nothing but brotherly equality, matchless temperance, frequent fasting, incessant prayer and preaching, continual watchings and labours in his ministry.'

(*d*) Finally Milton deals with ordination. The Laudian party maintained that a bishop is essential to the continued existence of the Church, since for centuries men had been ordained by bishops who laid their hands on ordinands and thereby conferred grace upon them. As for Milton he would have none of this.

> 'As for ordination what is it but the laying on of hands, an outward sign or symbol of admission? It creates nothing, it confers nothing; it is the inward calling of God that makes a man a minister and his own painful study that manures and improves his spiritual gifts. . . . It is but an orderly form of receiving a man already fitted, and committing to him a particular charge. . . .'

Here it seems to us Milton parts company with the Presbyterians and joins hands with the Sectaries.

All this has been said partly to show how John Milton fought with Joseph Hall; partly to show that whether he was called (as he was in succession) Anglican, Presbyterian, Sectary, Arian, Pantheist or 'Holist', he was (at bottom) essentially throughout his life a lover of liberty, especially liberty for John Milton to go whithersoever the spirit led him; but chiefly to remind our readers of the fact that but for this encounter Joseph Hall would have been long-since forgotten. A few might read his satires, a smaller number some of his innumerable devotional works; for the great majority of men he would be as though he had never lived at all. Instead of that he has joined the ranks of the immortals. The man who admitted him to membership of that august society was John Milton.

VII – LITERARY WORKS

(*a*) SATIRES (modernized spelling)

It is impossible in a book like this, which is primarily concerned with Hall as a writer on religious subjects, to devote the attention to his satires which they deserve. All we can do is to present a short summary – no easy matter – of what Hall has to say; and to call attention to the works in which the best commentary and criticism is to be found.

Before doing this, however, it may be well to say a word or two about some other verses which Hall wrote. The number of his Latin verses which have come down to us is but small; and they possess but little significance.

His last experiment in verse needs only to be mentioned to be dismissed. He wrote two sets of verses which, when set to music, were intended to be sung as anthems in Exeter Cathedral.

THE KING'S PROPHECIE *or* WEEPING JOY

Finally we must mention a lengthy poem – if so great a word may be used to describe such verse – one of many which were written to welcome King James of Scotland when he arrived in London to receive the English crown.

The verses were written in a hurry in order that they might reach London in time.

'Meanwhile this verse
Sawe too few days, to see too many years.'

This work is rarely mentioned by earlier critics, for the complete version was not discovered till 1882. As a poem its merits are but few: as a biographical source it is of considerable interest. In the fourth stanza the writer tells the king that he found no difficulty in writing verse.

'I wont to finde the willing Muse unsought
And vent my numbers in a plenteous vaine.'

From the seventeenth and eighteenth stanzas we learn that he had translated Vergil's Fourth Eclogue into English verse and applied the prophecy to the birth of Prince Henry. He also suggests that he had written pastoral poetry. Some critics suggest that such poetry had not only been written but published and that it is to this Marston refers in *Pygmalion's Image* (1598) when he says:

'Will not his pastorals indure for ever?'

As this pastoral poetry preceded the satires, it must have been written (and published?) when Hall was a mere stripling. There is a reference to the satires in stanza 39 and another in stanza 53 where the poet tells us he had abandoned satire for ever. Another point of interest is that Hall reveals himself as an ardent patriot. Of England he writes:

> 'Thou art the world's sole glory
> Earth's second Paradise.'

He also speaks of his great love for Suffolk.

> 'Then shall my *Suffolke* (England's Eden hight
> As England is the world's) . . .'

In dealing with his other works we have pointed out that Hall loved to pay a subtle compliment to a patron or a possible patron whenever opportunity offered. In this respect these congratulatory verses are true to type. James as the author of *Basilicon Doron* receives due praise. Allusion is made to his interest in religion. (It would have been more truthful if less tactful to have spoken of his interest in *theology*.)

> 'Purest religion hath his heart possessed.'

Two other statements need only be mentioned. In 1603 and for long years after Hall hated the Roman Catholic Church.

> 'And that stale strumpet of imperious Rome.'

He feared that on the death of Elizabeth England would be rent asunder by internecine strife; that the Wars of the Roses, or something like that would return. The coming of James meant the unification of the country and lasting peace. One further point. In view of the drunkenness and debauchery for which James's Court was notorious, it is rather pathetic to read Hall's prophecy that it was to be pure and noble.

> 'His Court shall be a church of Saints: quite free
> From filth, excess, and servile flattery.' (49.)
> 'The Courtier's only grace shall henceforth lie .
> In learning, wisdom, valour, honesty.' (50.)

THE SATIRES

On the title page we read *Virgidemiarum/Sixe Bookes/First Three Bookes/of/Tooth-lesse Satyrs/I. Poetical./II.Academicall./III. Morall.* The second volume is entitled *Virgidemiarum/The Three Last Bookes/ of/Byting Satyrs.*

'By Virgidemia,' says Warton, 'an uncouth and uncommon word, we are to understand a Gathering or Harvest of rods, in reference to the nature of the subject.'

The satires then are divided into two parts: the 'Toothless Satires' and the 'Biting Satires'. Neither volume is very easy to understand without assistance, or to put the matter in another way, few readers will fail to benefit by consulting the notes of commentators who have devoted considerable pains to explaining obscure passages in which the work abounds.

For more than a hundred years it seemed as if Hall's satires were doomed to oblivion. It is true that Pope[1] admired them. 'He esteemed them', it is said, 'the best poetry and truest satire in the English language', and toyed with the idea of modernizing them. The man, however, who rescued them from the grave and aroused fresh interest in them was Thomas Warton (1728–90).[2] In Warton's eyes 'Hall was a neglected writer of real genius'. Whilst recognizing their defects, he insisted that the satires were 'replete with animation of style and sentiment'. In them 'the thorns of severe invective are not unmixed with the flowers of pure poetry'. Warton pays tribute, as every reader is bound to do, to Hall's amazing ability in character-drawing. He finds in the satires 'masterly traces of genuine humour', and maintains that 'his versification is equally energetic and elegant'.

In contrast to Warton, who set out to reveal to others the merits he himself had discovered in Hall's satires, Milton wrote for the express purpose of holding Hall up to ridicule. Convinced that Hall enjoyed a reputation both as a man and as an author to which he was not entitled, Milton made it his business (if one may be forgiven the use of an expression borrowed from modern slang) to 'debunk' him. The *Apology for Smectymnuus* is primarily concerned with refuting Hall's views of Church government; but in order to undermine Hall's reputation for dignity and ability, he takes the opportunity of expressing his opinion of the satires. He does so in the following words:

> 'For this good hap I had from a careful education, to be inured and seasoned betimes with the best and elegantest authors of the learned tongues, and thereto brought an ear that could measure a just cadence, and scan without articulating: rather nice and humorous in what was tolerable, than patient to read every drawling versifier. Whence lighting upon the title of "toothless satires", I will not conceal ye what I thought, readers, that sure this must be some sucking satyr, who might have done better to have used his coral, and made an end of teething, ere he took upon him to wield a satire's whip. But when I heard him talking of "scouring the rusty swords of elvish knights", do not blame me if I changed my thought, and concluded him some desperate cutler. But why "his scornful muse could never abide with tragic shoes her ancles for to hide", the pace of the verse told me that her mawkin knuckles

[1] A. Davenport, *The Poems of Joseph Hall*, xxvii (n.).
[2] Thomas Warton, *History of English Poetry*, Hazlitt's edition, Vol. IV, page 364 ff.

> were never shapen to that royal buskin. And turning by chance to the sixth satire of his second book, I was confirmed; where having begun loftily "in heaven's universal alphabet", he falls down to that wretched poorness and frigidity, as to talk of "Bridge-street in heaven, and the ostler of heaven", and there wanting other matter to catch him a heat (for certain he was in the frozen zone miserably benumbed), with thoughts lower than any beadle betakes him to whip the signposts of Cambridge ale-houses, the ordinary subject of freshmen's tales, and in a strain as pitiful. Which for him who would be counted the first English satire, to abase himself to, who might have learned better among the Latin and Italian satirists, and in our own tongue from the "Vision and Creed of Pierce Plowman", besides others before him, manifested a presumptuous undertaking with a weak and unexamined shoulders. For a satire as it was born out of a tragedy, so ought to resemble his parentage, to strike high, and adventure dangerously at the most eminent vices among the greatest persons, and not to creep into every blind tap-house, that fears a constable more than a satire. But that such a poem should be toothless, I still affirm it to be a bull, taking away the essence of that which it calls itself. For if it bite neither the persons nor the vices, how is it a satire? And if it bite either, how is it toothless? So that toothless satires are as much as if he had said toothless teeth. What we should do, therefore, with this learned comment upon teeth and horns, which hath brought this confutant into his pedantic kingdom of cornucopia, to reward him for glossing upon horns even to the Hebrew root, I know not; unless. . . .'

Further on in the apology the following passage occurs:

> 'How hard is it when a man meets with a fool to keep his tongue from folly. . . . The Remonstrant (i.e. Hall) when he was as young as I, could
>
> "Teach each hollow grove to sound his love,
> Wearying echo with one changeless word."
> *Toothless Satires.*
>
> And so he well might and all his auditory besides, with his "teach each".'

Milton's warmest admirers cannot pretend that he was an expert in the use of a rapier: his favourite weapon was a bludgeon. Yet these words stung Hall to the quick. Here as elsewhere he condemns Hall's flippancy. He himself always wrote in the grand manner and almost always dealt with lofty and magnificent themes.[1] For choice he never read any but the greatest writers and he was confident that he was their peer. To him Hall was in very truth nothing more nor less than a 'drawling versifier'. Nay, more, he was a fool. Of all men who have written in the English tongue Milton had the most delicate ear. He loathed slovenliness as he abhorred discord. He found or thought he found plenty of both in Hall. No wonder he says that Hall bored

[1] 'It may even be doubted whether the grand style can be grander than Milton's or the heroic temper more sublime than his.' – C. M. Bowra, *From Virgil to Milton.*

his readers when he used such an expression as 'Teach each'. Milton's own standard of good writing was so high, that he failed to realize that the average writer and the average reader, then as now, is perfectly satisfied with work which to him was intolerable.

In the nineteenth century several editions of the satires were produced.[1] One of the best was that of Dr A. B. Grosart, who edited a number of Elizabethan works. He was not a professional philologist – indeed he was a busy minister of religion – but he called attention to many allusions in Hall's satires to the three great Roman writers Juvenal, Horace and Persius.

The man, however, to whom until recently we owed the greatest debt was Dr Konrad Schulze, of Berlin. In 1910 he published his fine edition of the satires under the title *Die Satiren Halls Ihre Abhängigkeit von den Altromischen Satirikern und ihre Realbeziehungen auf die Shakespeare-Zeit*. In this work Schulze gives a critical study of the text, and traces far more allusions in Hall than Grosart did, not only to Roman satirists but also to Ariosto, Regnier and other writers. From the standpoint of the general reader the chief value of this book consists in the splendid way in which Schulze illuminates the whole of the late Elizabethan period by quotations from contemporary writers. In the *Anatomy of Abuses in England*, by Philip Stubbes (1583), he found perhaps his richest source. No praise can be too high for the mass of illustrations he provides, or for the patient way in which he arranges under different headings the 'abuses' which in the satires Hall set out to attack.

In 1949 A. Davenport published *The Poems of Joseph Hall, Bishop of Exeter and Norwich*. This book is a credit to English scholarship. As we pointed out in our preface, it is likely to remain for many years the standard work on Hall's satires. It has all the minute attention to details which reminds one of the best type of German philologist. It seems to embody all the results obtained by previous scholars and includes what is of most value in the contributions of those who have put forth suggestions in the various journals which deal with English literature.

It is true that Davenport addresses himself in the first instance to scholars who specialize in late Elizabethan literature and to students in various universities at home and abroad who are reading for an honours degree. Much, therefore, that he says is of little interest to the general reader. At the same time the introduction and commentary to say nothing of the invaluable and illuminating notes, afford information which can be found nowhere else, and make it possible for any intelligent reader to understand and enjoy the satires in a way that would be otherwise impossible.

[1] See Davenport, op. cit, lxx ff.

Beyond all others Davenport has shown how deeply versed Hall was in the popular poetry of his time, how skilfully he laid his hand upon its many weaknesses, and what an active part he took in the guerilla warfare waged on one another by the leading satirists of those days. Davenport is a philologist. He does not deal with a question which has perplexed many a student of Hall's life and work: How was it possible for one who professed to feel at home in Emmanuel, that school of 'austere piety' as he put it, which existed expressly to prepare young Puritans for the sacred ministry to devote so much time and energy with a clear conscience to work of a very different kind? He prayed he tells us for divine assistance before he entered on a 'Disputation'. Did he ask a blessing on those other labours concerning which he kept such discreet silence in later life?

Before discussing the substance of the satires there are two points to which we must call attention. In the prologue to his first book these lines occur:

> 'I first adventure, follow me who list
> And be the second English Satyrist.'

As may be imagined these lines have given rise to much discussion. As a matter of fact Hall was *not* the first English satirist. Grosart says he was the fourth: Warton that he was the fifth. His predecessors were Wyatt (Snr.), Gascoigne, Donne, though his work was *published* much later, and Lodge. The difference in arrangement is probably due to the fact that satires like those of Hall and Donne were circulated in manuscript before they were published: that it is difficult, therefore, if not impossible, to determine the exact date at which they were composed. In any case there is no reason to doubt that Hall genuinely believed that he was the first Englishman who deliberately imitated and adapted the three great Roman satirists, Juvenal, Persius and Horace, 'hard of conceit and harsh of style'. Nor is there any reason to doubt his statement that the only modern satires he had ever seen were those of Ariosto (as yet untranslated) and Regnier, as yet unpublished. The other point is that with one exception Hall made no reference to any living person.

> 'If thou mayst spit upon a toad unvenomed, why mayst thou not speak of a vice without danger? Especially so warily as I have endeavoured: who, in the unpartial mention of so many vices, may safely profess to be altogether guiltless in myself to the intention of any guilty person who might be blemished by the likelihood of my conceived application.' *A Postscript to the Reader*.

The one exception to this rule is a gentleman named Labeo. Who was he? No two critics are agreed. Some say he was Nash; others Thomas Greene; others Chapman; others again that he was Marston,[1]

[1] E.g. *Cambridge History of English Literature*.

though least probable.[1] But the most interesting guess is that he was none other than Shakespeare. As may be imagined the Baconians run riot here. For instance, here is a book whose title speaks for itself.

> 'The hidden signatures of Francisco Colonna and Francis Bacon. A comparison of their methods with the evidence of Marston and Hall that Bacon was the Author of Venus and Adonis. William Stone Booth. Boston 1910.'

A much more interesting work is that of J. D. Parsons:

> 'William Shakespeare, "Another's name"; or, the suppressed [Labeo-Shakespeare] evidence of the Elizabethan satirists, Marston and Hall, concerning the Author of Venus and Adonis.' (1920.)

Here is a specimen of the evidence on which the theory rests. In the last satire (Book VI, I) the opening lines,

> 'Labeo reserves a long nayle for the nonce.
> To wound my margent thro' ten leaves at once;'

are supposed to prove that Shakespeare 'had helped Hall with kindly criticism of his satires', whilst in the same satire (lines 245–6),

> 'Tho' Labeo reaches right (who can deny?)
> The true strayness of Heroicke poesie'

Shakespeare is praised because he has now ceased to write such poems as *Venus and Adonis* and the *Rape of Lucrece* and has given to the world *Romeo*, *Richard II*, *Richard III* and *Henry IV*.

Still more curious is the work of William Henry Moore, of Birmingham who in his *Baconian Studies* (Vol. 44, 1939) finds by means of a curious kind of arithmetic that Bacon's cryptic signature is scattered far and wide throughout Hall's satires.

Content

There may be an allusion to the fact that Hall had written pastoral poetry in the eighteenth stanza of the *Defiance to Envy* which serves as an introduction to the satires:

> 'Speake, ye attentive swaynes that heard me late,
> Needs me give grasse unto the conquerors.
> At Colin's feet I throw my yeelding reed,
> But let the rest win homage by their deed.'

He then proceeds to develop the thought that only Spenser (Colin) is to escape criticism. Other writers merely profane 'the sacred hests' of the Muses: Hall will write nothing but satire.

> 'Only these refuse rhymes I here mispend
> To chide the world, that did my thoughts offend.'

The whole of the first book (and the first satire of the second book which Warton says should have been included in the first) is devoted

[1] Davenport (op. cit, lix) regards Labeo as 'the typical bad poet'.

to criticism of the forms of literature then in vogue and of the lives of the poets who produced them.

The Muses have ceased to be virgins: Parnassus is 'now turned to a stewes'. A strong attack is made on the writers of tragedy and especially Marlowe to whose genius Shakespeare owed so much; whose genius Hall failed to realize. He dislikes the 'big-sounding sentences' in *Tamburlaine*, which was very popular. He strongly objects to the use of blank verse in tragedy and to the introduction of the clown so characteristic of the Elizabethans, including Shakespeare. He objects to any writer who presents tragedy to the uneducated. Such fare is not for them.

> 'Shame that the Muses should be bought and sold,
> For every peasant's brasse, on each scaffold.'
>
> Sat. 3.

He lashes the intemperance of bohemian poets; the vicious life of men like Greene, Marlowe and Nash.

Hall has a rooted dislike of poetry written for money. He calls it 'hunger-starven, trencher-poetry'. He speaks with scorn of those who depend on a patron for financial assistance. A few years later when he himself set out to win the favour of a king he could not have written the haughty and somewhat contemptuous words which we meet with in the first satire:

> 'Nor can I crouch, and writhe my fauning tayle
> To some great patron, for my best avayle.'

Dramatic poetry is not the only kind which awakens our satirist's disdain. In 1579 a gentleman had attempted the impossible task of turning Vergil into English hexameters (1, 6). Many writers were so deeply influenced by the love of the Classics which came in with the revival of learning that they were prepared to carry the imitation of Roman writers to absurd lengths. This was one of them.

A very popular work of the time was Sackville's *Mirrour for Magistrates* first written in 1557, 'afterwards digested anew', says Ellis, 'and continued by several of the greatest wits of the Elizabethan age'. This book gives accounts of many men who rose to high estate and came to a miserable end. Hall found in this work nothing 'but notes of rufull plaint'.

Many attempts were made to produce a metrical version of the Hebrew psalter. In later days Hall made such an attempt himself. But many Puritans went farther and tried to turn the Commandments, the Creed, and various parts of Scripture into English verse. They met with no success. Hall disliked this sort of writing. But his contempt was not confined to doggerel. In 1595 Robert Southwell, who was something of a poet, wrote *St Peter's Complaint*. 'Now good St Peter weeps pure Helicon.'

Another writer, Markham, produced a work entitled *Sion's Muse*. It is based on the Canticles and was more like the product of a man who praised his mistress in a sonnet, than a piece of religious verse.

> 'Great Salomon, sings in the English Quire;
> And is become a newfound sonnetist,
> Singing his love, the Holy Spouse of Christ;
> Like as she were some light-skirts of the rest.'
> (I, 8.)

Such poets, Hall says, should be sent to Bedlam.

In Hall's time it was the fashion to write sonnets to one's mistress. Such poetry was often a mass of affectation which abounded in witty conceits and foolish sentiment. The gallantry was so laboured and artificial that to Hall it was at once ridiculous and rather nauseating.

> 'Great is the follie of a feeble braine,
> Ore-rul'd with love, and tyrranous disdaine.'
> (I, 7.)

Hall was perfectly justified in his contempt for the immorality of many poets of the time.

> 'What if some Shordich fury should incite
> Some lust-stung lecher, must he needs indite
> The beastly rites of hyred veneryе,
> The whole world's universall baud to bee?'
> (I, 9.)

Not content, however, with their own invention they went overseas to find and bring back filth; for example the *Facetiae* of Poggius Florentinus and the 'dronken revellings' of Rabelais. (II, 1.)

With the second satire of the second book Hall may be said to turn from criticism of contemporary literature to criticism of contemporary life. Out of the mass of references to various abuses we shall deal only with the most important.

Hall's picture of the sexual morality of his time is most depressing. He speaks as if he lived in an age

> 'When all, save toothlesse age or infancie,
> Are summoned to the court of Venerie.'
> (IV, 1, 92 ff.)

Gigolos, pederastrians, adulterers and adulteresses abound in every stratum of society. (IV, 1, 134 ff.)

Men waste their substance on such riotous living.

> 'Or if (O shame!) in hired harlot's bed
> Thy wealthy Heyre-dome thou have buried.'
> (IV, 3, 24.)

Stubbes (I, 31) assures us that in those days brothelry abounded.

Luxury in Dress

It was a time when those who aspired to be well dressed spent enormous sums on their wardrobes. According to Hall the fashionable dress of the day simply served to make men look ridiculous.

> 'But thou canst mask in garish gauderie,
> To suite a foole's far-fetched liverie.
> A French head joyn's to necke Italian:
> Thy thighs from Germanie, and brest fro Spaine;
> An Englishman in none, a fool in all.'
>
> (III, 1, 64 ff.)

Hall has much to say of pump-hose, corsets, laces, ruffs, ear-rings worn by men. He tells us that they carried mirrors, dyed their beards, chalked their faces, oiled their hair, took anise etc. to scent their breath.

He paints a picture of a typical gallant with his linen-collar 'labyrinthian set, whose thousand double turnings never met', his great sleeves, wasp-waist, and abbott's loin: and the result?

> 'Likst a strawne scar-crow in the new-sowne field
> Reared on some sticke, the tender corne to shield.'
>
> (III, 7, 47.)

Women's dress receives equal attention. In 1585 and 1595 certain foreigners recorded their impressions of the extraordinary luxury of Englishwomen's clothes. Women spent as much, perhaps even more on dress, than did the gallants of the Court. Hall thought their appearance was quite as ridiculous as that of the men.

The taste for expensive clothing was not confined to the gentry. The burgess and the peasant were eager to be accounted as something better than they were and dressed above their station. (Stubbes, I, 34.) Here for instance is the peasant:

> 'And, that men mought some Burgesse him repute
> With satten sleeves hath grac'd his sackcloth sute.'
>
> (III, 4, 30.)

> 'What broker's lousy wardrop cannot reach
> With tissued panes to prancke each peasant's breech?'
>
> (IV, 2, 60.)

Many a man ruined himself by excessive expenditure on dress.

> 'Who cannot shine in tissues and pure gold,
> That hath his lands and patrimonie sold?'
>
> (IV, 2, 17.)

In Elizabeth's time many who aspired to luxury came up to London and turned 400 or 500 acres of their best land into two or three trunks.

> 'Bearing his paune-layd lands upon his backe.'
>
> (IV, 2, 15.)

In IV, 7, there is a short but interesting account of a young farmer who has inherited £40 a year. His wife wants to spend £10 on a gown. He himself wishes to spend almost as much on a suit. His wife insists that she must have an idle man-servant to wait on her: that she must have a carriage, keep horses and hounds. The unfortunate couple speedily discover that all this cannot be done on £40 a year.

USURY

Although in Hall's time it was perfectly legal to charge interest on a loan (the maximum rate of interest was 10 per cent in Elizabeth's reign and 8 per cent in that of her successor), the old medieval feeling about usury continued. In the *Merchant of Venice* we find that whilst Shylock was a usurer Antonio 'lends out money gratis'. (*Merchant of Venice*, I, 3, 45.) Stubbes laments the fact that 'it is impossible for any to borrow money there (i.e. in England) without usure and loan'. Nash, in *Christ's Teares* (IV, 39), says: 'It is now growne a Proverbe that there is no merchandize but Usury.' (*Christ's Teares*, IV, 39.) Sometimes the usurer made his victim accept the loan partly in money, partly in goods which were not readily marketable. He was especially anxious to get hold of land and to inveigle a young heir into debt. The end of those who fell into the moneylender's clutches was sometimes imprisonment (Hall, IV, 2, 80); sometimes exile,

> 'So ships he to the wolvish westerne isle
> Among the savage kernes in sad exile'
> (IV, 5, 27 ff.)

sometimes enlistment in the army of a foreign power,

> 'Or in the Turkish wars, at Caesar's paye,
> To rub his life out till the latest day.'
> (IV, 5, 29.)

At times he was reduced to beggary:

> 'Whiles if he chance to breake his deare-bought day
> And forfait, for default of due repay,
> His late intangled lande; then, Fridoline,
> Buy thee a wallet, and go beg or pyne.'
> (IV, 5, 125 ff.)

Hall leaves us in no doubt of his opinion of the usurer:

> 'A pining gourmand, an imperious slave,
> A hors-leech, barren womb, and gaping grave;
> A legal theeve, a bloodlesse murtherer,
> A feind incarnate, a false usurer.'
> (IV, 5, 99 ff.)

It is true that the usurer seldom troubled his head about the poor: he flew at higher game.

> 'For, certes, no man of a low degree
> May bid two guestes, or gout, or usurie.'
> (IV, 5, 10.)

But there were exceptions to the rule.

'Who can despayre that sees another thrive
By lone of twelve-pence to an oyster-wive?'
(IV, 2, 3.)

Speculation

The form of speculation so much condemned by Elizabethan moralists was the attempt to make 'a corner in grain'. Men bought up crops in advance and held them till prices rose. Stubbes complains (2, 22) that 'they buy up, hoard and sell deare'. This sort of business flourished especially in times of dearth. Shortly before Hall wrote there had been three periods of famine: one in 1594, one in 1595, and one in 1596. On November 2nd Elizabeth issued an edict on this subject. The trouble was that there were 'Black Markets' in which 'Badgers' as they were termed, were holding back corn supplies and selling them secretly at very high prices.

On all such people Hall has much to say not only in his satires but later on in his sermons. Here he speaks of

'. . . some glozing merchant's feate
That laugheth at the cozened world's deceipt,
When as a hundred stocks ly in his fist,
He keakes and sinkes, and breaketh when he list.'
(IV, 5, 111 ff.)

Such speculators sometimes made mistakes and no one felt sorry when they burned their fingers.

'Each muck-worme will be rich with lawless gaine,
Altho' he smother up mowes of seven years' graine,
And hang'd himselfe when corn gows cheap again.'
(IV, 6, 23 ff.)

Land Enclosure

Schulze says that the process of enclosing common land had come to an end by the second half of Elizabeth's reign: but that the process had been renewed with fresh force in the year 1592. In any case when Hall was writing his biting satires feeling on the subject was very bitter. In addition, at that time, landlords were raising their rents. Often customary rent was replaced by competitive rent. A farmer was turned out of his holding without any compensation for improvements which he had effected on the land. Few of them were able to

'. . . defie
Such pilfering slips of pety land-lordie.'
(V, 1, 107.)

Meanwhile there were ejections.

'And might dislodge whole collonyes of poore,
And lay their roofe quite level with their floore.'

But not only did landlords enclose common land,

> 'They racke their rents unto a treble rate;
> And hedge in all their neighbour common lands';

they expected their tenants to pay heavy incoming dues, and to give presents:

> 'Yet must he haunt his greedy landlord's hall,
> With often presents at each festivall;
> With crammed capons every New-yeare's morne,
> Or with greene-cheeses when his sheepe are shorne;
> Or many maunds-full of his mellow fruite,
> To make some way to win his waighty suit.'

Even the entertainment which the landlord occasionally gave his tenants is criticized.

> 'As he, that, under name of Christmas cheere
> Can starve his tennants all th'ensuring year.'
> (IV, 5, 77.)

It has been pointed out that rents were raised partly no doubt because a different idea was coming into existence (competitive rent etc.) but also because the value of money had decreased through the debasement of the coinage by Henry VIII and Edward VI and through the great influx of gold and silver from America.

The Yeoman

This was the golden age for the Yeomen of England. In some cases their grandfathers had got hold of abbey land at the Dissolution of the Monasteries. More often they had profited by the great rise in prices. Hall devotes nearly a whole satire (IV, 2) to telling in an amusing way how Lollio tried to turn his son into a gentleman.

Like others of a similar snobbish disposition the son tells men that his forefathers came over with the Conqueror. He marries a squire's daughter and in some cases becomes a 'carpet-knight', i.e. one who had never seen military service. The sons of such upstart yeomen were sometimes called 'dunghill-gentlemen' even when they completed their education by going to one of the universities and one of the Inns of Court. In the graveyard scene Hamlet says: 'the age is grown so picked, that the toe of the peasant comes so near the heel of the courtier he galls his kibe.'

Hall refers to the same subject in another satire. (V, 1, 27 ff.)

> '... now his sonne sooups in a silken cote,
> Whose grandsire happily, a poor hungry swayne,
> Beg'd some cast abby in the churche's wayne.'

The Poorer Classes

It is obvious that the poor suffered a good deal by the Dissolution of the Monasteries. The new type of landlord spent lavishly on entertainments for his friends; he seemed to have little left to give to the poor. Elizabeth had something to say about this. Then, too, the brilliant Court was a magnet which drew many to London. The new country houses which the gentry built were beautiful and imposing but sometimes a gentleman would visit one of his manors only once in seven years. A vivid picture of such an empty house is given in V, 2. Anyone going to such a house in hope of entertainment might find a surly porter and a dog; he would find little more.

The old squire had kept open house; his son goes to live in Town.

> 'Plenty and hee dy'd in that same yeare
> When the sad sky sheed so many a teare.'

The satirist adjures the young gallant to stay at home and spend his money there, instead of wasting it in London.

> 'For shame, ye gallants! grow more hospitall,
> And turne your needlesse wardrope to your hall'.
> (V, 2.)

For as things are the poor suffer. Instead of generous assistance all they get is

> '. . . Some hungry gallant's dole,
> That in a dearth runs sneaking to a hole.
> And leaves his man and dog to keepe his hall'.
> (IV, 2, 39 ff.)

Even the small tenant farmer lived none too well. Here is a description of his house:

> 'God wot! a silly cote,
> Whose thatched sparres are furr'd with sluttish soote
> A whole inch thick, shining like black-moor's brows,
> Through smoke that down the head-les barrel blows:
> At his bed's feete feeden his stalled teme;
> His swine beneath, his pullen ore the beame.'
> (V, 1, 59 ff.)

Meat and Drink

In earlier chapters we have called attention to the fact that Hall was an ascetic. He ate to live; he did not live to eat. That, however, did not prevent him from making many references to meat and drink in his satires.

> 'O Nature! was the world ordain'd for nought
> But fill man's maw, and feed man's idle thought?
> Thy Grandsire's words savour'd of thriftie leekes,
> Or manly garlicke: but thy furnace reekes
> Hote steams of wine; and can aloofe descrie
> The drunken draughts of sweete Autumnitie.'
> (III, 1, 58.)

Satire III, 3, gives an interesting and amusing account of a meal at the house of a rich citizen. In those days the City was famous for lavish hospitality. Englishmen loved to see a well-covered table. In other satires Hall refers to the various dishes which were popular and to the great amount of drink that was consumed. Harrison tells us (I, 49) that Englishmen used fifty-six kinds of light wines together with thirty different kinds of 'Italian, Grecian, Spanish, Canarian wine'. Cecil lamented the fact that 'England spendeth more on wines in one year than it did in ancient times in four years'. Cambridge was famous for the number of public-houses it contained. In 1597 there were eighty; but in that year the number was reduced by royal edict to thirty.

To read Hall's satires is to get a liberal education in the manners and customs of his time. He is ready to take us to the theatre and the bear pit; to a cock-fight and to many kinds of sports. He tells us of the notices offering employment which were posted up in St Paul's Cathedral, of how men walked up and down the aisle in service time to study them. He takes us to the Exchange, to Cheapside which was the great business centre of the day, to Cole-harbour the refuge of debtors and thieves. With him we may watch the bear-baiting in Paris-garden or walk across London Bridge to see the heads of traitors. He is ready to show us the carriages which had been recently introduced; to point out the new system of street lighting which men admired. He knows Shoreditch, the 'red light' quarter of the day. Finally he will take us to some man's fireside where in winter evening the family gather to hear some traveller's tale, the more wonderful the better; for in those days men were more credulous than they are now. Hall had his own share of credulity; but there were two forms of what he regarded as credulity which always aroused his wrath. One was connected with alchemy and astrology.

> 'His feare or hope, for plenty or for lack,
> Hangs all uppon his New-Year's Almanack.'
>
> (II, 7, 23 ff.)
>
> 'But yet, if haply his third fornace hold,
> Devoted all his pots and pans to gold.'
>
> (IV. 3, 37.)

Hall did not believe that the Elixir of Life could be found. This is plain from II, 4, 39, where he speaks of the attempt to

> 'Bring Quintessence of Elixir pale,
> Out of sublimed spirits minerall'.

The other form of superstition which he detested even more strongly was that, as he conceived it, embodied in the Roman Catholic Church. The country which most truly represented Catholicism for him was Spain. And Spain was proud; very proud.

> 'And trace proud Castile that aspires to be
> In his old age a young fift monarchie.'
>
> (V, 3, 84 ff.)

In 1593 Philip completed his great palace, the Escurial. This is how Hall regarded it:

> 'Like the vaine bubble of Iberian pride,
> That over-croweth all the world beside.'
> (V, 2, 37.)

But there was worse than Spain; there was Rome. This is how he describes the Pope:

> 'To see an olde Lozell perched hy,
> Crossing beneath a golden Canopy;
> The whiles a thousand haireless crownes crouch low,
> To kiss the precious case of his proude toe.'
> (IV, 7, 13 ff.)

To him Rome represented lust for power.

> 'Or the red hat, that tries the lucklesse mayne
> For welthy Thames to change his lowly Rhene.'
> (V, 3, 86 ff.)

In any case Rome formed a magnificent target at which to aim his darts.

> 'Certes not all the worlde such matter wist
> As are the Seven Hills, for a Satyrist.'
> (IV, 7, 3 ff.)

As we have said Hall was a master hand in character painting. He introduces us to a number of types. We can only deal with a few. First of all there is the merchant. Hall says very little of merchants but that little is enough. He disliked them intensely. Stubbes tells us (2, 47) that corn merchants were wont, when they sent corn to market, to place good corn at the top of the sack and to fill up the bottom with bad. Hall tells us that the corn-merchant's premises were often so dark that a customer could not clearly see what he was buying. (IV, 6, 27 ff.) He was sometimes a usurer and often a cheat.

> 'But Nummius eas'd the needy gallant's care
> With a base bargaine of his blowen ware
> Of fusted hoppes, now lost for lack of sayle.'
> (IV, 5, 116.)

In satire VI, 1, having satirically described his age as the best,

> 'Sith now not one of a thousand does amisse,
> Was never age I weene as pure as this',
> (35, 36.)

he goes on in the same vein to say,

> 'Merchants are no whit covetous of late,
> Nor make no mart of time, gaine of deceit.'

The Clergy

In his sermons and meditations Hall often speaks of the small esteem in which the clergy were held. They had to submit to a lengthy training before they could take a degree; and even when they had acquired the necessary academic qualification had to woo the favour of some patron who could present them to a living. He did not always do this free of charge (Hall often laments what he called 'simonaical transactions'). Sometimes he 'gelded the living', i.e. kept back part of the stipend as Sir Robert Drury did at Halstead.

> 'Each home-bred science percheth in the chaire,
> Whiles sacred arts grovell on the groundsell bare.'
> (II, 3, 23 ff.)

> 'Fooles! they may feede with words and live by ayre,
> That climbe to honour by the pulpit's stayre:
> Sit seven years pining in an Anchore's cheyre,
> To win some patched shreds of Minivere;
> And seven more plod at a patron's tayle,
> To get a gelded chappel's cheaper sayle.'
> (IV, 2, 104 ff.)

Lawyers

In *Hamlet* (V, 3, 57 ff) the king contrasts the verdict of an earthly court with the Divine judgment:

> 'In the corrupted currents of this world,
> Offence's gilded hand may shove by justice;
> And oft 'tis seen, the wicked prize itself
> Buys out the law; but 'tis not so above:
> There is no shuffling, there the action lies
> In his true nature; and we ourselves compell'd,
> Even to the teeth and forehead of our faults,
> To give evidence.'

Hall devotes a whole satire (II, 3) to lawyers and he does not spare them. He makes use of the old saying that the client is the sheep, the lawyer the shearer. The wise man will leave law-suits alone. He is also convinced that lawyers are venal and can be bribed. The fifth satire in book IV begins thus:

> 'Would now that Matho were the Satyrist,
> That some fat bribe might greaze him in the fist;
> For which he neede not braule at any barre,
> Nor kisse the booke to be a perjurer:
> Who else would scorne his silence to have solde,
> And have his tongue tyed with stringes of gold?'

Lawyers were becoming rich in Hall's time and were buying up land. Hamlet refers to this in the grave-digging scene when the grave-digger turns up a skull that might have been a lawyer's.

> 'This fellow might be in 's time a great buyer of land, with his statutes, his recognizances, his fines . . .'

Hall sums up his view of lawyers in the words:

> 'Woe to the weale, where many lawiers bee;[1]
> For there is, sure, much store of maladie.'
> (IV, 3, 15 ff.)

[1] For the amazingly large incomes earned by lawyers, see J. S. Neale's *Elizabethan House of Commons*, page 306.

Doctors

One of the best satires is to be found in II, 4. It deals with doctors. Like the clergy they were despised and ill-paid.

> 'O Esculape! how rife is phisicke made,
> When each brasse-basen can professe the trade
> Of ridding pocky wretches from their paine,
> And does the beastly cure for ten-grotes' gaine.'
> (IV, 1, 162.)

It would unduly prolong this essay if one referred to the many other types which Hall introduces in his satires. He knew for instance, the braggart type of soldier like Pistol; he knew that tailors dressed well. Indeed he seems to have known something of almost every type to be met with in Elizabethan times. How he knew all this in view of the fact that he was only twenty-three or twenty-four and had spent almost the whole of his life at school or college, it is hard to explain. But we must end somewhere and we end with a reproduction of one of the shortest and wittiest of the satires.

The Private Tutor

It is said that Ariosto, in view of his wit, was invited to settle down at the court of Hippolito, Cardinal of Este. To this Hall refers when he says:

> 'Go, Ariost, and gape for what may fall
> From trencher of a flattering cardinall;
> And if thou gettest but a pedant's fee,
> Thy bed, thy board and coarser liverye.'
> (VI, 1, 200.)

Let this serve as introduction to satire II, 6, which sings the woes of the poor private tutor.

> 'A gentle squire would gladly intertaine
> Into his house some trencher-chaplaine;
> Some willing man, that might instruct his sons,
> And that would stand to good conditions.
> First, that he lie upon the truckle-bed,
> Whiles his young maister lieth ore his head.
> Second, that he do, on no default
> Ever presume to sit above the salt.
> Third, that he never change his trencher twise.
> Fourth, that he use all common courtesies;
> Sit bare at meales, and one halfe rise and wait.
> Last, that he never his yong master beat,
> But he must aske his mother to define,
> How manie jerkes she would his breech should line.
> All these observ'd, he could contented bee,
> To give five markes, and winter liverye.'

(*b*) LATIN SATIRE

MUNDUS ALTER ET IDEM (1605)

This Latin satire was published anonymously and dedicated to the fifth Earl of Huntingdon (of the Hastings creation). Four years later an English version appeared. It is certain that this translation was published without Hall's consent and against his wishes. (See Letter to Knight Wynter, Vol. VI, pp. 276–8 (Dec. V, Ep. 10)). Hall never acknowledged the authorship of *Mundus*. He knew that a witty cynic might have been proud to have written it; that an ambitious divine dared not claim it as his own.

Till recently those who read *Mundus* had either to be very good latinists – its vocabulary is full of words unfamiliar to those who only know the classics – or they had to go to one of the few libraries that possess a copy of Healey's translation. All that has been changed since the following pages were written, for in 1937 a book appeared in Cambridge, Massachusetts, published by Harvard University Press entitled *The Discovery of a New World*. This is Healey reprinted and splendidly edited by Huntington Brown. The editor is as one might expect much better as a philologist than as a theologian or he would never have described Hall's standpoint as 'that of a combined anti-Catholic and anti-Calvinist'. (P. XXIX.) An anti-Calvinist Hall never was.

Then, too, there are interpretations of *Mundus* that many will question. The editor maintains, for instance, that (amongst many other things) *Mundus* is an allegory, the story of man's (e.g. Hall's) journey through life. Surely the fact that the imaginary traveller spent thirty years in Australasia, and that Hall was thirty when he wrote *Mundus*, is a rather poor foundation on which to base such a claim. But as a philologist Huntington Brown is very good indeed. Introduction and glossary are worthy of all praise and the immense research that lies behind the notes is wholly admirable. Again and again he has traced Hall's ideas to their original sources, has shown how freely he borrowed from his predecessors especially perhaps from Rabelais. In doing this he has incidentally confirmed the suspicion of Schuckburgh that Hall did not devote all his attention to divinity whilst at Emmanuel. Far from it. He was widely read in books that had nothing whatever to do with theology and he was no mean linguist. That is one point which our editor has proved. The other is that Milton misjudged Hall when he suggested that he owed much of his apparent knowledge, much of the scholarship he (sarcastically) displays, to a cursory study of various polyglot dictionaries and certain encyclopaedias of the time. Hall's knowledge was at once broader and deeper than Milton supposed. The three main subjects to which the satirist directs attention are: the Roman Catholic Church; certain vices which prevailed in England in his day; and women, of whom as elsewhere, he has much of an unflattering character to say.

The satire contains a number of Rabelaisian passages, which ill become a clerical pen, a good deal of shrewd observation expressed in terms at times cynical, at times sarcastic. 'What fools these mortals be' may be regarded as the leitmotiv running through these pages. In them there is no pity for human frailty, no attempt to suggest how evil may be removed, no idealism, no vision of a better world. This it was which led Milton to pour out the vials of his wrath and to write as follows:

> 'That grave and noble invention, which the greatest and sublimest wits in sundry ages, Plato in Critias, and our two famous countrymen, the one in his "Utopia", the other in his "New Atlantis", chose, I may not say as a field, but as a mighty continent, wherein to display the largeness of their spirits, by teaching this our world better and exacter things than were yet known or used; this petty prevaricator of America, the zany of Columbus (for so he must be till his world's end), having rambled over the huge topography of his own vain thoughts, no marvel if he brought us home nothing but a mere tankard drollery, a venerous parjetory for stews. Certainly, he that could endure with a sober pen to sit and devise laws for drunkards to carous by, I doubt me whether the very soberness of such a one, like an unliquored Silenus, were not stark drunk. Let him now go and brand another man injuriously with the name of mime,[1] being himself the loosest and most extravagant mime that hath been heard of, whom no less than almost half the world could serve for stage-room to play the mime in. And let him advise again with Sir Francis Bacon, whom he cites to confute others, what it is "to turn the sins of Christendom into a mimical mockery, to rip up the saddest vices with a laughing countenance", especially where neither reproof nor better teaching is adjoined.' – *Apology for Smectymnuus*.

In his preface to *Mundus alter et idem*, Hall ('Mercurius Brittanicus' as he terms himself) tells us that he has no desire to visit European countries like France, Italy, Germany and Spain, since those who dwell there are so like ourselves. He therefore determines to visit Terra Australis *nondum cognita* and to this end embarks in the good ship *Fancie*. He first reaches the land of Tenter-Belly which borders on Terra del Fuego. The first canton he visits is Dressembourg in whose chief city save during Lent incense is continually burned on a thousand altars. He is now in the land of Eat-allia or Gluttonia. Thence he proceeds to Banquet-ois, famous for its forest of fruit trees, and the river Oil-brook which runs round the capital. The next canton to be visited is Pewter-platteria whose chief city is Victualla.

[1] Hall had previously called Milton a 'Mime'.

It is also known as Flesh-pasty-nople and is situated on the river Sauce. Its citizens are known as Gourmands. Every month a great feast is held in 'Gourmands' Hall' at which provisions are so plentiful 'that 100 Carthusians might have a Christmas dinner from thence at an hour's warning'. The city has a university; but the only lecture read there is the 'Munching Lecture' delivered by Dr Full-Gorge. The 'Gourmands' like venison; but prefer pork. At Christmas the rivers (i.e. the conduits into which the latrines empty themselves) are so full that they overflow their banks.

The traveller gives a satirical description of the laws and religion of this province. It is a rather coarse attack on the Roman Catholic Church, as may be gathered from the fact that the candidates for the Grand Dukedom (i.e. the Papacy) are drawn from one or other of the four classes: Treble-chins, Bacon-chops, Wool-sacks, Mumble-jaws.

The second province of Tenter-Belly is Drink-Allia. It consists of three parts: Wine-cester, Usque-bathe, Hop-sack or Strong-beer. The name of the metropolis is Carousi-kannikin. It is shaped like a tankard and on the city gate (the Flagon of Hospitality) is inscribed *Aut bibe aut abi.* The only clothing the inhabitants wear is a wreath of vine-leaves on their brows. At the banquet a bedroom chamber is set on one side of the reveller; a 'vomit-bowl' on the other. He who can empty the great tun (no doubt a reference to the celebrated cask in Heidelberg Castle) is knighted. The State has fifteen laws. The ninth runs as follows: 'He whom either nature or sickness hath made abstinent shall be banished the land.' The thirteenth: 'He that mixeth water with his wine shall be sent to sup among dogs.'

A chapter is devoted to a description of the arts and the military discipline of the Drink-Allians. Poets abound. They are a 'scurvy lot' who earn their living by writing elegies, epitaphs, epithalamiums, as they are required. The army has but one law: none must go sober to the field. Next follows a description of a funeral and a rather witty disquisition on epitaphs and the lies they contain.

After that we have an account of a pilgrimage in which Roman Catholic pilgrimages are caricatured, an account of Bacchus-Fiery-Face who has a Chapelle ardente, and to end the book, satirical allusions to the doctrine of Purgatory.

She-land or Womandecoia

The second book begins with an account of She-land. The chief province in this strange country is Tattlingen: its capital, Gossipingoa. Other important towns are Pratlingople, Talesborne, Lypswagg.

As we have said Hall had not a very high opinion of women; and here he satirizes them. He had a much poorer opinion of 'democracy' and here he deals with that. In a sense She-land is a democratic country. There political decisions are reached by a majority vote: the women who vote all shout at once. Parliament remains in *constant* session, in order that decrees made one day may be annulled the next. Few of the She-landers are native-born. Most of them are women who wanted 'to wear their husbands' breeches'; or the wives of jealous husbands who expelled them from their homes.

In Gygglot-tangire there are lovely perfumes and some beautiful women. Breast and face are bare: cheeks are so painted (as in Muscovy) that the women rather resemble a statue or a Westminster tomb than a living creature. The capital city is Shames-grave. The houses are made of glass. There women are always singing, laughing or dancing or engaged in *some such* employment of State. Hall tells us that it was a good thing he was not handsome: otherwise he might have been imprisoned and only set free when he was called upon to gratify the carnal desires of this or that woman.

Nearby is the Isle of Hermaphrodite, whose inhabitants possess 'both a man's wit and a woman's craft'.

The only defence against foreign invasion which She-land possesses is Shrews-burg. Here men are kept under the strictest control. It is said that once upon a time they 'plotted to escape subjection'; but one betrayed them. Hall says it was 'a beastly sight' to see 'a distaff and spindle in a man's hand, and a sword and buckler in a woman's'. But here, if any woman shows any tenderness to her husband she is held guilty of treason. Her head is shaved and she is put in the stocks; for in Shrews-burg no man rules in his own house. On the contrary women clip their hair and let their nails grow long. They are taught to box and to tear men's cheeks with their nails. All the houses are kept splendidly neat and clean, for housework is done by men. On the other hand the fields and walls 'are miserably attended to'; for this is the department of women.

Fooliana

This is the largest country that Hall had ever seen and the most densely peopled. Compared with Fooliana, China, with her seventy millions, is 'an uninhabitable desert'. *Stultorum plena sunt omnia.* Fooliana the Great is divided into Fooliana the Craggie, Fooliana the Fat, Fooliana the Fond and Fooliana the Devout.

The inhabitants of Fooliana are never met with alone. They are always talking and contending; and they have many sects – Fool-osophers. One sect is known as the Brownbacks; another as the Cluniacones, a third the Quadricornes who are Trinitarians and wear square caps. In addition there are 'societies' such as The Society of

St Paul del culo and the Society of St Gynny-come-home-at-noon, and so forth. They spend their time in begging, in bowing to painted stones, and they light tapers at noon. They regard it as sinful to eat flesh but gorge themselves on fish. They regard it as an unpardonable sin to touch gold or silver with bare hands. (No doubt this refers to the lifting of the Monstrance.) They scourge themselves for there is a tradition among them that calves' blood smells sweetly in the nostrils of their god. All this is a bitter satire on the Roman Catholic Church. But every man who lives in Fooliana is not a Catholic: and though there are more references to the papists in the pages which follow, the main attack is directed on England.

In Fooliana the fickle forms of government are constantly changing; for 'a Frenchman is naturally the weather-cock's ape and the Englishman is *his* ape'. Certain sarcastic observations are made on dress. Attention is called to the fact that in England there are many who make a great to-do about a stranger and then suddenly 'drop' him. Husbands and wives who once lived on affectionate terms drift apart. People do not keep their promises. The rules of life are 'mutable'. Once more we have a skit on epitaphs. This is what we read on Andrew Turncoat's tomb:

> 'Andrew Turncoat who was neither Slave nor Soldier, nor Cobler nor Filcher, nor Lawyer nor Usurer, but all; who lived neither in city nor country nor at home nor abroad, neither at sea nor at land, nor here nor elsewhere, but everywhere. . . .'

This is no doubt wit of a sort: to many it must seem rather laboured and not a little tedious.

Through the Valley Capricious, the travellers make their way to Fooliana the Craggie with its two Duchies Solitary and Sad, and Choleric-oye.

Solitary and Sad is a caricature of the Roman Church with its Duke (the Pope) and its hermits. The Duke lives in Hearts-grief-court.

> 'This is the place where sorrow dwells and care
> Fly far far hence, all you that mirthful are
> Live far apart from men – the life hermetical.'

The hermits whom Hall meets are like the Carthusians who only greet men on Thursdays. They spend their lives 'in imagining and framing fictions to themselves of things never done, nor never likely to be done; in believing these their fictions, and in following these their beliefs'.

The second Duchy of Fooliana is Choleric-oye. Here Duke Swash-buckler reigns. He is 'the model and emblem of all tyranny'. The dukedom has four divisions: Gallow-hew, Green-cheeks, Blue Brow, and Rougeux. The inhabitants are ever eager to kill. They have no laws: 'all goes by might and main'. Their only rule is 'Conquer and possess', and they are always eager for a duel.

The duke's palace is called Mount Scalpi; it is so lofty because of the human skulls on which it rests. The most famous mount in this grim palace is the Inquisition Chapel, i.e. Saint Shambles. There one finds every instrument of death: on every altar sacrifice is offered to the devil and the duke.

The next province to be visited is Fooliana the Fond. Here the parent puts out one eye of his child and men run hither and thither with marvellous distilled water. Alchemists abound. In the cities of Cockscombya, Asse-sex and Blocs-ford all the magnificoes are to be seen. Then we are introduced to the burgomasters of Blost-ford. This gives Hall the opportunity of expressing his views, by no means flattering, on English town councils and Parliament. Stupid views are put forth: men argue; but finally agree that everyone is to have a spire on his house, a weather-cock and a clock which strikes every hour. Next we come to the Marquisate of Spendall-ezza. Here everyone is in financial difficulties having squandered his substance on dogs, dice, hawks and cards. When they have lost everything, these people 'retire unto other men's tables' or else are maintained at the public expense. In Prodigal's Promontory all bankrupt debtors seek sanctuary.

In Claw-back-court we meet the flatterers. Each has two faces and two tongues, an ape's front and a dog's behind. They are a mixture of man-ape and dog. They simply copy others and are for the most part barbers, tailors, panders, etc. They are all toadies. They acknowledge no god but the man they serve and yet they turn back and retract all their flattery. The chief city of this region is Tutto-lodante (Praise all), the river on which the city stands, Fiction. To Shame-stead all wizards are banished and all those whom they call Bashful-orphans (for bashful modesty is the sworn foe of flattery).

The next province to be visited is Fooliana the Fat. Here everyone pretends to be better off than he is. The chief city is Hidalgo or Braggardie. Backbitembourg is not far distant and near it, Breakneck Cliffe, which looks rather like the Peak in Derbyshire. This is the place of execution. On the other side of the hill is the city of Bawdesden, Idle-berg and Holiday Hills on which are two towns Gamesware and Merry-cum-twang where people spend their lives in dancing.

One characteristic of the inhabitants of this place is that they all claim to be 'Gentlemen'. Most of them have pedigrees which date back to 10,000 years before the Creation: though their neighbours can easily prove that they had cobblers, carters or coster-mongers for grandfathers. However poor, they contrive to give one grand party a year even if they have to starve for weeks afterwards to pay for it. Others put all that they have on their backs, often go hungry though you will always find them picking their teeth as though they had just dined. This section ends with a bitter attack on Roman Catholic places like Loretto where miraculous cures are said to have taken place.

Finally we have a description of the Paradise of Fooliana the Fat. In the distance it seems to be a mountain of pure gold. When 'tested', however, the gold turns to dust. On the top of the mountain there is a castle of crystal. It belongs to the goddess of Fortune. Compared with the crowds which flock to this shrine the shrines of Our Lady of Loretto, St James of Compostello, Our Lady of Walsingham seem utterly neglected. Hither men come to pray for all manner of things: one to gain the favour of his wayward love, another to get a wife who is not a shrew. Some pray for honours; others for riches. This man prays that his uncle may die; that, that several churchmen who stand between him and a benefice which he covets, may be removed by death.

An amusing description is given of the way in which Fortune betrays her votaries, drugs them, promises them wealth; feeds them on luxurious fare, dresses them in costly raiment, puts them to sleep in a royal bed; drugs them once more and has them stripped of their grand attire, and carried out in their own old clothes and laid down penniless in the public highway.

In Fooliana the Devout, there are two provinces; Trust Fablia and Sectaryuoa. In the first, people neglect themselves and their land to serve their god 'by rotten ceremonies'. In this province you find hamlets like Mouldy Fragment, Wonders-field, Crepe-ham High Cross, Cringing Beck and Kissing All-up. Here there are as many monasteries as villages. Indeed all who are not 'professed cloisterers' are either slaves or beggars. They wear a melancholy look, tell beads, often make new gods, refuse to touch anything such as water, oil, salt, wax, iron, until it has been exorcized. They baptize bells and believe that stones and statues can weep.

In Sectaryuoa, on the other hand, one meets with all the old heretics, such as Gnostics, Ebionites, Severians (teetotallers, see Augustine de Haer), Montanists and Manichees.

Lately a new city has been built by 'a couple of damned vagabonds', the two founders of Anabaptism or 'The Family of Love'. Then, too, there are the 'Virginian Exiles' who 'laid a plot to erect themselves a body politic' (i.e. the Brownists). Hither kings send all heretics; for here they can do no harm.

The concluding paragraph of this section deals with the 'State politic of Fooliana in general'. The head of all, whether the government be aristocratic or democratic, is the Pope II Buffonio Ottimo Maximo who lives in Papagalli. He is at once emperor and priest and wears a mitre. Before him men carry a key and a sword: the key to show that all the wealth of the Foolianders is at his disposal; the sword to show that he can take from others and defend his own. Here follows a skit on the Pope who 'makes no laws nor keeps any'.

The fourth and last book is devoted entirely to England, Theeue-Inge, i.e. as the author explains *Theue* in English and *Ingenium* in Latin. It is a small country and consists of two signories, Robbers-Wald and Legerdemaine (i.e. thievery and cozenage). The Robbers-walders are of two kinds: Banditti and Pirates. In this little country you will find astrology schools. Tongue-Street is the rendezvous of lawyers. ('No nation is so overstocked with lawyers as this.') Pawns-brook is the resort of usurers, brokers and tailors. In a jeweller's shop the customer is always swindled. Inn-keepers are 'knaves rampant'. Then, too, this is the land of Lurtch-wit (the land of legerdemain). Scapula stole his Greek Lexicon from Steevens. Poets steal whole passages from the books of other men. Here too there are 'Benefice-brokers' and much coveteousness ('the old man's evil').

Such then is *Mundus alter et idem*. The present writer is not sufficiently erudite to assess the quality of Hall's latinity; though it is generally thought to be very good. Nor can he speak definitely of Hall's knowledge of modern languages. Report says that he was a good linguist. The book is full of made-up words apparently based on an adequate knowledge of several tongues. Milton maintained that Hall assumed linguistic knowledge he did not possess. He describes *Mundus alter et idem* as 'that wretched pilgrimage over Minsheu's dictionary'. (This was a polyglot dictionary which dealt largely with etymologies.) In matters of scholarship – himself one of the most finished scholars of the age – he was most exacting. He was also most bitterly prejudiced against Hall both as scholar and bishop. Indeed he set out with the express purpose of 'debunking' (as the moderns sometimes put it) Hall and of showing that he was neither the saint nor scholar he was generally supposed to be. In any case he described *Mundus alter et idem* as 'the idlest and the paltriest mime that ever mounted upon a bank'.

In fairness to Hall it must be remembered that he never wrote another book like *Mundus*. In later life he may have felt ashamed of it and must have blushed when he recalled certain passages it contains. In any case he did his best not only to forget it but also to have it forgotten. No one was more horrified than he when forty years later Milton dragged this anonymous production into the light of day and charged Hall, now a highly respected bishop and the most prolific producer of devotional literature, with its authorship.

(*c*) EPISTLES: VI DECADES

Intensely conservative though he was Hall claimed that in three of his works – the satires, the contemplations, the epistles – he broke entirely fresh ground. He admitted that letters similar in character to his own had been written in other languages; he maintained that he was the first to introduce this form of literature into England. At times he describes them as 'discourses': in point of fact they are essays written in the form of letters. Except in one instance, with which we shall deal later on, they are almost entirely impersonal. When, for instance, he writes to his father who is afraid to die, he writes as a spiritual expert, not as a son. When he writes to his sister, who is concerned about her 'sorrow for sin', he writes as one stranger to another. It is the matter with which he deals that interests Hall; not the person to whom the letter is addressed.

These sixty letters were written with a view to publication. They are dedicated to Prince Henry by his 'unworthy yet faithful and obsequious servant'. Evidently Hall thought well of them: the almost habitual self-depreciation, the disparaging terms in which he so often describes his writings, are entirely absent. In dedicating the last section to the prince, he says: 'These are my last and perhaps most material Letters wherein if I mistake not the pleasure of the variety shall strive with the importance of the matter.'

Of the sixty letters some forty deal with religious questions. In ten or more he criticizes the Roman Church on lines with which we are already familiar. In one he begins his celebrated controversy with Smith and Robinson, the leaders of that group of 'Independents' who had settled down in Holland. In another addressed to a Dutch divine – it is unusually mild in tone – he deals with Arminius to whom he gives this advice:

> 'Away with all new truths: fair and plausible they may be; sound, they cannot: some may admire thee for them; none shall bless thee. . . . Some quiet error may be better, than some unruly truth. Who binds us to speak all we think?' (VI, 7, 3.)

Some deal with the Church of England: we already know how he regarded it. In a yet greater number he seeks to minister consolation to people in distress. These vary from a man long imprisoned by the Inquisition to an English felon awaiting execution: from men who had lost friends to those who had lost money.

When Sir Edward Lucy asked him if we shall recognize each other in heaven, he gives an answer in the affirmative, though with some hesitation. He is certain, however, about another matter concerning which it had been well had he been more reticent.

> 'I fear not to say, we shall know, both our miseries past, and the present sufferings of the damned: it makes our happiness not a little the sweeter to know that we were miserable, to know that others are and must be miserable.'

It is possible that Hall derived this grim view of the future from Aquinas: it is almost certain that he did not obtain it through communion with Jesus Christ.

One or two of the letters deal with points of casuistry. 'Is it right', one correspondent asks, 'for a clergyman to desert his flock in time of plague?' 'Yes,' says Hall. 'I confess, I fear, not so much death, as want of warrant for death.' He believes that the innocent party should sue for divorce, and that the marriage of the clergy is legitimate. He does not believe that husband and wife should cease to cohabit, even though both are willing to do so. Duels – at that time so fashionable – are 'murderous, their nature, devilish'. A man may be at one and the same time a courtier and a Christian. (III, 10, 5.) 'The Court is as nigh to heaven as the Cell.' When one man ventured to suggest that Hall's view of the moral condition of the times in which he lived was unduly pessimistic, he replied by giving a long list of sins and shortcomings. He ended with these words: 'Look about you, and see if three great idols, Honour, Pleasure, Gain, have not shared the earth amongst them; and left Him least, whose all is.'

In view of this we are not surprised to find Hall congratulating one who had withdrawn from public life with all its temptations, to settle down in a quiet country district where he would be free to devote himself to study and 'observation'.

Apart from the description of the way in which Hall spends his time, with which this discussion of his letters will close, there are two points which because of the light they throw on the period deserve attention. Meanwhile it may be well to mention one or two of the *obiter dicta* which occur in these epistles. Hall had little respect for the Orthodox (Russian) Church. To him its members were 'the basest dregs of all Christians'. He believed that but for the Jesuits the Church of Rome would have ceased to exist. 'The brood of that lame Loyola shall have this miserable honour, without our envy: that if they had not been, Rome had not been.' (V, I.) Hall was a wit; not a humorist. There is, however, a touch of humour in the way in which he tells us that he was a bad sailor. 'The sea brooked not me, nor I it; an unquiet element, made only for wonder and use, not for pleasure.' (I, 5.) He believed in witches: he also believed in lycanthropy. (I, 5.) He was 'more rich in children than estate'. To him Henry of Navarre was 'that miscreant'. He claims that his letters are brief – they are.

'Brevity makes counsel more portable for memory, and readier for use.' His rule of life for himself and others ('To all readers', VI, 10) is 'Give way to the anger of the great: the thunder and cannon will abide no fence'.

(1) *The education of the gentry*

The grand tour of the young English noble did not reach its apogee until the eighteenth century: but even in the seventeenth century many young gentlemen completed their education by going abroad. Hall was convinced that this was a dangerous custom chiefly because Jesuit agents were lying in wait for all such travellers. In a letter to the young Earl of Essex (I, 8) he gives advice which reminds us of Polonius:

> 'Trust not strangers too much with your counsel, with your person: and in your greatest familiarities have an eye to their common disposition and infirmities . . . . The Italian, deep, close and crafty; the French, rash; the German, dull.'

Indeed, Hall was greatly perturbed when he thought of the sort of education a young aristocrat received. 'Our land', he says, 'hath no blemish comparable to the mis-education of our gentry.'

He begins with the home. 'Foolish mothers, admit tutors; but debar rods.' He goes on to consider the universities to which lads are sent at a far too early age. There 'they study in jest, and play in earnest'. Thence the young gentlemen proceed to the Inns of Court where 'too many learn to be lawless, and to forget their former little'. 'Paul's is their Westminster: their Study, an Ordinary, or Playhouse, or Dancing-school.' Then comes the time for marriage. 'The father enquires for wealth; the son, for beauty; perhaps the mother, for parentage; scarce any, for virtue, for religion.' When married, 'what is their care, their discourse, yea their trade; but either a hound, or a hawk? . . . and now, they so live, as if they had forgotten that there were books. Learning is for priests and pedants; for gentlemen, pleasure.'

In contrast to all this is the young noble who is to be met with abroad (he is thinking of France: he did not know Italy), who studied in academies and prized learning (which the young English noble despised). 'They travel with judgment, and return with experience: so do they follow the exercises of the body, that they neglect not the culture of the mind.'

When Hall wrote these words he had not been to France. After he had visited that country in the train of Lord Hay (1616) he wrote a tract *Quo Vadis*, with the subsidiary title, *A/Just Censure of Travel/ as it is commonly undertaken by the/Gentlemen of our Nation.*

In *Quo Vadis* these words occur: 'I am not ashamed to recant that, which my un-experience hath, out of hearsay, written in praise of the French education.' He now says that 'few of the foreign nobles are studious in comparison with ours'. Pratt's ed. (VII, 235). The only people who ought to go abroad are those who go to trade and those who are engaged in the diplomatic service. Certainly young gentlemen should stay at home. The only thing they can learn better abroad is 'civil law'. In all other respects the English Universities are immeasurably superior. As for the accomplishments which young gentlemen acquire such as dancing, fencing, music, vaulting, and the management of a horse, foreign experts are always willing to come and teach these arts in England. There are innumerable books about travel: from these the ways of the foreigner are better learned than from aimless travel. Above all the Jesuits, the most skilful agents Rome ever had, are lying in wait for the inexperienced youth. He is likely to lose his religion and to damage his morals. *Quo Vadis* ends with an appeal to parents and an appeal to the king. Great care should be taken to prevent those whom foreign travel is likely to injure, from receiving a passport without which they cannot go abroad. As we have seen before, Hall firmly believed that the manners and morals of the upper classes descend to the lower strata of society. That was why he wanted to prevent corruption in religion and morals from spreading, as he thought he saw it spread amongst the aristocracy. 'I well see, that either good or evil descends. In vain shall we hope for the reformation of the many, while the better are disordered.' (VII, 271.)

(2) *The metrical psalms*

In Julian's Dictionary of Hymnology there is a 'List of Complete and Partial Versions of the Psalms in English from 1414 to 1889'. The list consists of 326 names – some of them the names of very distinguished men. Yet of all the metrical psalters there are only three which have won popular approval and come into common use. These are (1) the 'Old Version' associated with the names of Sternhold and Hopkins; (2) the 'New Version', by Tate and Brady; (3) the version of Francis Rous. When the Westminster divines assembled to prepare a statement of doctrine, a directory of worship to supersede the Book of Common Prayer, a psalter which would be accepted by, or forced, upon the three kingdoms, the House of Commons accepted Rous's psalter, the Lords rejected it in favour of another. Thus it is that Rous's version was never used in England; in Scotland, so drastically revised that in most places the original text is unrecognizable, it has been used continuously ever since in the public worship of the Church. Throughout Hall's lifetime the 'old version' was universally used in England. We must remember that Calvin insisted that nothing which was not found in Scripture was to be used in public worship, and that his influence was so great throughout the Reformed Church (as distinct from the Lutheran which from the first used 'human hymns') that no hymns, save one or two like the Veni Creator, were used in England or Scotland for more than two hundred years. Even as late as 1820 when Heber 'tried to obtain from Archbishop Manners Sutton and the Bishop of London, authorization of his manuscript collection of hymns by the church, the authorization was refused'. The popular favour which hymns now enjoy was then bestowed on the metrical psalms. They were immensely popular in Elizabeth's time, thousands would gather outside St Paul's Cathedral to sing them; long afterwards, whilst men kept their hats on in church throughout the rest of the service, they uncovered their heads whilst they sat and sang the metrical psalms. Sternhold, who had been Groom of the Robes to Henry VIII was anxious to substitute something better for the bawdy songs the courtiers loved to sing. He was also eager to give the common people something which would appeal to them to sing, something moreover which would teach them religious truth. A dozen people combined to produce the 'old version'. But most of the psalms were written in the old ballad metre of Chevy Chase. These psalms, it is said, were faithful to the Hebrew text: but the metre was monotonous, the words at times undignified. Warton, no admirer of the psalter admitted that 'had they been more poetically translated, they would not have been acceptable to the common people'. We are not surprised therefore to learn that many men were eager to improve the 'old version'. One of them was Joseph Hall. He set to work and turned ten psalms into verse. These he sent to a friend asking him to criticize them. If his friend's verdict were favourable and if a number of competent critics agreed with it, Hall was willing – nay, more than willing – to complete the work. Evidently the verdict was not favourable; for Hall made no attempt to continue the work. Nonetheless his 'metaphrase', as he called it, if not as good as many is a great deal better than most. Abandoning the 'ballad metre' altogether he tries a variety of others: the best of them 66.66.88 has often been used by various composers as a fit vehicle for some noble hymn. Hall's own views are worth remembering. Some, he said, would find his verse harsh. There were they 'whose nice ear regards roundness more than sense'. To others who said that the tunes were too difficult to become popular he replied that he 'never could see good verse written in the wonted measures', that he 'ever thought them most easy, and least poetical'. If people reject them it is 'because our people will not take pains for any fit variety'. We could, if we were to try, do as well as the French and 'Dutch' who 'have given us worthy examples of diligence and exquisiteness, in this kind' (possibly the Lutheran Chorales).

> 'If the question be, whether our verse must descend to them, or they ascend to it; a wise moderation, I think, would determine it most equal, that each part should remit somewhat, and both meet in the midst. Thus I have endeavoured to do, with sincere intent of their good, rather than my own applause: for it had been easy to have reached to a higher strain; but I durst not; whether for the grave majesty of the subject, or benefit of the simplest reader. You shall note, that I have laboured to keep David's entire sense with numbers neither lofty, nor slubbered: which mean is so much more difficult to find, as the business is more sacred, and the liberty less.'

It is impossible within our limits to write a disquisition here on the Huguenot Psalter to which Hall refers. Its beginnings were the psalms made by courtiers and sung to the great delight of Francis and Henry II. These psalms at first approved by the Roman Church, afterwards placed on the index, were the nucleus of Huguenot psalmody. In 1932 Sir Richard Terry, himself a Catholic and at one time organist of Westminster Cathedral, published a facsimile of Calvin's first psalter. He had found the only surviving copy in Munich Library. He harmonized the airs and wrote a critique of each. The eighteen psalms in this collection are written in different metres, and set to a variety of airs. Sir Richard Terry speaks of them with enthusiasm. Of the complete Huguenot psalter which owes so much to the magnificent work of Louis Bourgeois much the same may be said. Sir Richard Terry admired Bourgeois (at one time Calvin's precentor), and Robert Bridges who did so much to restore Bourgeois to his proper place, once said: 'Historians who wish to give a true philosophical account of Calvin's influence at Geneva ought probably to refer a great part of it to the enthusiasm attendant on the singing of Bourgeois' melodies.'

To turn the Hebrew psalter into English verse successfully is a task beyond the power of man. The antithetical character of Hebrew poetry prevents it. But Hall was right. The metre used in the 'old version' was totally inadequate. It is a thousand pities that Rous wrote so much in common metre. Hall, who knew the Huguenot Church and admired its psalmody, would have done the work far better than Rous, and Scotland, which depends so largely on the psalter, might have had a far nobler version than that which replaced her first version which like the psalter of which Hall dreamed, owed much to France.

(3) *Self-portraiture*

One letter (VI, 1), as we have already said is purely personal. In it Hall gives an account of the way in which he spends his time. Rising early, he begins the day with prayer. Whilst his 'body is dressing, not with effeminate curiosity, nor yet with rude neglect', he maps out the day's work. Entering his library, he devotes some hours to the study of the Fathers, the most eminent of later divines, the Bible. Next comes family worship: then back to his books, to 'textual divinity, controversy or history, or a mixture of all three'. Then turning from what others have written, he gives rein to his own thoughts. He jots down the ideas that come into his mind; writes part of a sermon or part of a book. Then comes dinner. Hall tries to banish all thought of work since 'a full mind takes away the body's appetite, no less than a full body makes a dull and unwieldy mind'. 'Company, discourse, recreations are now seasonable and welcome.' He eats sparingly: his 'diet is not gluttonous, but medicinal'. If he sees a dish which tempts his palate he 'fears a Serpent in that "Apple" ' and declines it. After dinner he rests awhile, then returns to his book. After supper his 'thoughts are slight'; he tries to remember what he has learnt, examines himself on what he has done. Then, 'calling his family together, he ends the day with God'. On Sundays things are different. 'Prayer, meditation, reading, hearing, preaching, singing, good conference, are the businesses of this day; which I dare not bestow on any work or pleasure, but heavenly.' Though John Wesley knew German and translated Gerhardt (e.g. *Befiehl du deine Wege*) superbly, he spoke with his Moravian friends in Latin. It is probable that on his foreign travels Hall generally spoke in Latin, Nonetheless he had some knowledge of French, Spanish and Italian. When and how did he acquire it? If we accept the picture given in this letter as complete, it is hard to see how Hall found time to read anything but divinity. He does not tell us what his 'recreations' were. Did they include a little poetry and *belles lettres*? Unless we are mistaken he knew Hamlet. Did he ever read the classics after he left college? Surely he must have read and re-read his 'divine Seneca'. But when did he find time for French, Italian and Spanish? He makes no reference in this letter, though he does elsewhere, to pastoral visitation even though he had 'an auditory' of a thousand. Perhaps like the Lutheran clergy of the time, he did not regard this as part of his ministerial duty. We mention this because it is hard to escape the feeling that Hall was never entirely ingenuous – 'Who binds us to speak all we think?' – that there were deeds as well as thoughts which he carefully concealed. In this letter, as elsewhere, we have a self-painted portrait of Joseph Hall as he wished the world to regard him, rather than one of Joseph Hall as he actually was.

(4) *Characters of virtues and vices*

Between 373 and 284 B.C., if we may believe tradition, there lived in

Athens a man called Theophrastus. He had been a pupil of Aristotle, and, if once more we may trust tradition, produced a fascinating little book in his ninety-ninth year. He called it *Characters*, and it consisted of some thirty sketches.

At that time the citizens of Athens were not clearly divided into definite parties. Amongst them there was no such cleavage in regard to religion as we find in England between Puritan and Anglican in the time of Elizabeth: no such political cleavage as that between Whig and Tory in the days of Anne. To outward appearance the Athenian citizens dressed alike, lived alike and thought alike. Yet beneath this apparent uniformity there was difference. Theophrastus studied human idiocyncrasies and noted the difference between one man and another. He saw men who loved to flatter, men who were surly, men who were boorish or arrogant. To such qualities he paid close attention; defined the quality and then described it as embodied in a man and revealed in his actions. He had no particular man in view: he dealt with the species not with the individual. Yet so vivid and skilful is his description that instinctively we are led to think of some particular man of our acquaintance in whom the quality described is perfectly represented. In Sir Richard Jebb's opinion the most perfect specimen of such character-writing is to be found in Thackeray's *Book of Snobs*.

A simple illustration may serve to make all this a little clearer. We go, let us suppose, to a cinema. We see on the screen for a few moments the portrait of a man. He is 'the Flatterer'. Immediately afterwards, without caption or comment, we see this man perform a series of characteristic actions. That is exactly what Theophrastus tried to do and did so well. He begins with a brief description of the quality with which he deals; then he describes a series of actions in which that quality is expressed. He draws no moral but is content to let the picture tell its own story in its own way. Some may feel that these remarks are entirely superfluous for Jebb's edition of *The Characters of Theophrastus* has on one page the Greek text and over against it on the opposite page a translation distinguished by that splendid accuracy and felicity of expression which is the hall-mark of all Jebb's work. In addition this great scholar has provided us with a short but masterly account of the work of Theophrastus and the effect it had on his English imitators.

Here then are a few specimens taken from Jebb of the way in which Theophrastus defines the character he describes:

The surly man. – Surliness is discourtesy in words.

The arrogant man. – Arrogance is a certain scorn for all the world beside oneself.

The boor. – Boorishness would seem to be ignorance offending against propriety.

Whether or not the work of Theophrastus attracted the attention of English scholars before the seventeenth century we cannot say. The fact remains that in 1598 Casaubon produced a Latin version of the book and this had a deep effect on English scholars. In his *Elizabethan World Picture* (P. 80) Professor E. M. W. Tillyard says: 'The Elizabethans were interested in the nature of man with a fierceness rarely paralleled in other ages.' In his lectures on Shakespeare, A. C. Bradley was wont to contrast the Elizabethan Age with the Victorian as that of a youth with that of a middle-aged or elderly man. In the first we have ardent and adventurous youth described in immortal words in the glowing pages of *Areopagitica.* To this England nothing seems impossible. In the second we see the 'Titan weary' bowed down beneath the almost intolerable load of Empire. Of all periods in man's life youth is the most self-conscious. Never is one more tempted to ask the old, old question, 'What am I? What is man?'

To such men Casaubon's Theophrastus came as a godsend. Here was a new literary genre which readily yielded itself to imitation. Here was a kind of writing that was bound to make strong appeal to the love of ethical analysis in general and of self-analysis in particular, which was so pronounced in the England of that day.

Of those who determined to exploit the market for such novel and attractive wares, Joseph Hall was the first to attract attention. He had many successors who profited by his example. Of these the most distinguished was Earle (so much admired by Clarendon) who in Jebb's opinion was 'immeasurably superior' to Hall 'as an analyst of human nature though his reflections were not mingled so largely as those of Hall with bits of picturesque narrative which point their own moral'.

In his preface Hall says that 'it is no shame for us to learn wit out of heathens', informs us that he is one who 'in worthy examples, holds imitation better than invention' and that he had 'trod in their paths'. But he adds – and here we see the difference between himself and Theophrastus – he has followed 'with a higher and wider step; and out of their Tablets drawn these larger portraitures of both sorts'. Theophrastus had a priceless gift which Hall entirely lacked – a sense of humour. He painted the world as he saw it, ignored the darker sides of human character, and drew no moral. Hall was a preacher. 'Virtue', he said, 'is not loved enough; because she is not seen: and Vice loseth much detestation; because her ugliness is secret.' His aim, therefore, is to present 'Virtue and Vice stript naked to the open view; and despoiled, one of her rags, the other of her ornaments'. If men saw virtue and vice as they really are their attitude to life would be entirely different. 'This work', he said, 'shall save the labour of exhorting and disuasion.' The difference then between the aged Greek with his humorous tolerance of human frailty and the young English divine filled to overflowing with intense moral fervour, is pronounced. Theophrastus is the greater artist, and, within the narrow limits which he set himself achieved his purpose. Hall, who dealt with more serious subjects in a far graver manner, did not meet with such complete success. According to Jebb (P. 25) he was 'ingenious but not subtle' and had 'no special qualification for his task beyond a fancy fertile in illustration'. Yet he was, as he professed to be, not a creator but an imitator. Even in small details he borrowed freely from his Master. Of this Jebb has given us four excellent illustrations. Their number might be increased: Jebb's felicity of choice cannot be improved upon: they are as follows:

(*a*) Of *The Flatterer* Theophrastus says: 'The flatterer is a person who will say as he walks with another, Do you observe how people are looking at you?'

Hall's version runs as follows: 'When he walks with his friend he swears to him that no man else is looked at.'

(*b*) Of *The Penurious Man* Theophrastus says: 'When a servant has broken a pot or a plate, he will take the value out of his rations.' Hall repeats the same thought in these words: 'If his servant break but an earthen dish for want of light, he abates it out of his quarter's wages.'

(*c*) According to Theophrastus *The Officious Man* 'will undertake to show the path, and after all be unable to find the way'.

Of *The Busybody* Hall says: 'This man will also thrust himself forward to be the guide of the way he knows not'.

(*d*) *The Distrustful Man*, says Theophrastus, 'is one who, having sent his slave to market, will send another to ascertain what price he gave'.

Of *The Distrustful Man* Hall says: 'When he hath committed a message to his servant, he sends a second after him to listen how it is delivered'.

In two respects Hall's work and that of Theophrastus are at one. In each the sketches are short and there is great economy in the use of words. Each reveals not only careful craftsmanship but also the delight in skilful workmanship which every good craftsman enjoys.

Hall abounds – as was the manner of his time – in epigram, in paradox, in clever *mots*, in what the Elizabethan called 'conceits' – though these are often strained. Here as in all his other works he is never at a loss for an illustration. He is discursive as Theophrastus was not.

What manner of man Theophrastus was we know not: we know enough of Hall from his other writings to realize that he is often speaking of himself. There is no doubt, to take but one instance, of whom Hall is thinking when he describes *The Wise Man* in the following terms (Jebb's Edition, P. 86):

> 'He loves to be guessed at, not known; and to see the world unseen; and, when he is forced into the light, shows by his actions that his obscurity was neither from affectation nor weakness.'

As in his *Contemplations* Hall loves to arrest his reader's attention with his opening words.

> 'He looks not to what he might do, but what he should, Justice is his first guide: the second law of his actions, is Expedience.'

So he begins his description of *The Honest Man*.

> *The humble man* is a friendly enemy to himself.
> *The valiant man* undertakes, without rashness; and performs without fear.
> *The patient man* is made of a metal, not so hard as flexible.
> Of *the true friend* he says: His affections are both united and divided: united, to him he loveth; divided, betwixt another and himself.
> Of *the busy-body*. – His estate is too narrow for his mind; and, therefore, he is fain to make himself room in others' affairs.
> *The unconstant man* treads upon a moving earth, and keeps no pace.
> Of *the vain-glorious*. – All his humour rises up into the froth of ostentation, which, if it once settle, falls down into a narrow room.
> *Presumption* is nothing but hope out of his wits; a high house, upon weak pillars.
> *Ambition* is proud covetousness; a dry thirst of honour; the longing disease of reason; an aspiring and gallant madness.
> Of *the envious*. – He feeds on others' evils; and hath no disease, but his neighbour's welfare.
> *Superstition* is a godless religion, devout impiety.

Each sketch ends with a condensed summary of all which precedes it.

Here are a few examples:

> *The vain-glorious*. – He is a Spanish soldier on an Italian theatre; a bladder full of wind, a skin full of words; a fool's wonder, and a wise man's fool.
> *The unthrift*. – He is the living tomb of his forefathers, of his posterity and, when he hath swallowed both, is more empty than before he devoured them.
> *The busy-body*. – So then he labours, without thanks; talks, without credit; lives, without love; dies, without tears, without pity; save that some say, 'It was a pity he died no sooner'.
> *The honest man*. – He hates falsehood worse than death: he is a faithful client of truth; no man's enemy. . . . And if there were no heaven, yet he would be virtuous.'

We have already drawn attention to Hall's love of paradox. At times one gets a little tired of it. There are too many sentences in the book like this: 'The valiant man draws his sword with a willing kind of unwillingness.' At times there is over-statement. '*The Patient Man*', we are told, 'goes with the same mind to the shambles and to the fold', and of '*the Faithful*', i.e. the truly religious 'man', it is said, 'if his own parents lie in his way to God, his holy carelessness makes them his footsteps'.

One criticism remains to be passed. In this book Hall is seldom profound and often superficial.

One of his cleverest pieces is *The Ambitious*. It is virtually a skilfully painted picture of a courtier. But to say nothing of the Pyramids, as long ago as the fifth century Boethius had pointed out that in most great men perhaps to some extent in every great man, there is an inborn desire for fame that outlasts his lifetime. 'The one thing', said Boethius, 'that could allure geniuses outstanding but not yet quite perfected in virtue is the love of fame.' Never was that desire so prevalent as in the time of the Renaissance. Milton who himself possessed it has described it in words so often quoted as to become almost hackneyed as 'that last infirmity of noble minds'. To such ambition Hall's courtier was an utter stranger. Two more observations complete this survey.

(*a*) Throughout these sketches there runs that strain of stoicism so prevalent in the time of Elizabeth, so often met with in Hall's writings that it seems to have been part and parcel of his creed nay, more, of his very being. We see it perhaps most clearly in the 'character of *The Happy Man*' that 'knows the world, and cares not for it' who 'is not so engaged to any earthly thing, that they two cannot part on even terms'. 'Censures and applauses are passengers to him; not guests: his ear is their thoroughfare; not their harbour: he hath learned to fetch both his counsel and his sentence, from his own breast.'

(*b*) In one sketch, that of *The Good Magistrate*, Hall parts company with Theophrastus and breaks entirely new ground. In this he was followed by most of his successors and in particular by Overbury and Earle. In every other sketch Hall dealt as Theophrastus had done with character in general: now he describes the character of a man who holds a particular office, who occupies a specific place in society. It is a good sketch. It begins as follows:

> 'He is the faithful Deputy of his Maker; whose obedience is the rule, whereby he ruleth.'

It ends thus:

> 'He is the guard of good laws: the refuge of innocency; the comet of the guilty, the paymaster of good deserts; the champion of justice: the patron of peace; the tutor of the Church; the father of his Country; and, as it were, another God upon earth.'

There is little doubt as to who served as model for this picture. Strange though it may appear to us, it was James I; in Hall's opinion, the perfect representative of a good and great king.

LIST OF HALL'S WORKS

1598

March 30th	*Satires Virgidemiarum.* Three Books, or Second Part of the Satires containing three Biting Satires.

1599

June 1st	*Satires Virg. or Toothless Biting Satires.* 'That noe Satyres be printed hereafter.' Whitgift (Cantuar). Bancroft (London).
June 4th	Several satires burned. 'These were staied' (i.e. not burned).

1605

February 12th	*Meditations and Vows.* Two Books.
June 2nd	*Mundus alter et idem.* (Anonymous, Frankfort.)

1606

April 8th	*Heaven Upon Earth.*
April 14th	*Sermon: 'Redeeming the Time.'*
November 8th	*The Arte of Divine Meditation.*

1607

March 25th	*A Brief Sum of the Principal Points of Religion.*
November 20th	*Epistles: Vol. I Two Decades.*

1608

March 7th	*Characters of Virtues and Vices* in Two Books.
May 13th	*Sermon: Pharisaism and Christianity.*
October 17th	*Epistles: Vol. II.*
December 5th	*Solomon's Divine Arts of Ethics, Politics and Economics.*

1609

January	*English Version of Mundus alter et idem.*
April 24th	*Passion Sermon* (Good Friday, 14.4.09).
August 21st	*The Peace of Rome etc.*

1610

October 4th	*Epistles.* The Third and last part. Two Decades.

1612

September 9th	*Contemplations: Vol. I.*
December 5th	*Sermon on the Death of Prince Henry.*

1614	
March 8th	*Contemplations:* Vol. II (in Four Books).
July 14th	*Sermons (2): 'The Impress of God.'* Before this Hall published *Apology of C. of E. v. Brownists* and his *Brief Catechism.*
1615	
September 8th	*A Recollection of Treatises.*
September 8th	*Contemplations:* Vol. III.
1622	
May 11th	*Contemplations:* Vol. VI.
1623	
February 17th	*Sermon: 'The Great Impostor.'*
February 17th	*Sermon: 'The Deceit of Appearance.'*
June 20th	*Contemplations on the Old Testament.* Vol. VII. Two Books.
September 23rd	*Sermon: 'The Best Bargain.'*
1624	
January 14th	*Sermon: Exeter's Chapel Restored.* Preached 26.12.23.
February 20th	*Columba Noae:* Convocation Address.
September 22nd	*Sermon: 'The True Peacemaker.'*
1625	
November 17th	*Contemplations on Old Testament.* Vol. VIII and last.
1626	
February 1st	*Sermon: Thanksgiving.*
1627	(Hall Bishop Elect of Exeter.)
November 21st	*The Old Religion.* (Refd. *v.* Roman Catholic.)
1628	
April 8th	*Sermons* (2) *On the Fast:* (*a*) To the Lords; (*b*) Whitehall. (30.3.28.)
1629	
March 4th	*Sermon: Ash Wednesday Fast.* (19.2.29.)
March 4th	*Inurbanitati Pontificaae Responsio.* Latin and Eng. and *Bull* in Latin and Eng.

1630

March 3rd	*Sermon: 'The Hypocrite.'* (28.2.30.)
June 29th	*Occasional Meditations.*

1631

July 15th	(1) *An Apology Against the Slander of Puritanism.* (2) *A Discourse on the Unlawfulness of Marriage of the Uncle with the Niece.*
November 15th	*Paraphrase on Hard Places in the Old Testament.*

1632

April 30th	*Paraphrase on Hard Places in the New Testament.*
October 23rd	*Viginti Propositiones Catholicae.*
December 6th	*Twenty Catholic Propositions.*

1633

August 12th	*Contemplations: The Residue.*
December 9th	*Sermons* (4) in one Vol.: (1) '*The Beauty and unity of the Church.*' (2) '*The fashions of the world.*' (3) '*The estate of a Christian.*' (4) '*The fall of pride.*'

1634

January 17th	*Four Sermons:* (1) '*Christ and Caesar.*' (2) '*The defeat of cruelty.*' (Psalm lxviii. 30.) (3 and 4) '*St Paul's Combat.*' (1 Cor. xv. 32.)
October 23rd	*Meditatiunculae.*
October 23rd	*Henochismus.* (Latin and English.)

1635

March 10th	*Sermon* before the king.

1637

October 11th	*Sermon* on Consecration of a Burial Ground at Exeter. (Consecrated 24.8.37.)

1640

February 10th	*Episcopacy by Divine Right.*

1641

January 13th	'An humble remonstrance to the High Court of Parliament by a dutiful son of the Church.'
April 12th	'A defence of the humble Remonstrance against the frivolous and false exceptions of Smectymnuus.'

1641

July 28th	'A short answer to the tedious vindication of Smectymnuus by the Author of the humble remonstrance.'
August 17th	*A Sermon* preached before the king at Whitehall. (8.8.41.)

1645

June 27th	*The Remedy of Discontentment.* NOTE. – Sequestration and wives and children of delinquents. (8.9.45.)

1647

March 15th	*Satan's Fiery Darts Quenched or Temptations Repelled in three decades.*
December 9th	*Pax Terris* ('a small pamphlet').

1648

March 20th	*Select Thoughts* (*one century*), and *Breathings of the Devout Soul.*
November 3rd	*Resolutions and Decisions of Divers Practical Cases of Conscience in Continual Use Amongst Men* (*four decades*).

1650

July 6th	*Susurrium Cum Deo.* Soliloquies or holy self-conferences of the devout soul upon earth.

1651

October 15th	*The Great Mystery of Godliness.* *The Invisible World Discovered to Spiritual Eyes.* Three Books.

1653

November 4th	*The Holy Order, or Fraternity of the Mourners in Sion.*

1654

December 4th	*An Apologetical Letter.*

1662	Posthumously: *Contemplations on the New Testament.*

INDEX